REVIEW 6

REVIEW

Volume 6   1984

Edited by

James O. Hoge and
James L. W. West III

University Press of Virginia
Charlottesville

THE UNIVERSITY PRESS OF VIRGINIA
Copyright © 1984 by the Rector and Visitors
of the University of Virginia

This journal is a member of (CELJ) the Conference of Editors of Learned Journ

First published 1984

ISSN 0190-3233
ISBN 0-8139-1031-5

Printed in the United States of America

Major funding for *Review* is provided by the College of Arts and Sciences at Virginia Polytechnic Institute and State University.

Contents

Editorial Board

Faulkner and Race

Noel Polk

Thadious M. Davis. *Faulkner's "Negro": Art and the Southern Context*. Baton Rouge: Louisiana State University Press, 1983. xii, 266 pp.

Walter Taylor. *Faulkner's Search for a South*. Urbana: University of Illinois Press, 1983. x, 242 pp.

These are two of several recent books on Faulkner and the South/Negro.[1] Between them there are so many serious problems that it may be useful to reflect upon them as representative of some of the larger problems that have historically played significant roles in our perceptions of Faulkner's life and, more pertinently, his works. I am in fact only secondarily concerned here with the works themselves, and primarily about the larger problem. The works, however, first.

Thadious Davis's book is based upon her 1976 Boston College dissertation. Beyond a bibliography containing about twenty books (books: no articles) published after 1976, there is little evidence that the study has taken the subsequent six years of Faulkner scholarship into account. Davis does mention Lee Jenkins's 1981 study in her preface and in a footnote (p. 244), but only in a couple of footnotes (pp. 82 and 127) does another post-1976 work (Joseph Blotner's edition of *Selected Letters*) appear. The book's index is incomplete and frequently inaccurate; quotations are repeatedly marred by carelessness (sometimes whole lines are dropped); the prose is never very precise and is often formidably difficult to comprehend.

One could excuse the scholarly problems, however, if there were in the book something to learn. I fear there is not, or very little. Davis would have it that "The Negro" is at the center of everything Southern, a contention fair enough in certain specialized senses. But she is not content to argue the *importance* of "The Negro" to the southern experience; she must have it that Faulkner finds "signal inspiration in the life of blacks" and that "the Negro is part of Faulkner's creative impulse" (p. 15). Further, the Negro's "centrality" is responsible for Faulkner's narrative resourcefulness: forget Joyce, forget Eliot and Pound, forget the Modernist movement:

Faulkner writes with the weight of his culture upon him, and that culture centrally involves the Negro. Because the two parts of his society encompass values and attitudes that are essentially different, they constantly provoke tensions, which are intensified by a consciousness of southern history. The racially divided South presents, then, a unique problem of perception for Faulkner as artist. His awareness of the two separate worlds and his understanding of their mutual histories lead to an intense preoccupation with wholeness—with achieving a unified vision. Basically, it is an ongoing consideration of artistic integration, in which the artist attempts to bring about a fusion of fragmented parts. His art becomes an effort to transcend the tensions and divisions emanating from his cultural heritage, as well as from his position as artist in that culture, that divided world. Coming to terms with the Negro is essential to this process and, I believe, central to Faulkner's artistic achievement. [p. 4]

"The process of developing the Negro as an integral part of his artistic vision," she maintains in her discussion of *The Sound and the Fury*, "leads Faulkner to a technical breakthrough in his fourth novel" (p. 69). Surely this is overkill—can't "The Negro," or history, or sex, or Freud, or Joyce, or whatever, be a topic worthy of serious consideration without making it the *center*, the end-all and be-all of everything in Faulkner's work? Davis quotes, with approval, Nancy Tischler's contention that "the Southern Writer has very little choice—if he is to write about the South, he must write about the Negro" (p. 25), a contention flatly and irrevocably contradicted by the examples of Eudora Welty, Flannery O'Connor, Walker Percy, Barry Hannah, and Andrew Lytle, to name a few southern writers who write about "The South" without writing about "The Negro"; to be sure, there are Negroes in these writers' works, but they can be said in no sense to be writing about "The Negro." Such reductiveness vitiates Davis's book throughout, in chapters on *The Sound and the Fury, Light in August, Absalom, Absalom!*, and a predictable final chapter called "Set Patterns: *Go Down, Moses* and Beyond."

Walter Taylor's book is, like Davis's, replete with errors—
from a whopper in the first four words of the first line on the
first page (a reference to Faulkner's book of poems *"A Green
Bow"*: the title is correctly cited on the facing page of
abbreviations, but the designation there of "Random House,
1929" as publisher and date misses the mark on both counts) to
the statement that Faulkner and Estelle were married in 1927,
when *Sartoris* was still in manuscript (they were married in
1929, after *Sartoris* had been published; in 1927 *Sartoris* was still
known as *Flags in the Dust*) and to a mysterious reference in the
bibliography to a University Press of Mississippi in
Binghamton, New York. Taylor's first two chapters, describing
the cultural milieu into which Faulkner was born and in which
his social consciousness was set, and Chapter 11, "Doing
Something About It," discussing Faulkner's 1950s public
pronouncements on racial matters, are very much worth
consulting. Beyond these, however, there is very little to be
gained.

The organizational focus of this book is indicated by its title.
Faulkner's life, as recorded in his novels, was his attempt to find,
to create, "A South" which he, as southerner, did not have to be
ashamed of:

I suggest that each novel about "the South" is an effort to achieve "the capture
of that world and the feeling of it," arguing that Faulkner's protagonists—
Bayard Sartoris, Quentin Compson, and Isaac McCaslin—are not so much
surrogates for Faulkner as they are representatives of possible responses to that
world, responses from which Faulkner's art is an effort to exorcise himself,
failures from which he frees himself in order to move on to the next vision.

Faulkner's career thus reveals an inner dynamic in which each work may be
seen as part of a progressive effort to imagine what "the South" might have
been, or might become, in both its benign and nightmarish aspects—and to
imagine a series of protagonists who cope, or fail to cope, with it. This
dynamic identifies a lifelong psychodrama that had its beginnings before
Faulkner's birth and, to the degree that we are still struggling to understand it,
has yet to end. It offers certain answers to the questions raised by the
phenomenon that we describe as Faulkner's career and hence to the riddle of
Faulkner's southernness. It is to that riddle that the present study is addressed.
[p.x]

Faulkner was, in the beginning, Taylor writes, a man who
"virtually idealized John Sartoris as the epitome of *noblesse
oblige*" (p. 123). Only by the time of *Go Down, Moses*, was he,

in creating Carothers McCaslin, "ready to face the worst
implications of slavery" (p. 124); Isaac McCaslin is the
culmination of his "struggles" "to create a hero who could
transcend his heritage" (p. 136). But there were "difficulties"
with *Go Down, Moses*, Taylor reveals, "of which Faulkner
seemed unaware" (p. 138), particularly in regard to Lucas
Beauchamp and Sam Fathers:

Lucas had defended his manhood as few blacks in his time were able to, and
now he exuded a mature self-respect. His strength reinforced Isaac's claim that
blacks are "better" and "stronger" than whites; and Lucas himself seemed to
illustrate Isaac's belief [and Faulkner's?] that blacks had "learned pride
through the endurance which survived the suffering" of slavery. The trouble
with Lucas was that his presence, like Sam's, created difficulties of which
Faulkner seemed unaware. If Lucas's "suffering" as a black had taught him
any "humility," it was not visible, nor did this arrogant old man show any
signs of "pity and tolerance and forebearance." Even less visible was any
dramatic evidence of that primitive purity Roth Edmonds thought he saw in
Lucas. Lucas might be "indifferent" to his white blood, but, like Sam, he never
thought about himself as a black; he thought of himself as an aristocrat
deprived of his heritage by the accident of black ancestry. [p. 138]

Even though his portrait of Lucas was "one of his finest,"
Faulkner just could not completely overcome his inbred and
inevictable white Mississippi racist mentality, which *will out*,
apparently, no matter what, and inadvertently undermined his
own best intentions in regard to Lucas by having the racist
effrontery to make Lucas, a black Mississippian in the first half
of the twentieth century, a son of slavery, uneducated,
untravelled, speak in dialect!

Lucas's portrait was one of his finest, and it promised a reinforcement of
Isaac's ideas that would compensate for Faulkner's failure with Sam's.
    The first impression that "The Fire and the Hearth" gave, however, made
Lucas no more than another black clown. Readers were apparently meant to
laugh at his way of speaking. A divorce was a "voce" for Lucas, and a bill of
sale, a "billy sale." Lucas was never shy about playing darky; trying to pin him
down, Roth Edmonds found, was impossible, for the old man "became not
Negro but nigger"—he became "not secret so much as impenetrable, not
servile and not effacing, but enveloping himself in an aura of timeless and
stupid impassivity almost like a smell." [p. 137][2]

Why the assumption that Faulkner "apparently" wanted readers
to ridicule Lucas for his dialect? Do we assume that Taylor
laughs at it, or did at first reading? There is plenty to laugh at

Lucas about—is his language part of that parcel? But we need not wonder at Faulkner's failure in these and other matters, since, as we learn from Taylor in his discussion of *Intruder in the Dust*, "Faulkner had never been a master at tying up the loose ends of his plots" anyway (p. 162). This statement, reflecting as it does (1) the critical naiveté underlying the book and (2) the failure of its author to come to grips with all the implications of the last quarter-century of Faulkner criticism, is indicative of the entire book.

Faulkner's Search for a South ends, of course, with *The Reivers*, and it is convenient for Taylor's thesis that Faulkner cooperated by dying when he did:

The Mississippi Faulkner had known might be disappearing, dominated by Vardaman-style racists—soon, perhaps, to be ground under by Puritan liberals from the North. But entering the threshold of old age, Faulkner had at least learned how to recover that world: he had learned how to love it without feeling responsible for its faults. No wonder Faulkner had not been ready quite yet to "break my pencil and stop." The mellow nostalgia of his "reminiscence" had given him that "answer to the human condition" that had eluded him so long; it had given him, at last, the South for which he had been searching. [pp. 196-97]

That's a lovely thought and a nice peroration, and, as Jake Barnes might put it, "Wouldn't it be pretty to think so?" But if Faulkner, as Taylor would have it, was searching for "a South" through his works, and if "The Negro Problem" is at the center of his concerns, why did he write *Pylon*? *The Wild Palms*? *A Fable*?, not to mention numerous short stories in which neither Negroes nor the South are remotely concerned? These are questions which do not appear to concern Taylor, but they seem to me very much worth asking and worth trying to answer before we can hope to make any sense out of the entire *oeuvre*. Curiously, Taylor does not discuss the magnificent "Mississippi," a piece which seems to me absolutely central to any understanding of Faulkner's attitudes toward his homeland. Nor does he discuss any of the novels of the Snopes Trilogy, a series which seems to me more completely and deliberately *about* "The South" than anything else he wrote. Or perhaps this is not curious at all; perhaps it merely illustrates how completely Taylor means "race" when he says "South."

No question has been more troublesome in Faulkner studies than that of Faulkner's "southernness"; no question has been more completely responsible for misreadings of his work and of his life, misreadings which come equally from southern apologists who believe that Faulkner's strengths as a writer are a direct result of his southern heritage—the oral tradition, the sense of history, the agrarian culture, etc.—and from southern detractors who believe (1) that his genius emerges in spite of his southern heritage—racial turmoil and its accompanying heritage of guilt, rural backwardness, parochialism, etc.—and (2) that the ineluctable intellectual limitations of his "southernness" account for most of the perceived weaknesses in his work.[3] In its baldest terms, the question has perhaps more to do with politics than with literary criticism, as if there were some sort of need on the part of the apologists to offer Faulkner up as a justification or validation of certain qualities (racism not among them, of course) that are putatively unique to the "southern heritage" (he is one of us, and we are proud), and on the part of the detractors to find some way to "handle" Faulkner: it is, these argue, remarkable that he transcended his heritage to the degree that he did, but he is, after all, a white Mississippian, and it is unreasonable (isn't it?) to expect even a genius to transcend everything implied by *that* soubriquet (he wanted so badly to be one of us, but——).

I am, of course, describing the problem at its extremes; but these extremes do not, I believe, overstate the degree to which reactions to Faulkner's fiction have been colored by our responses to America's sorry and troublesome history of racial and regional antagonisms, or the degree to which those reactions are focussed on "The South" as symbol of all those antagonisms. And there indeed is part of the rub, since the insistence upon focussing solely upon the South's racial problems begs serious questions about racial antagonisms in *all* parts of the country (perhaps more subtle but, as Ralph Ellison's Invisible Man learned, no less insidious for being more hidden), and about a context for discussion of these problems which would include such racial problems as, for example, anti-Semitism, which abounds in the works of many major American writers. But let those questions remain begged here.

Part of the problem, of course, lies precisely in the power of the word "racism" to alter our capacity to judge, to discriminate, to criticize, or even to think clearly about so many political and social and personal issues. Even the otherwise most objective critic can be paralyzed by the fear of having the word "racist" hurled at him, since that is an accusation against which there simply is no defense; or, rather, no defense which can meliorate it, since in the eyes of the accuser, the accusation itself is at the same time judge, jury, and sentence; and so it (the accusation) is the first resort of the coward. After it is made, or implied, or even just feared, all dialogue is over, over really before it began, since the accuser was not interested in *dia*logue in the first place.

This statement obviously involves the immediate and, to some, more pertinent question: Can Faulkner, a white southerner, write about Negroes as human beings? My answer is an equivocal yes—equivocal because the question itself marks the limits to which any answer is sufficient. Can any writer imagine himself into the skin of another? It is fair—or relevant—to suggest analogically that I, at any rate, have no trouble with Edith Wharton's treatment of Newland Archer, with Willa Cather's treatment of Jim Burden, or with the numerous male characters of Eudora Welty and Flannery O'Connor? Are cultural differences between Blacks and Whites more pronounced—more important?—than sexual differences? Perhaps so. I, a WASP male, and a southerner, too, don't know. My answer to the question at the beginning of this paragraph is equivocal, too, because I do not think we have yet looked closely enough at black characters in Faulkner to be able to tell whether they are human beings rather than abstractions of one sort or another. They have generally been considered either as victims of white oppression or as representative of and so models for some quality of the "old verities" that his white Mississippi folks, because of their skins (white except for their necks), do not, but should, have. Critics wanting to find in Faulkner a concrete denunciation of racism, a transcendance of his heritage which would make his genius palatable, eagerly accepted Nancy Mannigoe in *Requiem for a Nun* (1951) as a sort of post-Dilsey savior who did more than merely endure: she actively and self-sacrificially intervened to save the white world from itself. Thus critics refused to look beyond those comfortable nearly allegorical categories to see that *Requiem* was a far more complex book than that sort of reading would allow and, worse, they failed to see that Nancy Mannigoe was a far more complex, interesting, and tragic human being than the savior they saw her as. This view seems to me prompted by a form of racism far more insidious than outright hatred because, though it does so with a smile, it just as surely dehumanizes all Negro characters. It is in some ways even more offensive than outright open and aboveboard redneck racism because it is invariably couched in pious truisms which force any Negro in Faulkner to be "The Negro" before he or she is anything else, and, because of its implied absolute sympathy with the Negro's plight, arrogates to itself an understanding of "The Negro" it denies to anybody who does not share its political or social sensibility. This is precisely the form of racism practised by Gavin Stevens in "Go Down, Moses." How many critics have noted Stevens' failure in this regard, and how many, attributing Stevens' failure to Faulkner, have believed that Faulkner did not understand the white man he had created?

Part of what seems to me so astonishing about Faulkner's depiction of black characters is his steadfast refusal to sentimentalize them; it is a significant part of the power and complexity of his mature fiction that his Negro characters are not accorded any sort of special treatment: they are always individualized, always people "in conflict with their environment" (an environment, to be sure, dominated by white people) and, most importantly, they are people who like his white characters must live in the real world and must, also like his white characters, bear the moral responsibility for their actions.

What makes "That Evening Sun" remarkable, for example, is not alone its depiction of Mr. Compson's abandonment of his responsibility to Nancy (see Taylor, p. 56) or of the Compson children's inability to understand what is happening, but rather the intensity and the complexity of the relationship between

Jesus and Nancy, which is thwarted by a variety of forces, some of which they have no control over, others of which they do. How victimized are Nancy and Jesus? Nancy is pregnant: by a white man? Apparently so, though there is no proof; Jesus certainly thinks so. Has Nancy been raped, forced? Apparently not, since she has at least one "customer," Mr. Stovall. Taylor tells us bluntly that Stovall had "made her his whore and got her pregnant" (p. 55), though there is no direct evidence in the story to support such a conclusion. Is Nancy here, as in *Requiem*, a "casual prostitute"? Does she entertain Mr. Stovall—and others?—for money to stay alive? for her own pleasure? in retaliation for Jesus's philandering? When Mr. Compson tries to comfort her by telling her that Jesus won't hurt her because he has probably "got another wife by now and forgot all about you," Nancy erupts with a macabre fantasy that surely reflects her agitation over her pregnancy: "If he has," she says, venomously, "I better not find out about it . . . . I'd stand there right over them, and every time he wropped her, I'd cut that arm off. I'd cut his head off and I'd slit her belly and I'd shove—".[4] Neither she nor her creator subscribe to the myths of sexual casualness among Negroes; in this story, at least, Jesus's love and sexual fidelity clearly are important to Nancy.

Is Jesus, by the same token, more outraged at a social structure which allows a white man to come into his house, for sexual and other purposes, but refuses him the corresponding right to the white man's house, or only at Nancy, for cuckolding him in the first place and then for compounding the cuckolding by publicly humiliating him when she attacked Mr. Stovall in front of the bank? Clearly his outrage and his frustration spring from very complex combinations of both of these things, and obviously there are significant ways in which he and Nancy are helpless victims of circumstance. Jesus is injured, yet impotent to strike back at the white world he blames, rightly or wrongly, for his troubles; so he takes all his frustrations out on Nancy, who is no less a victim of those same forces than he. He strikes out at the only thing he thinks he *can* strike out at, the woman he loves. Is that his only recourse? Nancy, for her part, strikes rather at herself—out of what combination of guilt or self-reproach—when she attempts suicide in the jail, and one can only assume that she got exactly what she wanted from Mr. Stovall: surely she knew that under the circumstances that good banker was more likely to beat her than pay her. Perhaps she thought her own pain, perhaps her death, was a small price to pay for such a public punishment of Stovall. Or was she simply so high on drugs she didn't know what she was doing?

But the chemistry of our deep sympathy with Nancy is seriously altered if we consider how dangerous it is for her to take the Compson children to her cabin to protect her: does she really think they can protect her? If Jesus decides to kill her, as she believes he will, does she think he will save the little ones? Even if she does believe Jesus will spare them, it is by no means responsible for her to try to hide behind them. Does she realize the danger, at any level? If, as some have suggested, Mr. Compson is the father of her child and so the author of her misery, does Nancy deliberately, consciously or unconsciously, put them in harm's way to avenge herself? This is the same Nancy Mannigoe, be it recalled, who in *Requiem for a Nun* murders an infant child of the people she works for, in what seems to me, at least on one level, a deliberate act of revenge.[5] It is very much worth suggesting, again, that if Faulkner had made the Nancy Mannigoe of *Requiem* white instead of black, critical reactions to her heinous act would have been very different. Perhaps the same is true of the Nancy of "That Evening Sun."

I do not know the answers to the questions posed in the preceding paragraphs, and I do not believe that the story itself provides answers. But I insist that the story *asks* these and other questions, and that much of the story's power is directly related to the complexity of the relationships between Nancy and Jesus, complexities which challenge the stereotypes and which force readers to the astonishing knowledge that Nancy's and Jesus's feelings are, well, *white*: when what readers are really astonished at, even if they do not know it, is that they recognize those feelings as *human*.

The same sorts of questions may legitimately be asked about the black Gibsons in *The Sound and the Fury*. In spite of a lot of lip service to the notion that Dilsey is no "plaster saint"

(Brooks's phrase), she has in fact been perceived and treated as a saint. Of course she looks good compared to the Compsons, and we cannot ever forget her incredible fortitude or Faulkner's lifelong admiration of her. I am far from trying to argue that Dilsey is not an admirable creation; but it will be useful to remind ourselves that Faulkner just *did not operate* by creating allegorical figures who were all "good" or all "evil," and it is at the very least critically irresponsible not to see even Dilsey, long-suffering, patient Dilsey, in all her magnificent complexity.

Into one of those interminable "quoils" the Compsons seem always to be having—this one over whether or not Caddy's baby should be accepted in the house after Caddy has sent her home—Dilsey peremptorily inserts herself: "And whar else do she belong?" she says. "Who else gwine raise her 'cep me? Aint I raised eve'y one of y'all?"[6] No one can argue with her on this point; Caroline and Jason Compson have long since abdicated their parental responsibilities. But however accurate it is, Jason *fils*'s retort should give the attentive reader pause: "And a damn fine job you made of it," he says (*SF*, p. 246). This is, granted, Jason speaking; but even Jason, as many commentators have been willing to note, is capable of truth occasionally. His comment is, at any rate, an interesting one, and even if we suspect Jason's motive in making the comment, the implication of the remark—that the Compson children have not, to put it mildly, turned out well—is very much to the point. It is, of course, unfair to blame Dilsey for their failures; but it is very interesting indeed to note that Dilsey should want to take credit for and even pride in such a dubious achievement.

Given her desire, then, to claim the *Compson* children, is it fair to ask what kind of job Dilsey has done with her *own*? We are never given much of a chance to see her at work rearing Frony and T. P. and Versh, but we do see her dealing with her grandson Luster, and I'm afraid the evidence of the novel suggests that Dilsey is not very grandmotherly when it comes to Luster. Indeed, she shows a decided partiality for Benjy and Miss Quentin—for her white "children," that is—which actually works against Luster, her own flesh and blood. She is *never* sympathetic with Luster, who seems to me in some ways the most put-upon, the most victimized, character in the novel; she never gives him any sense that he has any lot in life but to take care of Benjy. Even though she is ready to take up the cudgel against Jason in defense of Miss Quentin, she is not ready to do so to defend Luster. She is present in the kitchen throughout the scene in which Jason torments poor Luster with those extra tickets to the carnival; she does not, however, do one thing to help him. She does, of course, hector Jason from the sidelines; but she makes no move to get between him and Luster, as she gets physically between Jason and Miss Quentin. And she in fact contributes to Luster's misery by blaming *him* for losing the quarter in the first place, and, in the second, for standing there and letting Jason torture him. What grandmother, indeed what human being outside Jason, would not just simply give Luster another quarter and rescue him from Jason's insane cruelty? Dilsey does indeed finally tell Luster she'll get him another quarter from Frony (p. 318), but she does not: we learn later that it is Miss Quentin who gives him the quarter. In stark contrast, by her own testimony Dilsey has scrimped and saved her own money in order to buy the ingredients for Benjy's birthday cake—a cake, not incidentally, of which Luster, whose mouth aches for it, is allowed only a very small piece, while Benjy, who can't tell the difference between good cake and wood chips, is given the gigantic portion. Would readers and critics tolerate this type of behavior from Caroline Compson? Where, when, does Dilsey direct *any* of the love, compassion, honor, sacrifice, and pity—for which she so often stands as the prime example in Faulkner's work—toward her own family? Are Negro parents any less responsible to their own children, for being black? Can Nancy's helpless, hopeless, "I aint nothing but a nigger" excuse Dilsey too?

One can also note several things about Dilsey's trip to church that have more or less been obscured by readers' responses to her vision, as she walks home, of "de first en de last," of "de beginnin, en . . . de endin" (*SF*, p. 371). Dilsey goes to church regally dressed, in a maroon cape and purple gown and wearing "soiled white elbow-length gloves" (*SF*, p. 358). Perhaps this is condescension on Faulkner's part, perhaps his stooping to the stereotyped Negro's love of gaudiness: there is no way to know about that. What we can suggest, however, is that her dress is part of a pattern that emerges when we view Dilsey, in this scene, for the first time in a relationship to her peers— that is, to other Negroes—rather than in a relationship just to whites; the juxtaposition is startling. In the black community she is imperious, conscious of herself as a *grande dame*, and she makes the most of it: "And steadily the older people speaking to Dilsey, though, unless they were quite old, Dilsey *permitted Frony to respond*" (*SF*, p. 364, my emphasis). The scene at the end of the sermon is often quoted as a powerful index to the meaning of Rev. Shegog's sermon and so of the novel. Framing the scene, however, and part of it, is a brief conservation with Frony, about Dilsey's appearance:

> Dilsey made no sound, her face did not quiver as the tears took their sunken and devious courses, walking with her head up, making no effort to dry them away even.
> "Whyn't you quit dat, mammy?" Frony said. "Wid all dese people lookin. We be passin white folks soon."
> "I've seed de first en de last," Dilsey said. "Never you mind me."
> "First en last whut?" Frony said.
> "Never you mind," Dilsey said. "I seed de beginnin, en now I sees de endin."
> Before they reached the street, though, she stopped and lifted her skirt and dried her eyes on the hem of her topmost underskirt. Then they went on. [*SF*, p. 371]

The "though" in the final paragraph here, and in the preceding quotation, along with the imperiousness with which she disdains to speak to any but the eldest Negroes, "permitting" her minion Frony to handle that onerous chore, suggests that Dilsey's stand as regards her demeanour with members of her own race is considerably different from that regarding her white superiors. Clearly, behavior like this in a white person, in Mrs. Compson, say, would in the first instance be seen unmistakably as *hauteur*, plain rudeness, and in the second as pure hypocrisy. Why have these qualities never been recognized, or at least admitted, in Dilsey? Is it racist to suggest that Dilsey, too, can be guilty of overweening pride? Conversely, is it racism, on Faulkner's part, to have created a Negro character with moral flaws? Or on the white reader's for having noticed them? Have I imposed these flaws on Dilsey? Is she, in the book's, Quentin's, terms, an "obverse reflection" of the white people she lives among?

Further: is Quentin's observation in any way historically accurate? Does it in any way reflect historical reality for any period in this country's history? If we object to Faulkner's portraits of Simon Strother and Caspey in *Flags in the Dust* as stereotyped darky clowns, we must, it seems to me, argue that there never were Negroes who behaved as they did—no Simon Strother puttin' on ol' massa and no Caspey, returned from World War I bragging about his experiences and returned to his "place" by the likes of Colonel Sartoris. Can we argue that Caspey and Jason never existed? Can we argue that individual Negroes have never been irresponsible, have never *looked like* the stereotype even if they were deliberately putting on the mask for their own purposes? Have no Negroes ever played to their white bosses' prejudices either to save their skins or merely to keep their jobs? Is there no coin for verisimilitude, much less historical accuracy? Would we, as some tried to do a couple of decades ago, expunge the phrase "Nigger Jim" from new editions of *Huckleberry Finn*? Should we then revise Faulkner to make him more up-to-date, even as the doctors of the TV series *M*A*S*H*, practicing in Korea in the early 1950s, nevertheless have all the "proper" 1970s and 80s attitudes regarding blacks, homosexuals, women's rights, and war? That is, can we impose a 1970s and 80s social mentality upon folks of a bygone era who were simply trying to cope, the best of them, in the best way they knew how?

Was William Faulkner a racist? The question prompts more questions than answers. If by racist one means hatred of blacks, one can say, I think, clearly no: Faulkner seems never to have been any more intolerant of blacks than of whites. If, however, by racist one means a belief in the inferiority of blacks, one could probably answer that question with a Yes, but only by citing Faulkner's numerous invocations of historical, rather than biological, circumstances as being responsible for Negroes' social and economic and cultural differences. Is it racist to talk about facts? To describe Negroes or whites or Jews in their actual historical circumstances? Are the social and economic circumstances of Negroes in Faulkner significantly different from those of the poor whites in his work, or those in *Let Us Now Praise Famous Men*, for example? Was it racist to say, in 1950, that Negroes must work harder than whites in order to bring themselves up to the point where they can begin to take full part in American society? Or to aver that 300 years ago Negroes were eating rotten hippo meat in Africa, if he believed that was a fact? Faulkner said, in 1955, that if push came to shove he would fight in the streets to protect Mississippi from Northern invasion. Does that statement, made apparently while drinking, represent his *true* feelings about Negroes, reveal him for what, at bottom, he *really* is, a white Mississippian? Do his *true* feelings, then, cancel out a decade during which he spoke out against injustice in the public forum which he, as an artist, detested?

The fact is that William Faulkner did the best he could, and what he did was by no means bad or ineffective. Even if in his early work some of his generalizations about Negro intelligence, Negro odor, and Negro physical characteristics offend—even if, that is, he seems to us insensitive about such matters—we should not make more of such issues than can reasonably be made: clearly he was a product, in many ways, of his time and his place—as who of us isn't? But don't the works, even the early "Sunset," show him to be sympathetic to the individual Negro? And doesn't his concern with the problem express itself more eloquently and more profoundly in *Light in August, Absalom, Absalom!,* and *Go Down, Moses* than in any other book, by any other author, written anywhere, at any time, ever? What more could be expected of an artist?

If in his public declarations during the 1950s he expressed moderation, he was prominent on the firing line with other white moderates of his day. And even if black leaders were right in perceiving the cautious white moderates of the day as part of the problem rather than as part of the solution, let it at least not be forgotten that Faulkner made his public statements at a time in Mississippi when it was very dangerous to do so, and did so even though it cost him the contumely of his family and of his community and of his entire state. But he made them: he argued for equality of opportunity on all possible idealistic and pragmatic grounds. His rhetoric was, however, not designed to convince Northern black leaders or white critics of his good intentions toward "the cause," but rather, more pragmatically, to try to persuade his fellow southerners to do what was necessary. He did not waste time, in his public speeches, exhorting whites to give up their prejudices and love all Negroes; he knew that to be an idealistic but ineffective way to accomplish necessary and immediate ends. He instead tried to convince southerners to change their behavior, not their feelings: social equality is necessary not just because it is the *right* thing, but because it is the *practical* thing. He argued this, of course, out of a good deal of regional pride: the practical effects of continued southern insistence on racial segregation would be to invite outside interference. I suspect that his State's Rights stand to Russell Howe had less to do with racial bias than with a real fear of a second Civil War: there is no evidence that "State's Rights" was for him, as it was and continues to be for many, a code term for racial oppression.

Again, if he appears to the eyes of 1984 a "moderate," he certainly seemed to the eyes of white southerners of the 1950s a flaming, an absolutely blazing, liberal: "Weeping Willie Faulkner" he was called by at least one irate Memphian in more than one letter to the *Commercial Appeal* protesting his public statements. But even if it could be proven that in his very heart of hearts he was in fact a raging racist, that like his "southern" and "Mississippi" brothers and sisters of the stereotype he imbibed from his mother's milk an absolute hatred of all people with black skins, why can't we nevertheless still give him credit for the love and compassion and understanding with which he treated his black characters, his white ones too; for the courage with which he spoke out, publicly, in order to try to correct a situation which his intellect, if not his passions, found intolerable; and for the financial sacrifice he made in establishing with his Nobel Prize money—a "dedication for the money part of it commensurate with the purpose and significance of its origin"—a scholarship fund to help needy

Negro students go to college? One of his black characters opines that "Quality ain't *is*, it's *does*." The same is true, I submit, of racism: however ingrained they are, whatever their sources, whatever their objects, our prejudices, and their capacity to do mischief, can only be measured by what they force us to *do*. By this standard, William Faulkner measures up pretty well.

One more thing: "Pantaloon in Black" is, for many reasons, one of Faulkner's greatest stories. Most critics have, in my judgment, misunderstood it not because of Faulkner's treatment of Rider, but because of their inability to see the deputy of the second part of that story as anything but a stereotypical Southern Lawman, red neck and all. He is, of course, a redneck deputy, a southerner with all the prejudices, racial and otherwise, associated with that "type." Faulkner deliberately draws him that way. But if that is all he is, then "Pantaloon" is an unsuccessful story which rather clumsily juxtaposes the moving story of Rider's love for Manny, his grief, his suicidal murder of the white man, and then his lynching, with the story of the redneck deputy and his crass, unloving wife: the ironies are cheap and much too heavy to be effective.

Beyond those ironies, however, lies another story. Why does the deputy continue to tell his wife the story of Rider's lynching, in complete detail, long after she has made it clear, both by her indifference and by her general attitude, that she doesn't give one solitary damn about Rider, or about the deputy either, for that matter? One can only conclude that he isn't talking to her at all, but rather to himself. He has just experienced something, Rider's griefstricken and doomed humanness, which nothing in his background has prepared him for, and he is clumsily trying to talk it out, trying to explain to his own mind, using a completely inadequate redneck vocabulary and conceptual system, something it cannot quite grasp. He is trying to understand his actual experience of Rider, which has made that magnificent black man something devastatingly different from the stereotype he has come to think he knows.

That deputy seems to me, then, to reflect Faulkner's own position, as artist and citizen, far more acutely than, say, Quentin Compson in *Absalom, Absalom!*, certainly more acutely than Gavin Stevens, the smooth-talking intellectual, with whose voice Faulkner is most often identified. Michael Millgate and others have long argued that there are no answers in Faulkner's novels; their dialectical nature precludes answers, while of course they thrive on the questions. Like Faulkner, then, that deputy is at least asking the right questions. Thus he is far more educable than the more highly educated Gavin Stevens, whose presence at the end of *Go Down, Moses* serves, for the unwary, to muddy the racial waters of that novel. For with all the best intentions to be genuinely helpful, to demonstrate that he, at any rate, is civilized, Stevens is completely blind to Molly's real humanity. Most critics have, of course, noticed this, and many have thought Stevens' paternalism a weakness in the novel (how could Faulkner have done such a thing, unless there be sympathy with and approval of what Stevens is doing?). But I would suggest that Stevens is here set in opposition to the deputy. Both become privy to grief, to human passion, where they had least expected it, in a Negro. The deputy tries to understand it; Stevens thinks he does understand it, is arrogantly sure, in fact, that he understands "The Negro" completely. So if Stevens, with his liberal education, his broader cultural boundaries, is more likely to be among those in the forefront of civil rights "progress"—i.e. the outward and obviously very important manifestations of equality like voting rights and educational opportunities—it is nevertheless much more likely to be that deputy who will, one of these days, be able to meet black men and women as simple, complex, human beings. I do not think that Faulkner in either his fiction or his non-fiction would have denied the importance of either of those fronts in the war on racial discrimination. But I suspect he would hold that the surer, the long-range solution to racial problems, if there is one, lies in the direction that deputy is facing, even if he hasn't yet begun to move forward.

Notes

1. See also Lee Jenkins, *Faulkner and Black-White Relations: A Psychoanalytic Approach* (New York: Columbia Univ. Press, 1981); Jean Rouberol, *L'esprit du Sud dans l'Oeuvre de Faulkner* (Paris: Didier Erudition, Publications de la Sorbonne Littératures 13, 1982); Erskine Peters, *William*

Faulkner: The Yoknapatawpha World and Black Being (Darby, Pa.: Norwood Editions, 1983); Eric J. Sundquist, *Faulkner: The House Divided* (Baltimore: Johns Hopkins Univ. Press, 1983). Other, earlier, works which might also be consulted in this context are Charles H. Nilon's early monograph *Faulkner and the Negro*, University of Colorado Studies Series in Language and Literature No. 8 (Boulder: Univ. of Colorado Press, 1962); Elizabeth M. Kerr, *Yoknapatawpha: Faulkner's "Little Postage Stamp of Native Soil"* (New York: Fordham Univ. Press, 1969); Charles Peavy, *Go Slow Now: Faulkner and the Race Question* (Eugene: Univ. of Oregon Press, 1971); and Myra Jehlen, *Class and Character in Faulkner's South* (New York: Columbia Univ. Press, 1976).

2. Taylor also faults Faulkner's use of dialect in *The Sound and the Fury*, particularly in Reverend Shegog's Easter Sunday sermon: "It was one thing to suggest Shegog was rejecting 'civilized' sophisms for 'primitive' faith when his voice 'became negroid'; but in *The Sound and the Fury* the signal that Shegog was becoming 'negroid' came when he began to talk in dialect. The use of dialect was not the problem . . . . The problem was the way Faulkner used dialect . . . . Faulkner had given Shegog a moving sermon; but those *de's* and *dem dar's* operated on another level, calling attention to themselves, instead of to Shegog's words. Dilsey's speeches revealed similar problems" (pp. 48-49).

3. The classic statement of this attitude is Edmund Wilson's review of *Intruder in the Dust*, "William Faulkner's Reply to the Civil Rights Program," *New Yorker*, 23 October 1948, p. 121 ff. Nor should anybody miss Eudora Welty's equally classic reply, "Department of Amplification," *New Yorker*, 1 January 1949, pp. 50-51.

4. *Collected Stories* (New York: Random House, 1950), p. 295.

5. See my *Faulkner's* Requiem for a Nun: *A Critical Study* (Bloomington: Indiana Univ. Press, 1981).

6. *The Sound and the Fury* (New York: Cape & Smith, 1929), p. 246.

Shadows of Shadows: Biblical Typology and English Literature

George P. Landow

Paul J. Koshin. *Typologies in England, 1650-1820*. Princeton: Princeton University Press, 1982. xvii, 437 pp. 34 illustrations.

Herbert L. Sussman. *Fact into Figure: Typology in Carlyle, Ruskin, and the Pre-Raphaelite Brotherhood*. Columbus: Ohio State University Press, 1979. xix, 158 pp. 40 illustrations.

Leslie Tannenbaum. *Biblical Tradition in Blake's Early Prophecies: The Great Code of Art*. Princeton: Princeton University Press, 1982. xiii, 373 pp.

Ever since William Madsen and Northrop Frye discovered the importance of biblical typology to the study of Milton more than two decades ago, literary scholars have paid increasing attention to the way secular English and American culture has drawn upon this interpretive method and its corollary views of symbolism. This scholarly interest in typological symbolism has produced some exciting results, particularly in seventeenth-century studies. The writings of Barbara K. Lewalski, for example, have introduced new readings of individual poems and also new conceptions of poetic genres and literary interrelations. As scholars and critics with widely differing interests begin to consider the impact of this exetical and symbolic mode upon secular culture, the question arises how best to define and study it. By now all of us have probably encountered books or essays in which the author, having heard of typology, simply applies generalized notions of it to whatever work is under consideration. Others, we know, automatically infer that typological practice in one age, say, that of Milton, must obtain in any other. Fortunately, the three books I shall discuss in this review all relate typology to secular culture with more critical and scholarly rigor than that, but their varying approaches nonetheless raise crucial issues about the scholarly investigation of a set of related phenomena that are particularly important to understanding the writings of Donne, Herbert, Milton, Dryden, Blake, Ruskin, Rossetti, and Browning and the paintings of Memling, Van Eyck, Michaelangelo, and the English Pre-Raphaelites.

Paul Korshin's approach is to formulate a major overview of biblical typology, its secularized extensions, and their effect upon literature between 1650 and 1820. "My focus, the Enlightenment," he tells us, "means that I shall study the second rise of typology, the period of its first great secularization, and the phenomena in intellectual history that bring about these changes" (p. 36). *Typologies in England, 1650-1820* begins with an introduction concerning what Korshin terms "The Typological Propensity," by which he means the human tendency to seek signs and predictions of future events. A second brief chapter, "The Possibilities and Limits of Typology," sketches the history of this exegetical mode, though it does not define the orthodox or theological mode in any depth, and the following chapter on "Figural Change and the Survival of Typological Tradition" argues that although this symbolical mode came under attack in the period Korshin discusses, it survived in looser secularized forms because it provided "a logical imagistic system" (p. 65), "helped justify pagan symbolism," and "accorded so perfectly with the popular imagistic games of drawing parallels and making analogies" (p. 66). The next two chapters, "Typology as System" and "The Development of Abstracted Typology" examine the transference of structures originally derived from biblical interpretation to other, often secular, concerns, and with varying degrees of success the sixth through ninth chapters apply this general notion of abstracted typology to myth, satire, fiction, and prophecy. A final chapter on what he calls "The Typology of Everyday Life" stretches Korshin's notion of typology to its limit by arguing that many authors in secular genres attributed prefigurative qualities to many aspects of everyday life.

Korshin's volume provides a needed survey of a large body of difficult materials. Furthermore, his conception of abstracted typologies is a useful one, and he not only displays great ingenuity in seeking out the possible appearances of such secularized applications of biblical symbolism but he also perceives their complex relation to other patently nonreligious concerns. Drawing upon earlier students of typology, he is scrupulous about giving credit to them.

Although he succumbs to almost no fashionable jargon, Korshin has written what is essentially a structuralist approach to his subject, and his work displays the expected strengths and weaknesses of such a method. In other words, *Typologies in England, 1650-1820* works best when handling broad movements, patterns, and structures and relating them to each other, but despite its length the volume often seems curiously undetailed and abstract. I must admit that my reactions here may well be a matter of taste or even prejudice, since in my own work on the effects of scriptural typology upon secular Victorian culture I have chosen to examine both general conceptions of typology as symbolic and interpretive modes and also the specific ways in which exegetes, painters, and secular authors have employed them. My basic working assumption— which I suppose Professor Korshin, a student of the Augustan age, might term a Romantic prejudice in favor of particularity— is that acts of scholarly recovery have best chance of success when one tests them by investigating specific examples in detail. In this kind of an endeavour, I would argue, one must define precisely what orthodox scriptural typology meant in a particular age before examining the process of abstraction and secularization. Next, one must examine specific uses of individual biblical types, such as the directions for the Levitical sacrifices or Moses leading the Israelites forth from Eygpt, and then determine how they become applied in abstracted or secularized forms.

As I understand it, biblical typology has several defining claims: (1) that the individual types are each divinely ordained, not only because God placed them in his Scriptures but also more importantly because he made them prefigure Christ and the Christian dispensation; (2) nonetheless, despite the fact that individual types, such as David or Joseph, bear the stamp of God, they have their own historicity and within human time they have just as much reality as the beings or phenomena they prefigure; (3) types always prefigure a later antitype, which is said therefore to fulfill or complete the type (one important point here is that types do not in any way *cause* the antitype—Moses, Joseph, and the scapegoat do not cause Christ—but rather types are signifying elements in a complex gospel scheme or economy which God created to instruct fallen man); (4) strictly speaking, all types are situational, that is, Moses does not prefigure Christ but Moses leading the Israelites, the children of God, out of Eygptian slavery, guiding them through the desert, and giving them the moral law prefigures Christ's higher version of these actions. Authors secularize, abstract, or apply such biblical typology by manipulating any one of its essential elements, and perhaps the best means of charting such changes in this symbolic mode is by observing how its numerous elements vary.

Korshin, who concerns himself almost entirely with the predictive aspects of typology, pays little attention to any other, and he so concentrates upon loose or abstracted forms of typology, that he frequently empties the term of its imaginative force. For example, he argues that what have always been called stock or humor characters are properly considered typological because in a sense they predict how they will act later in the novel: "They are not so much *prefigurative personages* as they are *predictive structures*, a knowledge of which serves to foreshadow information about the novel to its audience. The *character type*, then, becomes a standard eighteenth-century fictive entity whose audience would probably understand without special authorial commentary. Such developments in the novel are a principal reason why abstracted typology flourished after 1700" (p. 114). I am not certain if one achieves anything of major critical value by so terming such forms of characterization "typological," and I am not sure precisely because, as other reviewers have pointed out, *Typologies in England, 1650-1820* does not offer any new readings of the novels it discusses or markedly change the way we experience them. Barbara Lewalski's investigations of typology in Donne, Milton, and other major seventeenth-century poets lead directly to new ways of looking at their works and the relations between them. Korshin's elaborate discussions of abstracted and secularized typologies unfortunately do not seem to lead to any such major discoveries, revaluations, or connections. One of the reasons I often find this learned volume a bit diffuse lies in the fact that instances of specific types do not illustrate its many careful definitions and distinctions.

A second serious problem with *Typologies in England, 1650-1820* stems directly from its initial assumption that the history of typology from the Restoration onwards is essentially the history of its dissolution, abstraction, and secularization. Beginning from this premise, Korshin assumes that one does not have to look at the changes taking place in scriptural typology during this period. According to him, "in the middle of the seventeenth century in England, typology slowly began to change, to become secular in its applications, and to involve genres of literature other than the strictly religious" (p. 5). He is correct as far as he goes, but unfortunately he does not take into account the crucial fact that the evangelical revival which began in the 1770s produced another major revival of complex, sophisticated applications of scriptural typology, and this revival greatly complicates the phenomena he tries to analyze, not least because late eighteenth- and nineteenth-century scriptural expositors and poets popularized new, yet orthodox, readings of individual types. For example, Moses striking the rock, which only becomes a particularly popular or commonplace type with the evangelical revival, frequently exchanges its traditional Pauline interpretation as a type of baptism for one as a type of the Crucifixion or of the believer's conversion experience. By ignoring the evangelical revival, which in some cases applied typology differently than did earlier exegetes, Korshin produces a very skewed picture of his subject. In fact, he resembles an observer who assiduously plots the effect of a stone dropped into a pond but has not noticed the impact of a second one: he accurately observes the splash made by the first stone, after which he carefully traces the ever widening circles that ripple outward from its point of impact, but failing to notice the splash of a second stone, he does not take into account a second set of ripples which sometimes magnify and somes intefere with the first set. Up to a certain point, such an observer's charts possess exact accuracy, but as the second set of unnoticed ripples have their effect, his partial observations, which necessarily become less reliable, begin to attribute to one stimulus the effects created by the other.

Korshin's method does not derive from any ignorance of this later revival of orthodox typological exegetics. When Professor Korshin delivered his paper on extended typologies at the 1974 Princeton conference on typology and literature, he assumed that orthodox typology ceased with the end of the seventeenth century, but since that time numerous works pointing to very different conclusions have appeared, and he himself cites these works. Korshin, who scrupulously acknowledges the work of others, advises the reader about studies of nineteenth-century typology both in his notes and in the bibliographical essay which concludes his volume. Nonetheless, although he cites such works, he does not take them into account in any meaningful way and he holds to his original emphasis on abstracted typology in isolation from the later eighteenth-century revival of interest in typology.

Unfortunately, Korshin's dual emphasis upon the dissolution of biblical typology and broad structures leads him to see little need either to define this hermeneutic method precisely or to examine closely the changing interpretations of individual scriptural types. The shortcomings of his method appear with particular clarity when he comments upon Blake, whom he discusses in his chapter on typology and prophecy. Despite some interesting observations on the general subject of eighteenth-century attitudes towards prophecy, his chapter never manages to establish any more than that Blake employs various forms of abstracted typology. In contrast, Leslie Tannenbaum's *Biblical Tradition in Blake's Early Prophecies: The Great Code of Art* succeeds in showing how Blake reworked various scriptural modes in order to create a new kind of poetry, and it succeeds precisely both because it defines traditions with care and because it argues from a wealth of individual examples as well as from more general patterns.

According to Tannenbaum, "we cannot talk meaningfully about Blake and the Bible without talking about Blake and Biblical tradition" (p. ix), and since he rightly observes that an "adequate account of eighteenth-century hermeneutics, exegesis, and biblical criticism has yet to be written" (p. 8), he sets out to provide an excellent summary one in his first chapter, "Blake and Biblical Tradition." Succeeding chapters cover the more specific influence upon Blake's poetry of Old Testament prophecy, the figurative language of Scripture, and scriptural typology, after which he devotes clear, strongly argued individual chapters each to Blake's *America, Europe, The Song of Los, The Book of Urizen, The Book of Ahania,* and *The Book of Los.* Adding the results of his own sound research to the works of many earlier scholars and critics, Tannenbaum convincingly demonstrates that "Blake's canon *was* an intentional imaginative recreation of the Bible, conditioned by his recognition of traditional interpretations of Scripture and by his own reworking of those interpretations, his reading of the Bible 'in its infernal or diabolical sense,'" and therefore to understand what he was trying to do, one must first perceive that "much of the shape and meaning of Blake's work is determined not only by his borrowings from the Bible but also by his borrowings and deviations from traditional uses and interpretations of that book" (p. 3). By looking closely at the various late-eighteenth-century approaches to Scripture, Tannenbaum clearly demonstrates Blake's dependence upon tradition and then shows with admirable clarity how he manipulates it. Far too many critics of Blake either treat the poet as virtually sui generis or else place him too firmly and too exclusively in some particularly eccentric tradition. Tannenbaum, in contrast, strikes precisely the proper balance between tradition and the individual talent, and I know of no interpretation of Blake's works which strikes me as more convincing. By showing how Blake drew in great detail upon commonplace beliefs about the Bible and attitudes toward it, which he then combined with his own reinterpretation of Christ and Christianity, Tannenbaum manages to do two essential things. First, he firmly roots Blake in the context of contemporary thought. Second, he can demonstrate with precision just how Blake manipulates such commonplaces to create such unique poems.

Like Tannenbaum's study of Blake, Sussman's *Fact into Figure* argues that biblical typology and its extensions provide the clue to a body of English art and literature. Like Korshin's *Typologies in England, 1650-1820*, Sussman's study of the role of this form of scriptural symbolism in Carlyle, Ruskin, and the Pre-Raphaelites begins with the assumption that one does not have to distinguish precisely among various forms of types. However, unlike Korshin, Sussman does not base his approach upon a stated theory about the development of such scriptural symbolism and its secularized analogues and influences. Furthermore, unlike Tannebaum, whose often brilliant interpretations of Blake depend upon his scholarly recovery of readings of individual types and passsages in the Bible commonly interpreted typologically, Sussman does not attempt to seek out the commonplace or traditional readings of individual types.

After a chapter which briefly sketches the role of typology in Carlyle and Ruskin, a second discusses Carlyle's *Past and Present* and Ruskin's *Stones of Venice* in terms of what Sussman calls figural history. Chapter 3, "The Brotherhood Aesthetic," argues that typology provides the basis of early Pre-Raphaelite art, and the fourth chapter, "Scripture as History," tests this hypothesis with reference to Millais's *Christ in the House of His Parents* and several of Rossetti's early works. "History as Scripture," which follows, discusses Pre-Raphaelite works which do not have explicitly religious subjects in terms of extended typology, and a long final chapter on "Literary Painting" examines the movement, by individual members of the Brotherhood, away from symbolic realism. An epilogue on *The Scapegoat* which claims that this work "epitomizes Brotherhood figuralism" closes the volume (p. 137).

Sussman's brief, well written study, which continually displays a perceptive, intelligent critic at work, has many virtues. Like several other recent authors, he performs an important act of scholarly recovery by suggesting some of the ways in which biblical typology informed form and content in Carlyle, Ruskin, and the Pre-Raphaelites. Similarly, he makes promising suggestions about the relation of Pre-Raphaelitism to early Victorian science and theories of scientific epistemology. Moreover, although the study of the Pre-Raphaelite painters requires a great deal of additional work with available primary materials (both visual works and manuscript materials) before one can arrive at a completely satisfactory overview, Sussman has obviously struck the right note. Finally, *Fact and Figure* certainly has the virtue of concision—it has less than 100 pages of text—and this very brevity makes it far more accessible than some more ponderous volumes.

Unfortunately, it purchases such brevity at a rather high cost, for this work generally proceeds by assertion rather than proof, something particularly annoying when Sussman perceives a point of major importance but fails to substantiate it. For example, I suspect that his assertion that pre-Darwinian science had a major influence upon both Ruskin and the Pre-Raphaelites is correct and well worth investigating, but the two pages (pp. 3-4) devoted to this crucial subject only cite books published more than a decade after the beginning of Pre-Raphaelitism, and his later citation of statements by F. G. Stephens and W. M. Rossetti (pp. 35-36) raises more problems than it solves. Since Sussman's manner of proceeding in this matter is representative of his general approach, it deserves a brief look. It is representative because Sussman, a perceptive, imaginative critic, does an excellent job of perceiving often unexpected relations and connections, but he does not do nearly as well in testing his hypotheses. In this case he accurately perceives that Stephens and W. M. Rossetti, both of whom we may characterize as typically forward looking Victorians, urged the importance of science and scientific observation as a guide to artistic styles. To what extent can one assume that their statements represent *the* Brotherhood position or even *a* Brotherhood position? I am not sure that I know how to answer that question, but other evidence clearly suggests that one cannot make easy assumptions about this matter. First of all, Dante Gabriel Rossetti, William's brother and the founder of aesthetic Pre-Raphaelitism, never displayed much interest in either science or naturalistic styles of painting. Second, their published criticism demonstrates that W. M. Rossetti and F. G. Stephens, who advanced a scientific naturalism as the appropriate style of painting for the nineteenth century, did not share Hunt, Millais, and Rossetti's early fascination with discovering or inventing a new pictorial symbolism. Furthermore, the evidence of Hunt's correspondence shows that when he had some control over Stephens's writings—as he did in *William Holman Hunt and His Works*, a pamphlet Stephens wrote for Gambart's exhibition of *The Finding of the Saviour in the Temple*—we can conclude that Hunt and Stephens agreed. Similarly, when Hunt informs a critic about his intentions in a work and then writes a letter thanking that critic for a published statement of these intentions—as he did with F. T. Palgrave in 1860—one can accept that the critic speaks for the artist more or less exactly. But when Stephens writes independently, he often demonstrates that his own conceptions of art do not necessarily match those of Hunt.

As this example suggests, Sussman sometimes creates problems for his thesis by his manner of handling evidence. Occasionally these problems stem from his basic assumptions. For instance, he too easily assumes that pre-Darwinian science and Pre-Raphaelitism have much in common and does not bother to define his terms carefully or demonstrate Pre-Raphaelite interest in such science.[1] Similarly, he rather too easily assumes that Stephens and W. M. Rossetti speak for the practicing artists in the group. Another evidentiary problem stems from Sussman's similar failure to determine the degree to which a particular writer can represent some general position. For example, in the midst of a successful discussion of Millais's *Autumn Leaves*, he claims: "Contemporary critics recognized the painting as repudiating the figural methods of the Brotherhood and yet accepted it as working within another well-defined mode, describing this rejection of narrative line and moral content for emotional suggestiveness as following the manner of Giorgione" (p. 113). The only contemporary critics he cites are W. M. Rossetti and John Ruskin, both of whom were at this time still close supporters of the artist and hence cannot be taken to represent the state of contemporary critical opinion. In fact, the anonymous reviewer of the *Art-Journal*, which was certainly the most influential art periodical of the time, demonstrated that he took Millais's painting as yet another instance of inexplicable Pre-Raphaelite symbolism when he mockingly inquired: "In what vein of mystic poetry will the picture be read? The artist awaits the assignment of the usual lofty attributes. The work is got up for the new trans-cendentalism, its essences are intensity and simplicity, and those who yield not to the penetration are insensible to Fine Art. . . . We are curious to learn the mystic interpretation that will be put upon this composition."[2] The hostile critic's suggestion that Millais (and by implication the other Pre-Raphaelites) first painted their pictures and then waited for someone else to assign "lofty" meanings points to two matters of importance. First, at least some of the contemporary critics who had access to a wide audience did not perceive the change in Millais's art which Sussman himself so accurately defines. Second, at least some of these same critics saw Ruskin as the source of fraudulent readings of an art which did not and could not have them; in this particular case, the critic obviously responds to Ruskin's recent letters to the *Times* defending Hunt's work.

In addition, Sussman introduces unnecessary minor awkwardnesses in the art historical portions of his book by departing from standard procedure in the field. Some of these divergences from usual practice are simply odd, such as his calling William Holman Hunt only "Holman Hunt" and John Everett Millais "John E. Millais" when he presents the full names of these artists in his list of plates. Similarly, his failure to provide the media and dimensions of individual works, either in his captions or list of plates, strikes one as amateurish, in large part because such a procedure essentially equalizes all the works and thereby makes it difficult to determine those which artist and audience granted special attention. He creates yet another problem for the art historical reader by choosing the term *figuralism* to refer to typology and other symbolic modes. In art historical writings *figural* and *figuralism* refer to the use of the human figure as a subject for painting, and to use a conventional term in an unconventional sense without first warning the reader leads to unnecessary confusion.

Other problems arise because he has not taken previous work or available primary materials sufficiently into account. For example, making a point essential to his interpretation of the artist's early career, Sussman asserts that "Hunt, the most authentically religious of the group, came from a firmly Protestant, deeply puritancial background" (p. 34), and he claims that, like Ruskin and Carlyle, he grew up within a family of Bible readers. Neither statement is supported by Hunt's own assertion that he was raised as a freethinker and that when he arrived at "manhood I had read most of the easy skeptical books and was a contemptuous unbeliever in any spiritual principles—but the development of talent—and Shelley and Lord Byron with Keats were my modern heroes—all read by the light of materialism or sensualism."[3] In fact, Hunt tells Ruskin in this same letter that *Modern Painters* "first arrested me in my downward course. It was the voice of God. I read this in rapture and it sowed some seed of shame." Although Sussman correctly describes Hunt as "the most authentically religious of the group" (p. 34), the painter himself pointed out that he had no religious convictions when he began his career as Pre-Raphaelite Brother, and this fact has important consequences for any interpretation of Hunt's development. In the first place, it explains better than Sussman has done why the artist abandoned work on *Christ and the Two Marys*, a work which is also known as *The Risen Christ with the Two Marys in the Garden of Joseph of Aramathea* (1847—c 1900). Hunt, who makes clear that sincerity was essential to his conception of Pre-Raphaelitism, states in his memoirs that he put the painting aside because it did not match his sincerest beliefs. Sussman only remarks that *Christ and the Two Marys* suggests "that in 1847 Hunt had not shed the Raphaelite manner" (p. 52)—in fact the style owes more to the Venetians—and from this assertion I assume that he believes Hunt gave it up because it did not match his artistic credo. A second, far more significant consequence follows when one recognizes that Hunt did not begin his Pre-Raphaelite career as a believer in Christianity, for one can no longer assume, as does Sussman, that works before *The Light of the World* have religious, much less typological, intentions. As I have suggested elsewhere, although Hunt found himself greatly attracted to the idea of symbolic realism which he encountered both in Ruskin's writings and in the works of the Early Netherlandish painters, his lack of sincere belief prevented him from employing biblical typology as the basis of such an artistic program until after 1853. Sincerely concerned to discover or create a new form of pictorial symbolism suited to the nineteenth century, he, like other members of the Pre-Raphaelite circle including Ford Madox Brown, turned to Hogarthian methods. Such a recognition also does much to explain both the nature of Hunt's iconological program in *A Converted British family sheltering a Christian Priest from the Persecution of the Druids* (1850) and why he did not cite the presence of types in this work when he described it to his patron, banker, and friend, the devout High Churchman, Thomas Combe of Oxford—someone who would readily have sympathized with such typological method.

Nonetheless, despite an abundance of such errors and problems, *Fact into Figure* provides an interesting, suggestive brief look at the influence of this symbolic mode upon a major movement in Victorian art and literature. The volumes by Korshin and Tannenbaum, on the other hand, make far more ambitious attempts to examine the effect of typological symbolism. Korshin has provided us with an important, if somewhat unbalanced, picture of eighteenth-century abstracted typologies, while Tannenbaum, who succeeds brilliantly in setting Blake within various exegetical traditions, has written a work which can stand as a model of how such investigations should be undertaken.

Notes

1. Sussman's interesting connection of pre-Darwinian science and early Pre-Raphaelite attitudes suggests that one might well investigate the influence upon the young artists of contemporary scientific draftsmanship and illustration. One focus of such an investigation could be John Lucas Tupper (1823?-1879), a member of the Pre-Raphaelite circle who contributed to *The Germ*. A lifelong friend of Hunt and Stephens, he earned a living as an anatomical draftsman at Guy's Hospital, London, while trying to make his way as a sculptor; from 1856 until his death fourteen years later, Tupper, a pioneer in art education, served as a drawing master at Rugby School.

2. "The Royal Academy. Exhibition the Eighty-Eighth: 1856," *Art-Journal* 18 (1856), 171.

3. Hunt's letter of 6 November 1880, which is in the possession of Cornell University, appears in George P. Landow, "'Your Good Influence on Me': The Correspondence of John Ruskin and William Holman Hunt," *Bulletin of the John Rylands University Library of Manchester*, 59 (1976-1977), 377.

Emily Dickinson and Feminist Criticism: Making a Place for Her

Suzanne Juhasz

Barbara Clarke Mossberg. *Emily Dickinson: When a Writer Is a Daughter*. Bloomington: Indiana University Press, 1982. 214 pp.

Wendy Martin. *An American Triptych: Anne Bradstreet, Emily Dickinson, Adrienne Rich*. Chapel Hill: University of North Carolina Press, 1984. 290 pp.

Joanne Feit Diehl. *Dickinson and the Romantic Imagination*. Princeton: Princeton University Press, 1981. 205 pp.

What we have begun to call the "new Dickinson criticism"—a flourishing of work since the mid-1970s on America's greatest woman poet—is dominated by the feminist perspective. Many recent studies of Dickinson make gender identity central to her poetic achievement. In addition to Mossberg's, Martin's, and Diehl's these studies include Jean Mudge's *Emily Dickinson and the Image of Home* (University of Massachusetts Press, 1975); Sandra Gilbert and Susan Gubar's *The Madwoman in the Attic: Women and the Nineteenth-Century Literary Imagination* (Yale University Press, 1979); Karl Keller's *The Only Kangaroo Among the Beauty: Emily Dickinson and America* (Johns Hopkins University Press, 1979); Margaret Homans's *Women Writers and Poetic Identity: Dorothy Wordsworth, Emily Brontë, and Emily Dickinson* (Princeton University Press, 1980); and my own *The Undiscovered Continent: Emily Dickinson and the Space of the Mind* (Indiana University Press, 1983). In the middle of so much critical energy, R. W. Franklin's two-volume *The Manuscript Books of Emily Dickinson* (Cambridge: The Belknap Press of Harvard University, 1981), has provided a much-needed addition to the primary source material, while Robert Weisbuch's *Emily Dickinson's Poetry* (University of Chicago Press, 1975) and Sharon Cameron's *Lyric Time: Dickinson and the Limits of Genre* (Johns Hopkins University Press, 1979), neither overtly interested in feminist issues, contribute excellent new readings of her poems. David Porter's *Dickinson: The Modern Idiom* (Harvard University Press, 1981) has proved a spur in many a feminist's side, because, while it purports to assess Dickinson as a woman poet, it often seems to belittle or disparge her for aspects of her poetry, like writing on the back of recipes, that feminists have found attractive and significant.[1] The strength of Porter's study lies in his new research on Dickinson's methods of composition and in his excellent analysis of her rhetorical structures.

Although the feminist "revolution" in Dickinson criticism is still very much in process, it is now possible to take a look at what it has so far produced, in order to have some understanding of its contributions to Dickinson criticism at large. In a previous essay, my introduction to *Feminist Critics Read Emily Dickinson* (Indiana University Press, 1983), I discuss the essential distinctions between the traditional and feminist approaches, examining "classic" Dickinson studies like George Whicher's *This Was a Poet: A Critical Biography of Emily Dickinson* (University of Michigan Press, 1983) as well as recent work by Weisbuch, Keller, Cameron, Gilbert and Gubar, Homans, and Porter. There I point out that when the traditional bifurcation of Dickinson into "woman" and "poet" (terms considered mutually exclusive) is bridged, so that she is viewed as a woman poet, a total shift occurs in the perspective from which the events of Dickinson's life and the acts of her poetry are viewed. The famous puzzle stops being one, because it starts making sense. Making sense and achieving power: this is what the feminist perspective sees in Dickinson's life and art.

Feminist criticism from the 1980s begins with these premises and continues to seek further definition of Dickinson's identity as a woman poet. Such definition demands in its process that a place be found for her from which she can be viewed. Dickinson's "mystery" has traditionally been associated with

her aloofness, her distance from everything deemed normal: her
lack in other words, of an appropriate "place." "Up in her
room" never seemed the right place to keep a poet who was one
of America's greatest, so traditional studies were always very
busy finding a place for her in the folds of Puritanism, or
Transcendentalism, or Romanticism, or even Modernism.
(David Porter seems to be arguing that her placelessness makes
her, in fact, the first Modern.) The new feminist studies are also
concerned with locating Dickinson, but they begin, as I have
indicated, by accepting and trying to understand the place where
she put herself.

For Barbara Mossberg, that place is most literally and most
centrally home. Mossberg investigates what it means for a poet
to be a woman who never stopped being a daughter: whose
primary relationships, therefore, were with her mother and her
father, inside her father's house. Mossberg uses the perspective
of psychology to study who Dickinson, the daughter, was—and
what that had to do with her art. Wendy Martin also places
Dickinson in her home—and, lest we forget its importance to
her, her garden—as she locates Dickinson as well in an
alternative American tradition of female poets. Linking this
tradition with the aesthetics of a co-existing female sphere,
Martin defines a place for Dickinson as hidden as her poems
were, a world of women and women's ways that, although its
significance was ignored and unacknowledged by the
patriarchy, defined female identity in the nineteenth century in
positive and admirable ways. Joanne Feit Diehl is not so
concerned with such literal contexts. The space where she places
Dickinson is what she terms a "crucial discontinuity,"
Dickinson's estrangement from the prevailing masculine
literary tradition, in this case, Romanticism: the conceptual
space that difference reveals. Diehl juxtaposes Dickinson against
the great Romantics precisely to show how, although sharing
many of their concerns, she is not like them and does not resolve
problems as they do. All three feminist critics, then, are situating
Dickinson in a context, or series of contexts, that female (rather
than male) needs and values have created. Thus Dickinson's
aloofness—her very special idiosyncracy and privacy—is not

taken away from her but is in fact reinforced as it is understood in relation to her womanhood.

Barbara Mossberg's *Emily Dickinson: When a Writer Is a Daughter* places Dickinson precisely where she kept herself: at home, in the bosom of her family. Mossberg convincingly insists upon the primacy of that position, of Dickinson's defining identity as daughter as it informed both her life and her poetics. Mossberg's approach, psychological in orientation, reinterprets Freud as well as Dickinson for us in terms both accurate and challenging. For Mossberg shows how a daughter who tells us she "never had a mother" is both rejecting the mother she does have and longing for the mother she needed, a mother who would not embody the traditional woman who was so completely at odds with Dickinson's own aspirations. "It was what Mrs. Dickinson *represented* as much as her actual behavior that made Dickinson into a self-declared orphan claiming to reject or not to have experienced maternal nurture," explains Mossberg. "The qualities that made Mrs. Dickinson a perfect wife and mother were the very qualities that made Dickinson believe she was not adequately nurtured and that being a wife was not a suitable occupation" (pp. 40, 41).

Mossberg shows as well how a daughter might both admire and resent her father, "aware of the absolute futility of the desire to emulate her father, an awareness that gives a self-mocking edge to her anger" (p. 71). "Her quarrel," continues Mossberg, "is not with her father personally so much as with a world which reveres her father at her expense. Therefore, to cut him down or otherwise satirize him in her letters is actually a way to attack a social structure which automatically confers on him (or any man) autonomy, power, and influence" (p. 73). Again, the particular, personal, and formative relationship becomes emblematic. "No matter what her age or their age, Dickinson approaches males . . . as a little girl seeking approval, advice, love, esteem, wisdom, sanction, forgiveness, and notice" (p. 82). In fact, Mossberg concludes, "Whenever she feels powerless and dependent, she conceptualizes the situation as an encounter between father and daughter: thus she takes secret pot-shots and irreverent jabs at dignified, sacred precepts, principles, and personages, including the seasons, time, God, and her country, all of which are seen trying to restrict her as a daughter and keep her from being 'great'" (p. 92).

This analysis of Dickinson's daughterly relation to her parents can help explain both her adult lifestyle and its connection to her concept and practice of poetry. The fact that she never left home, retained, in fact, her adolescent dress, hairstyle, behavior, and mannerisms, never developed a significant relationship that would take her away from home and projected onto all relationships her identity as a little girl, a daughter, makes sense when we see how her refusal to become an adult woman as she understood that role enabled her to become something else, a poet. For "She is by her own definition a rebellious, wicked daughter" (p. 49). Yet as a poet, Dickinson persists in being as well a daughter: "The daughter identity became a metaphor for her feelings and experience as an adult woman poet struggling to develop a voice in her patriarchal culture" (p. 11). Thus the poetic voice Dickinson develops articulates two sides of this daughter, sometimes dutiful—timid, eager to please, and vulnerable; sometimes rebellious—angry, scornful, and ironic. Most importantly, it is a voice persistently conscious of itself as a voice, conscious that the speaking itself constitutes the key to uniqueness and power.

Dickinson sets her poetry apart from the male literary tradition by emphasizing her problems in assuming her right to speak. Intensely self-conscious, deliberately so, Dickinson's words are attended with her anxiety about her inappropriate gender, and her consequent feelings of guilt, inadequacy, heresy, risk, and disobedience; these feelings permeate the poetry—in fact, constitute its central theme, and characterize its presentation. Refusal, defiance, risk, secrecy, sin, guilt, doubt: these are creative, purposeful ways of seeing her writing as a woman. Dickinson *chooses* to portray her art from these perspectives, rather than underplay any anxiety, or submerge her sexuality, in order to increase her reader's and perhaps her own, appreciation of the uniqueness of her art. [p. 167]

Mossberg's carefully detailed discussions of Dickinson's poems demonstrate the daughter construct at work. This perspective grants her repeated insight into the poems themselves, so that the whole becomes a compelling contribution to Dickinson criticism. The strengths of this study are situated in the understanding that, because she is a woman, Dickinson's home life is of crucial importance: it is for most women. The particular gestault that defined her living conditions and her relationship to those with whom she lived is not separate from the fact of her art. It is, rather, essential to her poetry, defining not only the shape it took and the themes it addressed but the very fact of its existence.

Wendy Martin's *An American Triptych: Anne Bradstreet, Emily Dickinson, Adrienne Rich* puts Dickinson in the center of a continuum that establishes an American tradition of women's poetry. In her concern with where to place Dickinson, Martin contends that the larger context is America. Her portraits of these poets focus on depicting them in a specific social and historical milieu. Nevertheless, what she shows for all three, what in fact defines the female tradition that they represent, is that "all three poets resisted the prevailing ethos of their time" and that each created "an alternative response to the patriarchal tradition in art and politics" (pp. 5, 6). Whereas Martin makes a convincing case for the connection between Puritan reformation (Bradstreet) and feminist revolution (Rich)—"both envision the creation of a new world whether it be the city upon a hill or the community of women" (p. 7)—Dickinson is necessarily excluded from this parallelism. Her rebellion was, after all, private and singular. However, Martin maintains that Dickinson's stance and situation is the necessary transition between Bradstreet and Rich: "There is a continuum from acceptance of traditional patriarchal values to passive resistance against convention to a deep alienation that has inspired the vision of a new society" (p. 10).

By placing the poets in history, in patriarchy, Martin succeeds in demonstrating how they worked against it and lived outside it. She defines a female poetic representative of an ongoing countertradition, one which does not, however, seem to me to be especially limited to American women poets.

All three poets have protested, to varying degrees, the disjunction of mind and nature that characterizes Judeo-Christian thought. The work of Bradstreet, Dickinson, and Rich suggests a female poetic in which nature is not subordinate to reason and in which genius, literary or otherwise, is not perceived as male energy uncontaminated by female matter. Replacing androcentric metaphors that define nature as a woman whose mysteries must be penetrated and whose body must be dominated by the male mind, or transcended by the male poet, the poetry of Dickinson and Rich often depicts the male principle as an intrusion on female process. In a reformulation of masculine hierarchies that create stratified order according to the principles of graduated power, or dominance and submission, the female counter-tradition postulates the co-existence of mutability—the disorderly, the unpredictable—with logos—the accountable, the knowable. With each of these poets, communal reciprocity and intersubjectivity increasingly takes the place of hierarchal authority. [p. 10]

In this countertradition, based on qualities and values engendered by traditional female socialization, Dickinson's strategic and successful use of her female identity is emphasized. For example, the perspective leads Martin to remind us of Dickinson's place not only in her house but her garden, viewed as emblematic of the female sphere which Dickinson supported in her decision to remain single. "The female sphere emphasized emotional rather than financial values," writes Martin. "Empathy and loyalty were regarded more highly than ambition or profit" (p. 154). In Dickinson's important network of female friends and relatives, her gifts of fruit and flowers, often accompanied by poem-notes, were associated with the nurturing values that Martin sees as defining Dickinson's poetic and experiential aesthetic. Home and domestic life, she argues, took on a sacramental quality for Dickinson, an allocation of value which is itself a rebellion against prevailing patriarchal norms.

Her appreciation of Dickinson in the context of the alternative female tradition leads Martin to see in Dickinson what she calls a "holistic" vision. Dickinson's understanding of experience, Martin argues, is defined by her disinterest in separating self and other or in perceiving the universe in terms of sequential opposites: "Instead of the hierarchical order, logical causality and abstraction characteristic of traditional masculinity, Dickinson concentrated on relationship, synchronicity, and textured details associated with feminine sensibility" (p. 125). Comparing Dickinson's work to Emerson and Whitman in particular and to Romantic poets in general, Martin points out that "the brooding alienation of much

Romantic poetry is absent in her work. Instead of willful individualism and an effort to transcend the temporal world, Dickinson evolved a nuturing vision based on a cyclical flux of interconnected life forms" (p. 138).

This position is diametrically opposed to Joanne Feit Diehl's in *Dickinson and the Romantic Tradition*, yet both are arguing Dickinson's difference from the masculine Romantic tradition. A comparison of the two studies indicates that the feminist perspective need not prove redundant: in fact, thoughtful differences can prove instructive. Diehl's book is based upon the premise that "no poet can develop in isolation from the word of his or her poetic predecessors and hope to achieve Dickinson's status" (p. 4), so that initially she seems also to contradict Mossberg, who stresses Dickinson's "apolitical, aworldly, microscopic, idiosyncratic and alienated vision" (p. 17). But, although Diehl begins by calling Dickinson's context the Romantic poetic tradition, it is, as in Martin's study, essentially for the purposes of establishing the nature of her difference within and from that context. For Diehl, as a feminist critic, maintains that the "crucial difference" of gender affects the course of poetic identity. What Diehl finds in Dickinson's relation to her romantic forbears is a discontinuity that may well have afforded opportunity as well as hardship: "By conceiving of herself as necessarily apart from this male line of poets, Dickinson creates a space, a crucial discontinuity, that provides her the freedom to experiment" (p. 7). However, Diehl's study more frequently shows how that "sense of estrangement" and "awareness of her own isolation" created not so much freedom as tension and torment—and an art, however experimental, that was produced from that torment.

Diehl posits a Dickinson aware of a "damning division" (p. 36) between herself and nature, so that she finds herself in competition with the external world. Diehl observes in Dickinson "the need to win dominance from a competing, potentially destructive province located in the land" (p. 35) and contrasts this attitude with a "reciprocity" that she observes in Wordsworth and Emerson, for example: "Not for her the wedding between the poet's ego and nature as bride" (p. 36). Yet

Martin finds the male poet to be the one interested in winning dominance, through aggression and ultimate mastery. Martin argues that for Emerson there is always a gap to be bridged, "and he maintains that it is the responsibility of the poet and the philosopher to leap over the chasm of the unknown; for him, the universe is the bride, the consciousness is the groom, and the two are never congruent" (p. 124). On the other hand, says Martin, Dickinson feels no need to strive to attain the universe, for she, as a woman poet, is grounded already—in the present moment, in the quotidian, in mundane experience.

The issue Martin and Diehl are circling, albeit coming towards it from different directions, is one made explicit in Margaret Homans's *Women Writers and Poetic Identity*. If, Homans asks, nature is traditionally female and the Other, while the poet is the self and male, how can a woman write poetry, since she is supposed to be subject, not author? Diehl's answer to this underlying question is that, while the male poet sees nature, and his muse, as female, so that his poetry becomes an engagement with them, a penetration that can result in union (one which, however, many women would see as a clearly aggressive act, an act of dominance), the woman poet does not see nature as female but as male, since for her the other is, by definition, the not-me, and hence masculine. Thus too, from Diehl's perspective, the muse (and precursor) is an aspect of the psyche that also seems "male." Sexual politics between the two (or between the woman poet and the outside world, a version of this same interaction), is not the same as between the male poet and his female muse. For example, "the essential difference between Keats's muse and Dickinson's," writes Diehl, in agreement with Mossberg, "is that for her the other is father, poet, lover, and Christ. His existence is coextensive with Dickinson's own; she cannot, like Keats, separate female lover from precursor poet" (p. 82).[2] "The problem Dickinson faces," Diehl continues, "is how to maintain a dialogue with this projected other—composite precursor and internal adversary— while at the same time protecting herself from him lest she be overwhelmed" (p. 83). Hence all the ambivalence, as well as anxiety and aggression, that both Diehl and Mossberg see in Dickinson.

But Diehl understands full well that for Dickinson this dominance over the external world (or indeed, over her internal muse, identified as an aspect of her own self) is well nigh impossible. The "fluidity" Diehl finds in Emerson's relationship with nature, the "reciprocity" that characterizes the Wordsworthian attitude, are achieved by means of their masculine ability to dominate and conquer and satisfy "the Romantic ambition of bridging the distance between world and imagination" (p. 185). Consequently, Diehl observes that Dickinson's actual solution becomes the positing of "an alternative, internal landscape, created and controlled by her imagination" (p. 42). "Dickinson," observes Diehl, "will either appropriate the landscape by internalizing it, or, obversely, deny the boundaries between self and nature by describing the landscape in the anatomical language of arteries and veins, impressing herself upon the land" (p. 35).

It is precisely this appropriation, what Diehl calls "the aggrandizement of the mind" (p. 48), that Martin observes (and which is in fact the subject of my own study, *The Undiscovered Continent*). Martin does not dwell on the anxiety that may well have produced it, even as, indeed, she posits a Dickinson who may have gone through some initial period of stress but who clearly resolved it. "Before achieving autonomy, Dickinson alternated between the extremes of abject helplessness and scornful superiority," writes Martin, identifying two positions or attitudes reminiscent of Mossberg's dutiful and rebellious daughter, but locating them in a "before." When Martin notices a lack of boundaries and a flux of interconnected life forms, she sees the results of what I have called living in the space of the mind and, in consequence, altering external reality to suit one's own needs. What Martin observes in Dickinson is really there, and it is something that Diehl sees too. Their interpretations sound so different because they are focusing on different stages of a process that seems to have repeated itself over and over. I do not believe that Dickinson ever moved beyond her patriarchally-induced anxiety to a state of comfortable autonomy in the alternative female sphere, although at the same time I think that Martin is correct in noticing how that world and mode helped to influence Dickinson's strategies and achievements. Mossberg shows Dickinson as a "daughter" to the end of her life, and I think that Mossberg is right.

Circling the same issues as well as the same poet, these studies offer interpretations with both similarities and differences, at least partially due to the fact that the feminist perspective is allied with other critical perspectives, such as psychology, history, and genre. From my point of view the weaknesses in these books (accompanying their clear strengths) have less to do with which critical approach and more to do with how that approach ultimately encounters Dickinson's poetry. *An American Triptych*, for example, is most impressive to me in its ability to relate historical and biographical material to a female aesthetic that is spiritual in implication. On the other hand, analysis of the poetry is both minimal and predominately thematic, supporting the epistemological claims of the author rather than enlarging or enriching them. Diehl makes a more careful attempt to read the poems, and comparing them with well-known Romantic lyrics provides many helpful insights. Yet the contrasts with the major Romantic figures so consistently repeat Diehl's basic ideas about Dickinson viv-á-vis nature and the muse that finally they all blend into one poet, a generic male Romantic poet. This may well be an underlying truth about them, but it contradicts the book's assumption that there is something special to be learned from Shelley, from Emerson. Mossberg is very good on the poems. Naturally, the ones she chooses are used to demonstrate her theory (a tendency critics can hardly avoid), but, perhaps because many of the poems she has included are nearly unfamiliar, or perhaps because of the three she is the closest reader of the texts, or perhaps because I am sympathetic to her ideas about daughters and poems, I like her readings best. Whatever the approach, it seems important to examine the poems themselves with much care, because they are never, after all, self-evident; that is their glory and their challenge.

Finally, in their concern with identifying Dickinson's place, these three studies indicate an important interest, not in whether she put herself in the right or the wrong place (they all assume she knew what she was doing, unlike traditional critics, who too often bemoan her mistakes and failures in judgment), but in what happened to her in the place she made for herself. We all know she became a great poet there; what we need to find out is how she did it, and what it did to her. Was she satisfied, comfortable, in control; or was she tortured, frustrated, erratic? When we look to Dickinson as forebear, we are concerned not only with her greatness but with how she won it. Both Mossberg and Diehl attest to the idea that Dickinson's triumph never made her comfortable. Both show her as, finally, too much a woman of her own time and place, no matter how critical and rebellious, to be at ease with an achievement that a part of her still believed was inappropriate. Her methods for poetic success made victories, or rather poems, out of conflict—whether that conflict be interpreted as being a "good" or "bad" daughter of Edward and Emily Norcross Dickinson, or between being a "good" or "bad" daughter of the Romantic tradition.

What makes for comfort, it seems, is feeling at home in one's context or place—one is not so much of a rebel, really, if others have gone before or beside. Only in a footnote does Diehl remark on Dickinson's "other" reading—of the Brontës, George Eliot, and Elizabeth Barrett Browning, yet Dickinson's letters contain more references to these precursors, this tradition, than to the male English romantic poets. As Martin points out, not only was there a female literary tradition, but right at home there was a sister, Vinnie; across the hedge there was a sister-in-law, Sue: there was a female world within (or without) the patriarchy that had its own rules. These traditions for writing and for living both influenced Dickinson and nurtured her, so that another aspect of her complexity is that she could find some access to comfort and safety, through channels that, as Martin demonstrates, were peculiarly and especially female. That Dickinson experienced both comfort and conflict does not seem an untenable idea.

The growing contribution of feminist criticism to Dickinson studies has most to do, as these books demonstrate, with the way in which it can appreciate Emily Dickinson. As she grows more and more believable, her art becomes, never simpler, but more and more available to those who are endlessly attracted to her genius.

Notes

1. In *An American Triptych* Wendy Martin writes, "David Porter asserts Dickinson's poetry is impoverished by a lack of 'controlling architecture' or system of beliefs that would enable her to reconcile the contradictory extremes of her experiences . . . But her poetry, and especially her letters, demonstrate that she deliberately avoided a system of categories that would prestructure or limit her perceptions. Dickinson's disjunctive states of awareness were the necessary concomitant to psychological and artistic autonomy" (p. 83).

2. Harold Bloom's theory of anxiety of influence would have the male poet needing to agress against his male predecessors, but this is not the same force as his muse, or nature, who are blessedly female and much more readily subdued.

Editorial Presence in the
Variorum Chaucer

Christian K. Zacher

The Miller's Tale, ed. Thomas W. Ross. Norman: University of Oklahoma Press, 1983. Part Three, Volume II of *A Variorum Edition of the Works of Geoffrey Chaucer*. xxix, 273 pp.

One modern way to make more manageable the great body of scholarship that in our time has grown up around an important author is to organize and digest it in a variorum edition, a work that represents in convenient miniature whole shelves of textual and interpretive commentary. A bibliography is only an itinerary, showing the progression of scholarship; a variorum can reflect in a fuller if condensed manner the many directions of that scholarship. Although a variorum must scatter in pieces scholarly studies that are sometimes better read whole, there is a value to making available in compressed form on a single page a variety of past responses to a line or a passage. A variorum provides users with core samples of textual and critical study; it promises more than an annotated bibliography but less than chronologically arranged collections of criticism or, of course, the mass of sampled scholarship itself. Scholars and teachers go to a variorum because it saves time.

The editors of a variorum must possess humility as well as a talent for abstracting, however, for their enterprise is caught up in paradox. As a work of reference, the variorum is intended to stand above or to the side of the scholarship it encapsulates, yet it can turn out to be but another contribution to that scholarship. As a retrospective summary of what has been said, a variorum is built to endure, although as soon as it appears it begins to be dated by the scholarship that follows it. A variorum audience commonly expects of the editors a nonpartisan detachment, but rhetoric and editorial will often thwart such objectivity.

Probably the most troubling problem variorum editors have to face is one of self-definition and focus: does a variorum exist to digest the commentary (and how neutrally) or to present a literary text (and which one), or both? Can a variorum insist on one text over another and still function as an impartial record of other, previous textual choices? What is the relationship of the commentary at the bottom of the page to the particular text set above it? Answers vary. A century ago Horace Howard Furness, in issuing *A New Variorum Edition of Shakespeare* with both text and commentary, announced his decision not to borrow the familiar Cambridge edition text of Shakespeare but instead to piece together a text from various editions, "since, in such an edition as the present, it makes very little difference what text is printed *in extenso,* since every other text is also presented with it on the same page." As for the commentary, he had decided his new variorum "should contain all the notes [from the 1821 variorum], except such as the united judgments of all the editors since that date have decided to be valueless, together with all the original notes of these editors themselves."[1] By the time of his second variorum volume Furness relaxed that limitation on the commentary and with the third volume he further expanded the commentary to embrace all sorts of critical notes, even though some might seem of "little or no value, except as hints of the progress or of the madness of Shakespearian criticism."[2] Furness changed his mind about the text as well, telling users of the fifth variorum volume that he was now substituting the First Folio text for the "modernised" one he had earlier adopted. Small wonder this buffeted variorum editor ended his preface to that volume by saying, "The next play in this edition, if there ever be one, will be, probably, *The Merchant of Venice.*"[3]

The original editors of the Spenser variorum chose to offer both text and commentary, declaring simply that they were going to furnish "an accurate text" and "all the significant scholarship and literary criticism" on the poet.[4] Editors of the variorum edition of Milton's poetry have avoided problems that the choice of text occasions by deciding to provide no text at all, only the commentary (tied to an already existing Milton edition). And the remaining possibility—no commentary, only text—can be found in *The Variorum Edition of the Poems of William Butler Yeats.*

Chaucer, as much as these writers, has deserved such a retrospective, and, in a period that has seen the inauguration of other large projects devoted to him such as the Chaucer Library and the Chaucer Bibliographies (and perhaps a Chaucer Encyclopedia), *A Variorum Edition of the Works of Geoffrey Chaucer* has begun to be published, under the courageous general editorship of Paul G. Ruggiers and Donald C. Baker. In 1977 there appeared Volume I, *Geoffrey Chaucer*: The Canterbury Tales: *A Facsimile and Transcription of the Hengwrt Manuscript, with Variants from the Ellesmere Manuscript*; in 1982, Volume V, *The Minor Poems*, edited by George B. Pace and Alfred David; and now, Part Three of the twenty-five parts that will comprise *The Canterbury Tales*, Thomas W. Ross's edition of *The Miller's Tale*. (A fourth fascicle of the variorum, Derek Pearsall's edition of *The Nun's Priest's Tale*, has now been announced.) How has the *Variorum Chaucer* approached the questions of text and commentary?

The general editors note in the prefaces to the two latest volumes that although the variorum was "originally projected exclusively as a commentary upon the entire canon of Chaucer's poetry and prose," it "was expanded in 1979 to include a series of facsimiles representing the tradition upon which subsequent editors of the printed editions of his work have based their texts. Thus the *Variorum Chaucer* rests upon the two great foundations of text and commentary" (Pace and David, p. xiii; Ross, p. xiii). These facsimiles heralded the decision to produce for the variorum not only commentary but a series of in effect critical editions of Chaucer's works, dependent on "newly established texts for the poems" (Ross, p. xiv), a decision stemming from the general editors' conviction that a fuller understanding of Chaucer's writings (and particularly "the evolving text of *The Canterbury Tales*") could be best served by a fresh reliance on "those manuscripts that have borne the commentary of past scholarship" (Ross, p. xvi). What this judgment in turn depends on, in the case of the *Tales*, is the editors' firm belief that as a "base-text" for Chaucer's most important work, the Hengwrt manuscript is superior to the Ellesmere. They acknowledge that many might doubt the need for a new text of the *Tales* and that a variorum edition ought to be less a text and more "a means of sorting and organizing the mass of commentary" (*Facsimile*, p. xvii). But some text was thought needed, and because the widely used Robinson edition is "too committed to the Ellesmere manuscript" and the authoritative Manly-Rickert text, "not being punctuated, is almost never cited for purposes of quotation" (*Facsmile*, p. xvii), they elected to settle on a new copy-text, one that would be generally accepted by all the variorum editors. There is, they admit, a more fundamental reason for developing a new text for the variorum: "Clearly, the chief reason for not selecting an existing printed text is that it would present a single reading, or a single statistic in the larger body of evidence, and the very fact that our new text had not been cited would free the new text from too close an association with other texts and it would therefore provide a structure around which all other readings and the commentary bearing upon those readings could be grouped without the danger of bias arising." (*Facsimile*, p. xviii). The *Variorum Chaucer* thus has placed equal emphasis on the text, a new one, and the commentary that attaches to it.

Thomas Ross, author of *Chaucer's Bawdy* and a consulting editor for the *Facsimile*, was a logical editor for *The Miller's Tale*. At the outset he says his purpose is to present the tale "in a form that may approach the poet's final version" (p. 4), and he then outlines the organization of the volume:

The "Critical Commentary" offers brief discussions of sources, analogues, and date. The survey of criticism is organized into topics, and, within these subdivisions, critics' views are presented, usually in chronological order. The "Textual Commentary" deals in detail with the ten manuscripts and twenty printed editions that have been selected as the basis for the Variorum Edition. It explains the use I have made of these materials in my construction of the best possible text. The text of *The Miller's Tale* then follows. It is accompanied by collations of both manuscripts and printed editions and by notes that incorporate comments by Chaucer's critics and explain meanings and allusions. [p. 4].

The Critical Commentary is an efficient if at times judgmental reprise of the criticism, assessing studies of sources and analogues (there is no evidence of a direct source), the date (uncertain), the fabliau nature of the tale, its morality (is it more *solaas* or *sentence?*), the portrayal of the teller and the four main characters, the relation of the tale to other ones (especially the Knight's), and its style and structure. This long summary accounts for all important criticism, and Ross's occasional partiality as he sifts it is here more pardonable than it will be later in the running notes to the text. It is difficult in an essay to summarize numerous critics in one's own voice without at least tacitly preferring some to others (so, Bolton's gloss on Nicholas's name sways Ross less than Bennett's or Gardner's [p. 32]). However, Ross could have merely mentioned rather than quoted Bateson's silly remark, "Chaucer criticism has multiplied recently, but apart from Dryden . . . and Aldous Huxley . . . no first-rate literary critic has ventured into the field except C. S. Lewis (not quite first-rate?)" (p. 7). He also might have given less space to Robert Graves's odd opinions (Chaucer "reveals how strong [the Miller's] criminal sympathies are" and he "lets the prize for the best story be awarded to the Knight") which then provoke Ross to say, "Graves perhaps had access to manuscript materials no longer available" (p. 27). Ross's two paragraphs of "Conclusions" (pp. 48-49) do not really conclude much about the criticism just summarized, and the second one, in fact, seems to belong elsewhere.

The latter half of the introduction, a "Textual Commentary," is an engaging, learned guide through the forest of the tale's textual history which describes and evaluates the reliability of the "base-group" manuscripts and printed editions that underlie this edition. Like the variorum's general editors, Ross believes in the primacy of the Hengwrt and convincingly argues its merits, concluding that Hengwrt "had access to what must have been one of Chaucer's near-final revisions or something very close to it" (p. 75). He thinks a combination of "the incomparable beauty" of the Ellesmere and "the vastly influential editions of [Skeat] and [Robinson]" (pp. 53-54), who based their editions on it, has kept most modern editors of

Chaucer from giving their full allegiance to the Hengwrt. "The
dazzling El," moralizes Ross, "is a showy (and demanding)
mistress; the drab and 'rat-gnawn' Hg is a dependable wife" (p.
54). Ross's knowledgeable survey of printed editions highlights
villains (like John Urry, whose "execrable" enterprise was "the
worst edition of *The Canterbury Tales* ever printed" [pp. 87,
108]) and influences (Caxton's two editions, with their "outré"
appearance and "swash type" [pp. 95, 96], and Robinson's pair),
and it directs readers to the modern edition most acceptable
textually to the variorum editors (Pratt's, which is "closer to the
present edition than any of the previous printed editions—and
also closer than are the editions published after [Pratt]" [p. 82]).
The entire Textual Commentary is a mighty brief for the
variorum editors' trust in the Hengwrt, and Ross closes the
section by noting with satisfaction that "the history of modern
editions demonstrates the gradual recognition of the superiority
of Hg to El" (p. 113).

The rest of the volume contains Ross's text of *The Miller's
Tale* and the associated commentary. Beneath the text on each
page appear in collation all manuscript and printed edition
readings that differ from Ross's copy-text readings, and they add
up to a handy historical index of the textual vicissitudes of *The
Miller's Tale*. The remainder of each page is taken up with what
is the meat of any variorum, the line by line textual and critical
notes. One might quibble that Ross's statement—"Explanatory
notes follow the textual notes separated by the symbol §" (p.
114)—does not precisely enough tell the reader that some line
notes will be only textual and others only explanatory; Pace and
David in their edition offer a clearer account of the handling of
these notes (pp. xxii, 46). A far more crucial matter, however, is
the role Ross decided to play in composing the notes. Pace and
David say openly in their introduction that they plan "to
evaluate [the commentary of previous editors and critics],
especially where disagreement exists, and we have introduced
new evidence and new interpretations of old evidence wherever
appropriate" (p. 46). Ross will also evaluate—most notably in
the explanatory, critical notes—but he does not so forewarn the
reader.

It is apparent the *Variorum Chaucer* editors were not persuaded by the opposite view of their function, recently best expressed by Emerson Brown, Jr., that a variorum editor "should not 'editorialize' at all," that "the main obligation of the variorum editor is not to tell us what his author wrote and meant but to show us, fully and impartially, the history of what people have *thought* that his author wrote and meant."[5] It surely is true that the confining nature of variorum notes might lead any reporter of scholarship, however much committed to objectivity, into a show of prejudice: quoting a little rather than a lot from one critic, summarizing rather than quoting at all from another, mentioning this critic before rather than after that one—these and other subtle choices will raise in some minds suspicions about the compiler's neutrality. Perhaps Brown's ideal editor does not exist in practice. Yet the general and individual editors of the *Variorum Chaucer* seem to have assumed that such neutrality is unattainable (or undesirable) without articulating their view for the reader. Is it their bias toward the Hengwrt and their consequent vested interest in a new Chaucer text that nourishes in them a proprietary concern about the criticism as well? Whatever the reason, a reader of this volume of the series will find that Ross often acts as governor and judge of the assembled critics, not merely as their detached reporter, and this partiality has the effect of turning Ross the editor into another of the critics.

Some of his judgments of critical contributions are made implicitly. For instance, not every critic listed in the "Bibliographical Index" at the rear of the book is quoted or mentioned in the explanatory notes. Studies by Biggins, Bowker, Bratcher-von Kreisler, Fletcher and Frese, one notices, are entered in that index; but according to the final, general index to the volume these critics do not appear in the notes or in the Critical Commentary. Should one take such omissions of these critics' offerings as Ross's silent verdict on their worth? The label "Bibliographical Index" itself implies not necessarily that all known scholarship on *The Miller's Tale* is reflected in this variorum edition but rather that what is reported in the notes and Critical Commentary will be indexed in that list.

Some critics are more visible in the explanatory notes than others: a tally of those most mentioned or quoted in the notes shows that Ross himself leads the list, followed by Rowland, Robertson, Kaske and Bennett. These prominent critics deserve the attention the variorum gives them, but Ross's reports of their views are not in every case thorough. For example, in the note to line 3207 he refers the reader to his own *Chaucer's Bawdy* (pages 132-33) for a discussion of "the richly suggestive cluster *lycorys-likerous-leccherous*," but it turns out Ross there discusses only the last two words (and one finds no entry for *lycorys* in *Chaucer's Bawdy*). Paull Baum's work could have been appropriately cited in this note (for, also on page 132 of *Chaucer's Bawdy*, Ross cites Baum on the pun *likerous-leccherous*); indeed, Baum is unrepresentatively cited only once in Ross's edition. On the other hand, Ross can be too humble in citing his own work: in his treatment of *likerous* in *Chaucer's Bawdy*, he refers the reader to line 3244 of *The Miller's Tale*, but in his variorum explanatory notes on that line he omits what would be a proper citation of his own discussion in *Chaucer's Bawdy*.

There is a related, more general problem reflected in the explanatory notes: Ross nowhere mentions a cut-off date for scholarship accounted for by the variorum. Some comment about it—or about the difficulty of imposing a date—would seem essential for users of the volume, since most of them will be consulting it for the generally chronological gathering of commentary in a given explanatory note. (Notice, in contrast, David's remarks on this matter in his preface to *The Minor Poems*, p. xvii.) As it is, a reader must examine publication dates in the notes and Bibliographical Index, locating one recorded item from 1982 (Ramsey's valuable analysis of the Hengwrt and Ellesmere scribes), two from 1981, three from 1980 (one of which, by Dane, is also not cited in the notes or Critical Commentary), and then several from 1979, in order to determine that 1978 or 1979 must have been the last year systematically searched for relevant scholarship. If Ross had better indicated which of these years was his cut-off date, readers would know, once they had finished with this volume, which year's bibliographies they must next turn to.

More obvious than the implicit evaluations are the examples of Ross's explicit agreement or disagreement with assorted critics. Robertson and Kaske are often cited without editorial comment, but not always: at one point we are told that Robertson "makes Nicholas' rude act bear the burden of moral significance" (p. 154), in a few other places Ross disputes Robertson's interpretations (pp. 155, 205, 222-23), and more than once he casts doubt on Kaske's translation or interpretation of passages from Canticles (pp. 150, 161, 173). Half of the time that Ross cites Howard he quarrels with his views (pp. 127, 129, 155, 192). After quoting Haskell's depiction of Alison, Nicholas and John up in the tubs, "wearing only their expressions of fatigue and adultery," Ross gamily adds that "it is not easy to imagine what an expression of adultery might be" (p. 211). Donaldson, whom Ross praised in the Critical Commentary for "breaking new ground and providing the most nearly complete analysis of the diction of *The Miller's Tale*" (p. 46), is cited with approval throughout the explanatory notes, especially so in one of the longest excerpted comments in the variorum (pp. 206-07).

Ross the critic is present not only in his discriminations among others' interpretations but in his own volunteered observations about the tale. In his Critical Commentary he said he would be critic as well as editor—"There is still a need for an analysis of the poetic effects other than diction in the tale. In some of the Notes I try to fill that need" (p. 48)—but he ends up remarking on much else besides. He suggests a possible echo of a line from Canticles (p. 145); proposes a time scheme for the tale (pp. 177-78); gives three explanations for readers who might wonder "why Alison and Nicholas did not go to bed together as soon as John left Oxford on business" (p. 178); tells us concerning the word *storial* that "Chaucer's notion of what was fiction and what historical fact probably differed from ours; he might have included *PrT* and *MLT* among the 'storial thyng' in *CT*, for instance" (p. 129); and responds to other critics' interpretations of the narrator's apology at the end of the Miller's prologue by asserting that "It is perhaps best not to concern ourselves with problems of narrative voice or persona here: the passage is a traditional disclaimer, the actual effect of which is to attract us to this coarse (and masterful) tale" (p. 127). Ross observes, "It may be said that as *hende* is the epithet for Nicholas and *ioly* for Absolon, *sely* is John's" (p. 179). He offers the opinion that "Many readers would choose line 3740 as their favorite in all of Chaucer; it certainly includes the cruelest titter" (p. 229). He sometimes reminds us of his own previous study of Chaucer by quoting critics' reactions to it, once with apparent good humor (p. 168), once without comment (p. 193), and once with an objection (p. 215). There is even a point at which Ross the editor forgets that Ross the critic should remain an alter ego; he says that "I have suggested a double meaning for the Latin lines . . ." (p. 137).

Whether or not other readers concur with Ross's reactions to the critics and countenance his decision to be present amid the commentary, they will find his note by note distribution of criticism on the tale enormously helpful. A gathering of variorum criticism should both recall for us what has been said and emphasize as yet unsolved problems. Throughout his account of the criticism and in his explanatory notes and general index Ross underscores outstanding cruxes of *The Miller's Tale*. He shows us we still do not know the exact meaning of *gnof* or *Kynges Note* or the puzzling *viritoot* (about which Ross provides a superb note). What does the Ovidian marginalis at line 3382 mean? Is it (in Ross's words) "our craving for mathematical symmetry" (p. 42) that makes us find fault with Alison's not being punished at the end of the tale? And in at least a dozen places Ross draws attention to alliterative phrases (all but two of them catalogued by Oakden) and implies their presence in the tale needs more study.

Before returning to the vexing problem of editorial neutrality, let it be said that the volume is impressively free of mechanical errors and inconsistencies but that in a few places the logic of Ross's argument needs reappraisal.[6] Two remarks made by Brewer five years apart are quoted on page 25: since the first remark does not clearly enough reveal Brewer's attitude toward modern critical stress on the morality of the tale, it does not seem accurate to characterize the second remark as a sign that Brewer "is still unwilling to find a serious moral in the tale." In discussing the manuscripts, Ross says of the two couplets present in the Ellesmere but absent from the Hengwrt (lines 3155-56, 3721-22) that both "are possibly Chaucer's—the second couplet more certainly so" (p. 75); "certainly" does not sound right, since Ross's earlier (quite sensitive) examination of the problem with the second couplet made it clear that "modern taste" rather than firm textual support had convinced Manly and Rickert that this couplet was more authentic than the other one. Finally, Ross twice mentions Ramsey's evidence that the Ellesmere and the Hengwrt were written by different scribes (pp. 53, 203); yet, without saying why he would disagree with the evidence, he concludes that the two manuscripts were written, "probably by the same scribe" (p. 54).

Variorum editions are produced by people, not by machines. As much as one might agree with Emerson Brown's and others' understandable desire to possess a textually and critically unbiased *Variorum Chaucer*, it does not seem practical to hope for one. At times in the notes we hear Ross more than the critics and there are moments of harsh engagement with critics whose views Ross rejects. The whole project's tilt toward the Hengwrt, along with its promulgation of what really is a new edition, has very likely created an ambience which allows participating editors to feel they may acknowledge the scholarship in a manner more like the Host's than, say, Chaucer the pilgrim's. In assigning *The Miller's Tale* to Ross, the general editors must have realized that this critic with an interest in special Chaucerian language would find it hard to disengage himself from aspects of the commentary on this tale. In the end, the *Variorum Chaucer* editorial committee is as responsible as this one editor for the non-neutrality.

The general editors' prefatory remarks in the volumes so far published and especially Donald C. Baker's response to Brown's call for editorial objectivity suggest that in fact the sponsors of the project have long agonized over this problem. Baker agrees that variorum editors should be constrained from improperly inserting themselves into the variorum; but he argues that "in determining the text [the variorum editor] will inevitably discover errors" (perhaps textual misjudgments that derive from prior critical biases) and the variorum notes are the proper place for such errors to be rehearsed and rebutted. The variorum editor "is, after all, in most cases himself creating a text which has never existed before in all its details. This is certainly original. He must therefore be prepared to give his arguments in support of his reading of the evidence, even if it runs counter to the published opinions of some or all scholars."[7] Baker is right: having chosen to offer a new text in this variorum, the editors have the responsibility to defend it. However, Baker's argument cannot reach out to justify a variorum editor's transformation from authorized textual expert into critic in the explanatory notes. The text presumes an editor, the commentary only a reader. What the *Variorum Chaucer* still lacks, then, is a rationale for the unexpected shifts from textual to critical analysis that users of these volumes will encounter.

However effective such an explanation might be, there remains the complicated fact that the *Variorum Chaucer's* sanction of commentary on the commentary, together with its adoption of a fresh text for Chaucer, makes it inescapable that post-variorum study—and later some *Variorum Chaucer* II— must critically assess this effort as a contribution to the very stream of Chaucer scholarship the variorum exists to measure. Immediately, and finally, these volumes themselves will become what the general editors correctly wanted to stand apart from, "statistic[s] in the larger body of evidence." Yet perhaps everyone expects this to happen to variorums anyway. As the years age their contents, they come to serve less as a quick summary for users and more as a monument to be scrutinized by future historians of literary scholarship. Furness's wondrous project rests on the shelf now as a monument. Over time the forty-some volumes of the *Variorum Chaucer* will solidify that way, although the existence of a number of separate editors completing different editions with differing cut-off dates for their commentaries will guarantee this series of volumes a varying utility for some years.

One way to preserve it all from decay, of course, would be to follow the suggestion of Emerson Brown, the project's gadfly; he has urged the variorum editors to computerize the enterprise, thus making it "constantly available, on a computer screen or in a print-out" to both its editors and readers for continual revision and easy updating. This vision of an ultimate, never to be finished, Borgesian variorum has its appeals. It would ensure a tool rather than an eventual monument; and, among other things, it might allay the fears of some that "anything not included in [the present *Variorum Chaucer*] will be forgotten and anything included will be necessarily incomplete and possibly even distorted."[8] As part of some totally bookless future scholarly world it would become the final arena of arbitration for all "published" Chaucer scholarship, replacing individually edited volumes of a variorum with an omniorum built by all.

Until and unless that happens, we will have the present, growing *Variorum Chaucer*. Ross's volume is evidence that it is less purely an observor of the scholarship, too much a participant in it; but it reflects God's plenty and we will not be able to get along without it.

Notes

1. *A New Variorum Edition of Shakespeare*, Vol. 1 (Philadelphia: J. B. Lippincott Co., 1871), p. vii.

2. Ibid., Vol. 3 (1877), p. v.

3. Ibid., Vol. 5 (1886), p. viii.

4. Edwin Greenlaw, Charles Grosvenor Osgood and Frederick Morgan Padelford, eds. *The Works of Edmund Spenser: A Variorum Edition*, Vol. I (Baltimore: Johns Hopkins Univ. Press, 1932), p. v.

5. "Thoughts on the Variorum Chaucer: Editorial Intervention in the Explanatory Notes," *The Chaucer Newsletter*, 2, i (Winter 1980), 4.

6. On page 8, in the sentence about Kittredge, the third comma is not needed; on page 14, in the sentence introducing Wedderburn's poem, a comma is needed before "writes"; on page 23, in the sentence about Nykrog, the comma is not needed; on page 94, line 5, "manuscripts" is misspelled; on page 224, in the note to lines 3709-10, a comma seems necessary before "who." A random check of the general index shows the entry for Cline should include a reference to her having been cited on page 153.

The word *vita* in the title of Walter Burley's book is translated on page 140 as *Lives* and on page 186 as *Life*. The passage of quoted Middle English in the note to line 3655 is translated but other ME quoted in the volume is not. In the

Bibliographical Index, since the second entry for Donaldson is cited in its original place of publication as well as in its reprinted place, the first entry for Donaldson and the first one for Howard ought to include the original places of publication. The date of Siegel's article, mistakenly given as 1961 in the Bibliographical Index and elsewhere in the volume, should be 1960. On page 25 appears a reference to an essay by Brewer ("The Criticism of Chaucer in the Twentieth Century," printed in Cawley's collection) which is not listed under Brewer's name in the Bibliographical Index.

7. "Editorial Animadversion," *The Chaucer Newsletter*, 4, ii (Fall 1982), 3.

8. "Thoughts on Editing Chaucer: The 'Electronic-Information Revolution' and a Proposal for the Future," *The Chaucer Newsletter*, 2, ii, (Summer 1980), 2.

Self-Writing

Paul Connolly

Avrom Fleishman. *Figures of Autobiography: The Language of Self-Writing in Victorian and Modern England.* Berkeley: University of California Press, 1983. xiv, 486 pp.

Janet Varner Gunn. *Autobiography: Toward a Poetics of Experience.* Philadelphia: University of Pennsylvania Press, 1982. x, 154 pp.

Albert E. Stone. *Autobiographical Occasions and Original Acts: Versions of American Identity from Henry Adams to Nate Shaw.* Philadelphia: University of Pennsylvania Press, 1982. xvi, 349 pp.

Albert Stone's informed estimate is that Americans have now produced upwards of ten thousand autobiographies. Some are classics; others sell by the hundreds of thousands from the racks of drugstores and supermarkets. Autobiography, he maintains, is "firmly rooted in our culture—and . . . not simply in high literary culture" (p. 3). It is best undestood, therefore, not simply as a literary genre but as a complex cultural activity, particularly when one considers further that "in endlessly different ways all autobiographers are anthropologists returned from sojourns in the countries of their own pasts" (p. 7).

To appreciate why autobiography is so popular a form of democratic expression, one must recall, Stone suggests, three basic features of the American culture in which it flourishes. First, "Americans have confirmed and celebrated the individual, as few other cultures in history have done." The cultural impulse animating both the writing and reading of American personal history is "belief in the validity and importance of every single life" (p. 9). If belief in *individualism* is the first article in the American creed, then the achievement of personal *identity* is the second. In autobiographies, democrats bear witness to their personal identities. "Discovering and asserting the self . . . is the 'original' achievement autobiography affords and our culture applauds" (p. 10). Thus, this study of "Versions of American Identity" has as a fitting epigraph Erich Fromm's observation that "The sense of 'I,' or the sense of self, means that I experience myself as the true center of my world, as the true originator of my acts. This is what it means to be original."

The third feature of American culture deserving attention is our initial lack of a historical identity. When Tocqueville took stock of America in 1831, one of the places he peered into was our bookstores. There he noted many American books on the shelves, few of them by known authors; America, particularly its aristocratic readers, borrowed its literature from England. In autobiography, however, the country began to create both a literature and a historical consciousness, for "[the] impulse to find order and meaning in past experience is the initial motive behind autobiography, as it is for other modes of history-making" (p. 10). Appropriately, then, the other epigraph to Stone's book is an observation by Alfred Kazin: "The deepest side of being an American is the sense of being like nothing before us in history . . . the experience of being so *much* a 'self'—constantly explaining oneself and telling one's own story—is as traditional in the greatest American writing as it is in a barroom."

Albert Stone relishes the fecundity of American autobiography as the natural expression of a free democratic society. Avrom Fleishman, on the other hand, though equally open to the protean possibilities of autobiography, must be less sanguine, I suspect, about the prospect of barroom biography— and not only because his own book aims to "set out the most telling evidence for the study of some important autobiographies in nineteenth- and twentieth-century England" (p. 39). To tell the story of one's life, writes Fleishman, "may seem as unmediated an action as a writer can perform, given his experience in the subject and the singular authority he can exert over it" (p. 43). Given a self and a language, to write a life may seem a simple act of will. But Fleishman's study of "The Language of Self-Writing" is an argument for "inter-textual relations, if not historical continuity, in autobiography," and he advises students of the subject to "emulate the autobiographers in their sense of tradition" and to "speculate that the books an autobiographer is most likely to be reading are other autobiographies and that these will make an appearance of some kind in the work of his hand" (p. 2). Americans may — or may not — be an exception to the rule, but Fleishman maintains that "A man does not sit down to write his autobiography in cold blood, without a language somewhere at hand for the enterprise" (p. 113). Where, then, does the language of self-writing come from? "From the community's narrative discourse, to be sure," concludes Fleishman, "especially from those authoritative texts which embody the prevailing schemas of a life—whether simply human, heroic, or divine." And where autobiography is written by nonliterary or barely literate men and women, "Life stories, like lives, are modeled after idols of the tribe"; the distinction of individual lives "is traceable to their variation of the community's sense of the sequence and shape of individual life itself, a communal sense, which they by turns enforce and help to modify" (p. 479). Both Stone and Fleishman recognize the complex interaction between culture and autobiography, but whereas Stone focuses on how the individual story contributes to the cultural narrative, Fleishman focuses on how the cultural narrative helps define the individual story.

The particular task that Fleishman sets himself, then, is to examine the "verbal formulas, iconographic images, and intellectual commonplaces . . . . I shall use the term *figure* as most supple in its applications . . . that show a high incidence in autobiographical writing down through Western history," providing many self-writers with language for their lives (p. 49). His study opens with a survey of six modern approaches to autobiography—attending to the Truth, Meaning, Convention, Expression, Myth, or Structure in autobiography—but concludes "on a note resembling the research report of a negative outcome of an experimental design" (p. 37). Each approach, taken singly and simply, is inadequate to this complex genre; "all are broadly enlightening but are useful only operationally in exhibiting the behavior of one or another self-writing" (p. 36). The bulk of the book, therefore, is a series of essays that begins with a study of Augustine's *Confessions*.

"When we say that an autobiography presents the *figure* of a man, we dwell on a mental image of him along with the linguistic strategies by which that image has been conveyed" (p. 50). Augustine is the "father of autobiographical figuration," for he modeled his life on the lives of Adam, Moses, Jesus, and Paul, and most comprehensively assembled the phases of life on which later writers focus: Natural Childhood, Fall and Exile, Wandering-Journey-Pilgrimage, Crisis, Epiphany and Conversion, Renewal and Return. In so doing, Augustine creates "a rhetoric of the possibilities of self-writing" (p. 52) and "demonstrates the power of figurative narration to order the chronicle of this-worldly events by a set of traditional figures, the chain of metaphors assuming the shape of myth" (p. 57). Augustine becomes, in Fleishman's reading of intellectual history, "the enduring figure of autobiography, and his/its presence will be discovered in a number of nineteenth- and twentieth-century works—some as inevitable as Newman's apology, others as unexpected as Gosse's family romance" (p. 72).

Before turning to the Victorians, however, Fleishman examines the spiritual figures that arose from the Reformation, particularly in the writings of Bunyan and Fox, in order to show how "The cultural basis for the emergence of a popular set of autobiographical conventions was the struggle for and limited success in establishing an experientially tested religion" (p. 76). He considers also the figures of Romantic autobiography, again demonstrating, particularly in *The Prelude*, how "the stages of spiritual autobiography are placed in the foreground of these poems of intellectual prodigals on pilgrimage for self-discovery and poetic power" (p. 98).

In the second section of his five-part book, Fleishman examines the "great age of English autobiography" and the figures of its prophets: Carlyle, Mill, Newman, and Ruskin. I cannot dwell, as I should, upon particular premises of Fleishman's learned and coherent argument, for more general issues deserve greater attention. Here I can only indicate that he extends his study of "shared religious concerns, figurative language, and narrative imperatives" (p. 39) into the autobiographical fiction of Dickens, Brontë, Eliot, and Butler; into the extended autobiography of Yeats, Sassoon, O'Casey, and Muir; and finally, into the modern autobiographical fiction of Lawrence, Joyce, Dorothy Richardson, and Virginia Woolf. "Before it comes to provide possibilities of individuality," writes Fleishman, "language learning is a socializing process" (p. 414), and no autobiographer, however eccentric or egocentric, writes without some resonance of the communal figures of language. Thus, toward the end of his book Fleishman can claim: "In autobiographers from Augustine to modern times, we have learned to see the co-presence of personal experience and literary convention as no contradiction but a confirmation of the ways in which autobiography transforms experience into art" (p. 424).

A question the student of autobiography must inevitably ponder, though it has not been addressed thus far, is what makes an autobiography better or worse, successful or unsuccessful. "No prescriptions for procedure or estimation will be forthcoming here," states Fleishman (p. 37). But this is not entirely true, despite the fact that he takes obvious pains throughout his book to qualify every descriptive or evaluative statement that might become normative. Autobiography is, for example, a more sophisticated art than mere memoirs, for while in the latter the "focus of attention is almost always on the I-past," the former "derives much of its interest from the complications generated by the interplay of I-past and I-present" (p. 192). Later, Fleishman writes: "The self-writings we recall as especially readable are those which venture more than a dignified statement of the facts—which become memorable by the mediation of their prose," particularly prose which fully utilizes "the traditional figures of autobiography, even in the act of casting off the weight of inherited religious and social commitments" (pp. 275-76). Edwin Muir's *An Autobiography* wins particular praise for "the self-awareness of the self-writer in foregrounding the traditional autobiographical figures": its array of "biblical figures, archetypal patterns and prophetic... rhetoric continues to give *An Autobiography* the kind of luminous power we associate with *The Prelude* as a definitive autobiography" (p. 369).

"The self-conscious autobiographer," writes Fleishman, "may ask himself: What am I doing in the act of writing this? His book becomes an answer to this question" (p. 37) and, one might add, "self-consciousness," of a particular kind, becomes a criterion of autobiographical achievement. For further on Fleishman adds that "the answer to such queries is sometimes framed—by those writers with a lively sense of their predecessors—in terms of that question posed and answers given by previous writers" (p. 37), thereby establishing not a "generic code" but "an ongoing and ever-changing stream of influence and originality." Indeed, it is this sense of tradition that makes autobiography, for Fleishman, "one of the most sensitive registers of the idea of human existence and the pattern of individual life in a given society" (p. 43).

But where does barroom biography fit into all this—the distinctively modern American form of swash-buckling self-assertion? Albert Stone is as interested as Avrom Fleishman in the "self-consciousness" of autobiography, but these two scholars, each of whose books is the culmination of a decade's work, do not see eye to eye because they are not looking at the same thing. The personal history reported in autobiography is "consciously lived history" (p. 12), writes Stone, and it is the consciousness a self-writer achieves when "life is brought to language" (p. 11) that gives autobiography its value both for an individual and a culture. Fleishman is not insensitive to the valorous act of the autobiographer "writing for his life" (p. 36), but what, he might ask, of the informing "figures" that a culture's language brings to the individual life. "To stress the self as the creator of history . . . maximizes one's freedom from circumstances and social stereotypes" (p. 13), writes Stone, but what about the liberating force of cultural circumstance and stereotype, against which we define our individuality and personal identity, Fleishman might ask.

"[E]ven eccentric or experimental autobiographies recreate a self-in-its-world" (p. 15), assumes Stone, but it remains necessary then to "see beyond and around as well as *into* each singular life" (pp. 15-16), in order to transform the individual story into a cultural narrative. Such transformation does no violence to the story, insists Stone; indeed, "Autobiographers intend such uses of their private lives" (p. 16). Thus, the particular task Stone sets himself is that of the cultural critic, who seeks to "identify and connect the mythic and ideological components of an individual's story, noting the distinctive ways each author manipulates ideas to make bridges beween public life and private experience, past and present, and between writer and reader" (p. 16).

Like Fleishman, Stone grounds his generalizations about autobiography in essays on individual autobiographers, and, again like Fleishman, he does his work admirably well. More specifically, Stone examines "seven characteristic occasions or situations which a number of modern American autobiographers have found themselves in, to speak both metaphorically and literally" (p. 19): the situation of "an old man looking back over a long career" (W. E. B. DuBois and Henry Adams); the situation of "holy men who relate their soul's experience" (Black Elk and Thomas Merton); the situation of writers whose gaze is fixed upon "the self as child and youth" (Louis Sullivan and Richard Wright); the situation of "a long list of autobiographers who have witnessed or endured family and psychic violence" (Alexander Berkman and Conrad Aiken); the situation of "becoming a woman in male America" (Margaret Mead and Anais Nin); the situation of "the creative act of collaboration between a subject and a professional writer" (Ossie Guffy, Nate Shaw, and Malcolm X); and the situation of "experimental narratives of modern experience" (Norman Mailer, Frank Conroy, and Lillian Hellman).

One of the six modern approaches to autobiography that Fleishman found unsatisfactory, in and of itself, was the preoccupation with the "Meaning" that an autobiographer imposes upon the events of life, particularly when the self is conceived of "as a process rather than a determinate structure" (p. 11). Stone also recognizes limitations in this approach, and yet it is one he favors in defining "Versions of American Identity." While an autobiographer inevitably communicates information and may openly express an ideology, "the ultimate aim," writes Stone, "remains identity and not historical messages" (p. 17). The issue Fleishman raises is the extent to which historical messages, embedded in the figures of language, are a vital part of identity. It is not surprising, therefore, that Stone prefers to "compare synchronically works which deal with similar themes, social situations, or strategies of self-construction" (p. 19), construing a cultural narrative in the individual stories, while Fleishman expresses admiration for Paul Ricoeur's "intention to return a diachronic dimension to the study of narrative" (p. 476). Nor should it be surprising, therefore, that Stone attends to the "the whole oratorio . . . of separate Songs of Myself" (p. 27) in American autobiography, while Fleishman focuses on those firm voices of English autobiography that are not only self-conscious but whose self-consciousness is already informed by a sense of cultural history, evident in the figures of language they employ in their self-writing.

While I have said that Fleishman and Stone do not see eye to eye because they are looking in different directions, I would not be understood to imply that either of these readers is blind in one eye. These are, each in its own way, two extraordinarily learned and balanced books that correct more simple- and single-minded views of autobiography. The ship of "self" sails on perilous seas, between the Scylla of the solipsistic notion that history is what the self makes of it and the Charybdis of the positivistic notion that the self is what history makes of it. Fleishman and Stone both aim to chart a middle course of understanding those who read and write lives by closely examining what T. S. Eliot called, in another context, "Tradition and the Individual Talent."

Janet Varner Gunn's *Autobiography* expresses a similar regard for balance that she casts not in terms of Scylla and Charybdis but of Narcissus and Antaeus: "Interpretation has its risks: the risk of drowning, like Narcissus, in ideological certainty; or the risk of being strangled in the air by some brand of Herculean deconstruction when, like Antaeus, the autobiographer loses contact with the 'spot of time' which grounds his or her life, and *autos* is severed from *bios*" (p. 145). Or, to restate the two dangers directly again, without figures: "Just as the idealistic self might threaten to engorge the world in the direction of solipsism, the empirical world might engulf the self in the direction of positivism" (p. 72).

While Gunn assays the particular autobiographical writings of Thoreau, Wordsworth, Proust, Augustine, and Black Elk, her book, more than the other two, offers a theory of autobiography, "A Poetics of Experience." Whereas Stone studies specific autobiographical "occasions" or situations, Gunn examines "the autobiographical situation," defined as "the autobiographical impulse, the autobiographical perspective, and the autobiographical response" (p. 12). Her central argument is that it is possible to report a life in narrative time without sacrificing depth to surface, contrary to the opinion of Cartesian "essentialists" who maintain that autobiography can be no more than "a failed version of the autobiographer's real self, which is presumed buried under its various and changing appearances and therefore ineffable" (p. 30). It is Gunn's position, as a professor of religious studies, that "The issues at the heart of narrative theory . . . are religious issues having to do with the sense we can make out of our experience in the world" (p. 37).

In making her case, the first problem to which Gunn responds is "the idealistic tendency of the self's over-projection on the world" (p. 68). "Rather than starting from the private act of a self writing," however, Gunn begins "from the cultural act of a self reading" (p. 8). Autobiographical "readings" of lives are constructed by "selves who *inhabit* worlds, not by a subject who has had to pay the price of world-habitation for access to itself" (pp. 8-9). In a phrase reminiscent of Fleishman, Gunn notes that the self's entry into history "makes it impossible to assume an unmediated relation to the world" (p. 9). When an autobiographer brings a life to language, "he or she always adumbrates a perspective from somewhere—namely, from a world whose meanings and codes and even whose burden of unintelligibility serve to locate and ground that perspective" (p. 9). As will be evident momentarily, however, the paths of Fleishman and Gunn soon diverge.

The other side of the autobiographer's problem is "his or her relation with the world: namely, the problem that the *world* presents in leveling the poet's perceptions in his or her entanglement with it" (p. 68). Borrowing from Karl Popper and E. H. Gombrich, Gunn maintains that all cognitive processes involve schema and corrections: "The schema are the habits of perception, the mental sets with which the artist, as a member of his or her society, necessarily begins, and which, in the process of 'making and matching,' he or she goes on to correct" (p. 70). A mental set necessarily "inclines us toward a particular way of understanding the present," but correction, on the other hand, is also needed "since new experience necessarily fails to fit our expectations" (p. 71). Such correction preserves individual perception in the face of the world's leveling influence.

"Many of the most popular and innovative forms of autobiographical literature today are, then," writes Albert Stone, "attempts to recreate a self amid and against a variety of cultural cross currents and forces which limit or deny that possibility" (p. 276). Janet Gunn agrees, for she writes: "Although there is no denying the continuing convention in modern autobiography, there is greater insistence on what Ortega calls man's 'ontological perspective,' the necessity of being the 'novelist' of oneself, itself a convention in much autobiographical writing of recent times" (p. 73). Indeed, she goes on to say, "It is the *success* of autobiography, not its failure, that becomes the problem—one of over-orientation rather than alienation, of completing not losing the self" (p. 119). Autobiography can become ideology, she adds, "when the multidimensionality of lived meaning, with its inescapable burden of unintelligibility, is abandoned for the unambiguous clarity of monochromatic truth" (p. 120).

So, in attending particularly to contemporary autobiography, Gunn values the "corrections" of what Fleishman calls "figures of language." More recent autobiographies, she observes, "no longer utilize so comfortably the trope of religious pilgrimage," preferring more naturally, "if more nervously," the trope of the stage, which "allows for the variety of roles that a less fixed social structure and a more heteronomous set of religious views both permit and, in fact, enjoin" (p. 57). In her own reading of Augustine's *Confessions*, Gunn finds that "the religious hermeneutic of *credo ut intelligam*, restored to temporality, can be paradigmatic of all acts of autobiography, indeed of all interpretive activity. The 'I' that understands," she concludes, "is the 'I' that is *committed* to understanding; the 'I' that believes is the 'I' that belongs" (p. 134).

In their studies of modern culture, Stone and Gunn celebrate the fact that, in Stone's phrase, "autobiography today remains vital as an individuating language act and shared cultural activity" (p. 26). Fleishman, too, examining more "traditional" works of English autobiography, values the individuating power of self-writing, while emphasizing the enduring importance of schematic figures of language. Each reader will decide for himself, therefore, the unresolved question of where the greater danger lies in 1984: From the fire of ideology that leaves ash in the mouth of the self-writer; or from the ice of egocentricity that freezes the self-writer's tongue. Gunn and Stone remark the perils of fire, but Fleishman reminds us, to borrow from Robert Frost, "that for destruction ice / Is also great / And would suffice."

In Memoriam, **Complete**

Jacob Korg

Susan Shatto and Marion Shaw, eds. Alfred Lord Tennyson. *In Memoriam.* Oxford: Clarendon Press, 1982. 397 pp.

The primary aim of this edition is completeness. Its introduction and notes bring together the scientific, religious, literary, and biographical backgrounds of Tennyson's poem, and record the comments made about it by Tennyson, his friends, his contemporaries and his critics in a thoroughly comprehensive way. Since the editors aim to include everything of possible relevance, some will feel that many of the echoes and parallels they cite are not especially relevant, and the repetition of previous annotations is, of course, unavoidable.

The edition's distinctive feature is its exhaustive textual apparatus, which records all the variants in the numerous manuscripts and printed editions of *In Memoriam.* Tennyson transcribed most of the poems in his sequence into two large notebooks which are now in the possession of the Tennyson Research Centre at the Lincoln Central Library and Trinity College, Cambridge. But there are many other notebooks, stray leaves, and records of impromptu composition and correction. One of these is a notebook of prayers copied by Tennyson's sister, Emily, which contains four stanzas of the introduction to *In Memoriam.* Another is an envelope on which Tennyson wrote some lines that occurred to him eighteen years after the first publication of the poem; the envelope was apparently lost at the back of a desk for a time, but it was recovered, and the new poem was inserted in 1870 as number 39 in the sequence. When it went to press, *In Memoriam* had first, a trial edition, and then many further issues which were more or less revised. The present edition gives full descriptions of all these sources in an appendix, and records every variant in them, generating a large and complex textual apparatus. The magnitude of this editorial project may be suggested by the fact that the list of minor variants—those too unimportant to be included as textual footnotes—occupies 67 pages, while the annotated text of the poem itself is 117 pages long.

There can be no doubt about the diligence and professional competence that have gone into this work. (There is one exception—a glaring and uncorrectable printer's error, the reversal of the first two pages of the text, duly acknowledged by an erratum slip.) But in choosing to develop their textual apparatus in a perfectly mechanical way that excludes the possibility of editorial judgment, Shatto and Shaw have entered on controversial ground. When the editors of the Ohio edition of Browning's works (now the Ohio-Baylor edition) decided to ignore the accepted distinction between substantive and accidental variants, and to record all the changes in punctuation and spelling Browning had made in the many editions of his works, they produced a textual apparatus that was attacked as unwieldy, unreadable and unnecessary. Yet, as one of the editors, Park Honan, asserts in a recent review of a rival edition, the Clarendon Press Browning (*Browning Society Notes,* Vol. 13, No. 2), no change of punctuation is entirely without meaning, some are very significant indeed, and future critics may find even trivial changes interesting. He also implies that editors who set out to record the development of a text must record all variants, without making distinctions among them. Such arguments as these no doubt can be taken as justifying Shatto and Shaw in their effort to be complete. But the effort turns out to be, in a measure, self-defeating because the vast majority of the variants in *In Memoriam* really have little or no bearing on the sense of the poem, and do not reconstruct "the growth of the poem" (one of the aims of this edition), but show Tennyson tinkering with poetry that is already formed, or correcting spelling and printer's errors. By failing to select the handful of significant variants from among the hundreds of others, Shatto and Shaw have obscured, rather than illuminated, the process of composition.

In assessing the value of recording variants, we must first

remember that the text of *In Memoriam* has been fixed since 1884, and no emendations have been made to it since that time, in this or any other edition. Shatto and Shaw's elaborate textual apparatus is entirely concerned with readings that Tennyson himself corrected or rejected. Further, their effort to achieve completeness in tracing "the growth of the poem" through these is compromised by two unfortunate facts. First, the two main manuscripts and most of the minor ones are fair copies whose corrections tell little about the poem's development. The earlier manuscripts in which, as the editors reasonably speculate, the poet wrote and revised his first drafts have been lost. Second, the text of the first printing was set not from any of the manuscripts now known, but from a fair copy made by Mrs. Coventry Patmore, which has also been lost. The differences between the surviving manuscripts and the printed version show that Tennyson continued the process of revision in this intermediate manuscript, and that there is an irremediable gap in the record of "the growth of the poem."

The volume of Tennyson's poems edited by Christopher Ricks for the Longman's Annotated English Poets Series in 1969 includes an edition of *In Memoriam* with explanatory and textual notes which are often cited by Shatto and Shaw. They observe, in their preface, that Ricks was not allowed full use of the Trinity Manuscript, which was made available later; this statement implies that their edition's textual annotation could be more nearly complete. The manuscript given to Trinity College bore an inscription written by Tennyson's son, but signed by the poet himself forbidding the copying of any portion of it, and this condition was attached when the library received it. As a result, Ricks was able to read, but not to record, the variants it contained. The ban was lifted in 1969 (and it would be interesting to learn how the poet's wish was set aside), so that it became possible to produce a "full-scale" edition of the poem.

But examination shows that the accessibility of the manuscript has added little to Ricks' annotation. Of the seven full stanzas found in the Trinity manuscript which did not reach publication, five were published by Ricks, who found them in sources not affected by the ban, one was paraphrased, and the other was noted. The local variants Ricks could not record are, like most of the variants, of little importance.

The urge for thoroughness that may be considered inappropriate for textual annotations has led Shatto and Shaw to compile an informative set of explanatory notes. Not many of these are original; the aim here is rather to bring together annotations and comments from scattered sources, together with such material as parallel passages in other works and the sources of Tennyson's religious and scientific ideas. Like other commentators on *In Memoriam*, the editors have found it hard to resist citing as parallels passages that have some faint resemblance to Tennyson's lines. Many of these echoes seem to reflect the editors' erudition rather than the poet's consciousness. They can be extremely arbitrary, as when Shatto and Shaw connect one passage with Virgil's account of Aeneas' descent to Hades and also cite a parallel for the same passage from Carlyle's *French Revolution* suggested by Ricks. Tennyson objected to this kind of commentary; as the notes to this edition show, he once read an article which offered similar parallels and put some such notation as "Nonsense" in the margin next to them.

The apparatus offers a number of things that have not been done, or not done so thoroughly, elsewhere. Shatto and Shaw bring together a short, but interesting list of variants that show how Tennyson revised the poem to give it a less personal tone. For each section of the poem they discuss the problem of dating, carefully reviewing all the relevant evidence. They show that various parts of it correspond to certain classical *genres*, and even to specific examples, demonstrating that it is more strongly influenced by Tennyson's classical background than has generally been realized.

But the main value of the commentary rests on the details gathered from a wide range of sources, beginning with the observations Tennyson himself made about his poem. It appears that he believed Hallam's body to have been set ashore at Bristol after its voyage from Vienna when he wrote "The Danube to the Severn gave / The darken'd heart that beat no more," and that he did not learn until many years later that it had been landed at Dover. Hallam himself emerges a little more clearly as we are given some facts about his interest in Italian literature and some passages from his own poetry that display his tendency to melancholy. The editors suggest, quite plausibly, that in writing the group of poems dealing with Lazarus, Tennyson had a favorite picture in mind, Sebastiano del Piombo's *Raising of Lazarus.* They show that when he lamented the decline of "the grand old name of gentleman," he was echoing the words of a popular song, and that the allusion struck at least one of his contemporaries as discordant.

The vocabulary of *In Memoriam* is, in general, unremarkable, but the notes alert the reader to overtones that tend to be lost with the passage of time, and trace some of the less common words to their probable sources in Tennyson's reading. When he wrote of "Aeonian hills," the poet was using a word that had been coined as recently as 1768, and was probably as unfamiliar to his public as it is today. The "roaring wells" that are imagined as engulfing Hallam's body are identified as a dialect term for whirlpools that Tennyson found in one of Scott's novels. Section 56, after raising the poem's most crucial spiritual questions, famously concludes that their answers lie "Behind the veil, behind the veil." The notes present the many comments that have been made about this image, including those that locate the veil in specific contexts. In his *Victorian Devotional Poetry,* G. B. Tennyson shows that the image of the veil was used by the Tractarians to express the idea that man was, for his own benefit, shielded from direct knowledge of God. The poet used the image in this sense when he suggested, in a letter, that revelation itself might be "a veil" meant to conceal the naked glory of God's love. The veil was a way of preserving mystery and persuading the believer to rely on faith instead of seeking spurious knowledge. To the modern ear, "Behind the veil" sounds like a cry of despair from one who has given up the possibility of resolving his spiritual dilemmas. When its background is considered, it sounds much more like an expression of thanks for deliverance from a state of mind that made true devotion impossible.

Reasonable people will no doubt continue to differ about the style of textual annotation represented by Shatto and Shaw's *In Memoriam*. The theory of critical editing has become a subject of fundamental disagreement, and nothing like a consensus can be expected until the general controversy is resolved. The question of how variants should be recorded is only a minor issue within the larger ones. Conventional editors feel that it is their duty to exercise discrimination in recording variants as well as in shaping the text itself. This, of course, leaves the door open to differences of opinion, and even to charges that important material has been suppressed. Shatto and Shaw belong to the school of editors who feel that they should locate and record every reading, without presuming to evaluate its importance. It is hard to argue with the cold logic of this position, even if one feels that it leads to the inclusion of much that is superfluous, or that the contributions made to the understanding of the text do not match the effort and expense involved. Shatto and Shaw have not given much consideration to questions of economy, convenience, or readability; rather they have aimed at producing a final, complete edition that contains all the relevant information and that will be permanently useful. There is no doubt that they have succeeded in accomplishing what they set out to do.

Wolfe's Literary Agent and Her "Profession"

James L. W. West III

Richard S. Kennedy, ed. *Beyond Love and Loyalty: The Letters of Thomas Wolfe and Elizabeth Nowell*. Chapel Hill: University of North Carolina Press, 1983. xxvi, 164 pp.

> Among all those quasi-professional businesses which like to refer to their customers as clients the business of literary agenting is probably the most enduring and the most adhesive. Technically, you can fire your agent; it is a sticky operation, but a determined man can achieve it. It really ends nothing. Years after you speak to him you will, if you are a writer for publication, be finding mud tracks across the carpet. He will have been there in the night doing what he calls "representing" you, and you will wake up in the morning with that tired feeling as if a Doberman pinscher had been sleeping on your chest.
>
> Raymond Chandler
> "Ten Per Cent of Your Life"
> (*Atlantic Monthly*, Feb. 1952)

All authors do not dislike literary agents as much as Raymond Chandler did, but most authors do have ambivalent feelings about them. Who are these people who take ten per cent off the top, and what do they do to deserve their money? Any producer or creator will always have a fair amount of contempt for the middleman, the broker, who after all is just one more person making a living off his blood and sweat. Hence the large dog on Chandler's chest.

Thomas Wolfe was as cranky as Chandler in his dealings with agents, editors, and publishers. It took a gifted literary agent to handle his work and his ego—someone self-effacing enough to endure his cantankerousness but still spunky enough to back him down on occasion. And, if that agent were a woman, she had to resist his amorous advances as well. Elizabeth Nowell was such an agent, and such a woman. Under review here is an edition of her correspondence with Wolfe; the volume, entitled *Beyond Love and Loyalty*, reveals the crucial part she played in Wolfe's career. She was nearly as important to him as Maxwell Perkins, his discoverer and editor at Charles Scribner's Sons. Wolfe's *The Story of a Novel* (1936) and Bernard De Voto's nasty reaction to that small book ("Genius Is Not Enough," *Saturday Review of Literature*, 25 April 1936) have directed attention to Perkins as the shaper of Wolfe's books, but we can now see that Nowell had almost as much influence on Wolfe as Perkins. Certainly she had more to do with turning him into a successful professional writer.

Like most other industries, publishing was dominated by men before 1950. Today it is still largely controlled by males, but women have made significant inroads in the business, and many of them now hold positions of responsibility and authority. One of the earliest and best modes of entry into publishing for a woman was to work as a literary agent. Women faced less discrimination in this field than in any other branch of publishing, and they quickly proved themselves adept and successful. Nowell's road into the profession was as typical as any. She was born near New Bedford, Massachusetts, in 1904; she graduated from Ethel Walker School in 1922; and she attended Bryn Mawr on a scholarship. After graduating in 1926, she took a course in writing at Columbia and published some pseudonymous short fiction in *Harper's Bazaar* and *Redbook*. In 1928 she began work as a manuscript reader at *Scribner's Magazine* where she stayed for five years, learning a good deal about book and magazine publication during her tenure there. In 1933 she left Scribners to work in Maxim Lieber's literary agency, and late that year she began to handle manuscripts by Wolfe, who had been sent to the agency by Perkins. Wolfe, who was struggling to complete *Of Time and the River*, had exhausted most of his sources of advance income and needed to publish some short fiction in order to remain solvent. His problem, as always, was length. Most of the promising material in his fabled trunk of manuscripts was in units of from 12,000 to 20,000 words—not an attractive or saleable length on the periodical market since most magazine editors wanted short stories of no more than 7,000 or 8,000 words.

Nowell assumed the task not only of cutting these manuscripts down to marketable size, but also of turning Wolfe into a more disciplined writer. Perkins had been pursuing the same end since 1928, with mixed results, but Perkins had been working with Wolfe on novels. The novel is an expandable form; there is no length past which it absolutely cannot go, and its saleability is not necessarily affected by its page count. Perkins's efforts to stem Wolfe's flow of verbiage could only be backed by aesthetic reasoning. Nowell had the stronger weapon of economics. Wolfe needed money and would earn it only if he put his short stories into marketable length and shape.

Nowell went beyond the normal duties of an agent in her work with Wolfe. She edited his typescripts paragraph by paragraph, sometimes making block cuts, sometimes pruning within sentences, and she gave useful advice about narrative tone and descriptive detail. She understood that magazine fiction, if it was to sell quickly and for a good price, needed a clearly stated or implied theme—a point that the reader could readily grasp. Wolfe had a tendency to stray into autobiographical ramblings and oratorical prose, and she worked tirelessly with him to break these habits. Her method was to mark the number of words tentatively cut from each paragraph in the margin of the typescript beside the paragraph. Then she would total the marginal numbers at the bottom of each page. Wolfe usually took her advice, and eventually it had a positive effect on his writing. Gradually his manuscripts became shorter and more compact, less autobiographical and more didactic. By 1936, Nowell no longer had to prune his work nearly so stringently.

Wolfe's ability to adapt his work to magazine standards and Nowell's energy in marketing the manuscripts yielded good income. Her first sales for him were to low-paying journals like the *American Mercury*, which paid $200 for "Boom Town" in

1934. By 1936, however, she was having much more success and was selling Wolfe's work with some regularity to the *Saturday Evening Post* and *Redbook* for fees as high as $1,200 and $1,500. By this time she had left Lieber's agency to set up in business on her own, and Wolfe had come with her. He came to depend on her for all kinds of personal services, especially after his break with Perkins and Scribners in 1937. Nowell had to do his banking, handle his foreign rights, and even deal with his cleaning woman while he was out of the country. And there was something else: she had to believe in him and his work. Fortunately this part came easily to Nowell, who seems to have had genuine enthusiasm for Wolfe's writing. After reading the typescript of "The Party at Jack's" for the first time, she wrote him an excited letter in which she used "swell" seven times (and "sweller" once). She knew how to quiet his fretting over magazine editors: "But you know I know you've got more talent and poetry and sincerity and greatness in your little finger than all the other writers I can think of put together," she wrote him in March 1935. "It's fallen on me to pick on you about all the nasty little details that magazine editors carp at, and I'm afraid you'll always think of me as dragging you out of the Chatham bar or waving a blue pencil in your face. But underneath all that I always get a tremendous inspiration out of your things and out of working with you" (p. 17). She encouraged Wolfe to do the writing and leave the marketing to her. "Dearie," she wrote him in August 1937, "I wouldn't worry about the big magazines at all, if I were you. Don't try to play the slot machine, but just go ahead and write the best you know how, with your eye on Mount Parnassus" (p. 72).

But Nowell could also be tough. In April 1936, she stood up for herself and insisted on a ten per cent commission for the work she had done on *The Story of a Novel,* a book which would probably not have seen print had it not been for her efforts. That fact is ironic, for *The Story of a Novel,* and De Voto's reaction to it, helped precipitate Wolfe's break with Scribners. Nowell steered him to Edward Aswell at Harpers, but Wolfe died before the two men could carve a book from the "mess" of a manuscript that then constituted "The Web and the

Rock." Aswell's editing of Wolfe's three posthumously-published volumes has been a subject of much recent controversy. One scholar, John Halberstadt, has argued that these three books were in effect fabricated by Aswell, who took extraordinary and even unethical liberties with Wolfe's manuscripts. Most Wolfe scholars—including Richard S. Kennedy, the editor of *Beyond Love and Loyalty*—have attacked Halberstadt for his assertions, but no one has been able to erase the suspicion that he may be right. Wolfe's last three books are beginning to look tainted.[1] The Nowell-Wolfe letters may add fuel to the controversy, for they reveal clearly the give-and-take that occurs when a gifted author tries to write for the magazines. Length, subject matter, style, sex—all must be "negotiated" with editors by a clumsy, unpredictable system of submission and rejection, inference and suggestion. The agent is called upon to be the dispassionate intermediary, the medium through which the commercial pressures of the literary marketplace are conveyed to the author.[2]

When Elizabeth Nowell became a literary agent in 1933, she was entering a relatively young profession in America. The background of that profession (or quasi-profession, if one accepts Chandler's terminology) is interesting. Informal literary agents were operating in America as early as the 1820s. James Lawson, a Scot by birth, came to New York City in 1815 where he worked as an accountant for his uncle. He devoted substantial amounts of time to literary matters and shortly became unofficial representative for such writers as Bryant, Paulding, Poe, Simms, and Whittier. He was also friendly with the actor Edwin Forrest, and through Lawson many plays were submitted for Forrest's consideration. Lawson built up a network of friendships by doing favors and making small loans to publishers and editors. His negotiating powers were strengthened by these connections and by the fact that he charged no fee from his authors. He sought to be "gentlemanly" in all dealings, an approach that made him the more effective. The appearance of leisure and detachment has always been one of the qualities an agent must cultivate. The publisher much prefers dealing with a relaxed, objective agent rather than a debt-pressed, importunate author.[3]

By the 1840s Park Benjamin was also functioning as a literary agent in New York. Today Benjamin is most frequently remembered as one of the editors of the cheap weekly *Brother Jonathan*, a newspaper that pirated the work of established British novelists and caused great difficulties for more dignified but no less piratical American publishers. Benjamin lost his inheritance in the Panic of 1837 and thereafter turned to newspaper work, journalism, and occasional publishing for his livelihood. He operated an informal literary agency during the 1840s and handled some of the work of Longfellow, among others. Benjamin also ran a lecture bureau for authors. Initially he charged no fee or commission for these services; his rewards were the goodwill of authors, editors, and publishers. By the early 1860s, however, he had begun to ask for remuneration. His 1863 advertising flyer promised that for a fee of ten dollars he would "assist authors" by reading their manuscripts critically and giving a "candid opinion." If he approved the manuscript, he would recommend it to a publisher. "Letters of inquiry or asking advice," he added, "should always cover a small fee, to compensate time and trouble in replies."[4]

In the 1870s and 1880s there were several literary agencies in New York, including the Athenaeum Bureau of Literature, the New York Bureau of Literary Revision, and the Writer's Literary Bureau. American authors' societies also performed some of the services of literary agencies. The Association of American Authors, for example, published a journal, offered information on the costs of publication, arbitrated disagreements between authors and publishers, and supplied funds to needy members. All of these early agents, paid and unpaid, offered writers the advantage of having a representative in New York, which had by then become established as the publishing center of the country. The author could live and write elsewhere but enjoy the advantage of face-to-face bargaining through his agent.[5]

The first successful and influential literary agent in America was Paul Revere Reynolds. He was born in Boston in 1864; his father and paternal grandfather were prosperous physicians, and the family had impeccable New England roots. Reynolds attended Harvard, where he was a classmate of George Pierce Baker and a student of William James. He took his baccalaureate in 1887 and worked briefly for the Boston publishing firm D. Lothrop & Co. before returning to Harvard in 1888 to study for the M.A. under James. Reynolds was much influenced by James, who once said that the young Bostonian had the most honest mind he had ever taught. The years under James's tutelage were perhaps the most satisfying and stimulating in Reynolds's life (one of his fellow students was George Santayana), and he took his master's degree with honors in 1891.

Reynolds went to New York that same year and almost by accident became the American agent for the books of the English publisher Cassell. His duties were to place Cassell's books with American publishers and to dispose of plates or printed sheets from a list supplied by the London office. He also served as a scout for Cassell and attempted to secure English rights to promising books or magazine material for his employer. For his services he was paid five hundred dollars annually. Reynolds was a vigorous worker who went out of his way to meet many of the prominent American writers, editors, and publishers of the day. By 1893 he had become American agent for William Heinemann and for Sampson, Low; and he had begun to work on commission for individual authors, handling their book and magazine submissions from his office at 70 Fifth Avenue.[6]

Reynolds, and the agents who followed him, were not readily accepted by New York publishers. Both Charles Scribner and Henry Holt refused for a time to deal with any author who employed an agent, and other publishers were scarcely more hospitable. Publishers had always enjoyed an advantage in face-to-face dealings with authors, and they did not wish to lose their edge. They disliked being forced to bid against one another for an author's work and argued that the author should accept a lower royalty in order to keep all his work "under one roof," where it could be promoted in such a way that each book would help sell its fellows. Publishers also resented the implication that they were sharp or dishonest dealers. They maintained that the publisher's interests were identical to the author's: both wanted to produce a good book that would sell to as many readers as possible. But the publisher neglected to mention, or failed to realize, that all author-publisher dealings are initially of an adversary nature. Within reason, the publisher wishes to secure the right to manufacture and sell the work on terms most advantageous to his house. The author wishes to receive the highest payment possible for his labor and to retain as many of the subsidiary rights (or percentages of them) as he can. By the early decades of this century, publishing had become so complicated and potentially profitable that the author badly needed a representative who was principally loyal to him.

Only a few decades before, authors had dealt directly with printer-publishers in all details of manufacture and sales. The results were usually unsatisfactory from a financial standpoint, but the writer could exert immediate influence over production and marketing of his work. When publishers began to function separately and to job out the manufacturing of books, they became middlemen. And by the 1880s and 1890s heads of publishing houses had begun to employ editors and other subordinates to insulate themselves further from authors. Faced with this situation, the author had no choice but to employ his own intermediary—the agent.

Agents became more useful as the possible ways for an author to republish his work increased in number, but the agent had to be energetic, persistent, and imaginative in his efforts to exploit the earning potential of a given literary property. Most of all he needed experience and a wide circle of contacts. Agents, like publishers and editors, went through no training program and passed no certification exam. They were not really "professionals": anyone could become an agent, simply by declaring himself to be one. The temptation was great to make the easy and expected sales, collect the ten percent commission, and leave the difficult work alone. Most agents insisted on handling a writer's entire output. Everything had to pass through the agent's hands, and he received ten percent of the entire literary income of the writer, even when the writer occasionally handled a sale himself. Many authors balked at this condition, and agents accordingly began to require written contracts to stipulate the conditions of the relationship. Only occasionally would an agent make an exception for a big-name author because being known as that author's agent provided prestige and helped bring in other business.

It was not long before agents began to manage the literary careers of their authors, to advise them on the directions in which they should take their work, the genres they should develop, and the material they should exploit. Agents also began to read, critique, and even revise manuscripts. In giving advice and working on manuscripts, the agent naturally could be counted on to keep commercial possibilities in mind since his livelihood depended on his success in marketing the author's work. The agent became a means by which commercial considerations and popular taste exerted influence on the author's work, a way in which the tension between art and commerce was communicated to the author. And since much of the agent's work was with mass-circulation magazines, he was usually in closer and more immediate touch with middlebrow tastes than were editors at book publishing houses.

Many agents began to function as editors, offering criticism and suggesting cuts and revisions, often refusing to offer a manuscript to a publisher or a periodical until it had been revised and rewritten. The agent's role here was crucial and probably useful. A good agent wanted every manuscript to sell to the first buyer to whom he sent it. This was an unrealistic goal, of course, but the agent aimed for it nevertheless. The author would receive his payment more quickly, and the agent would collect his commission immediately. Too, the agent would not waste time for which, in effect, he would not be paid. The agent wanted his offerings to come to publishers and magazines as clean, crisp typescripts, with no lifeless characters, confused chronological schemes, or blurry plots. The agent wanted to develop a reputation for offering goods which could be put into print with a minimum of editorial effort. That kind of reputation would help sell later work by the same author to the same market, and it would help sell work by other authors in the agent's stable to the market. This was an additional reason for insisting that an author channel his entire literary output through the agent. If it passed muster with the agent, it was likely to sell more quickly, and for a higher price.

Most publishers were quick to realize that the agent could be useful—that he could, in fact, take over many time-consuming duties for the editor in return for the ten percent commission he charged. Agents came to function more and more as editors had once functioned. They answered mail, secured books and research materials, performed errands, and assisted authors with their tax returns. Indeed the functions of the editor and the agent eventually became almost identical, and many persons moved easily from one position to the other. The only real adjustment was to transfer one's primary loyalty from author to publishing house, or vice versa. Some persons even managed to free-lance or work part-time simultaneously in both capacities. Book publishers and magazine editors came to rely heavily on agents for materials; eventually some publishing houses and periodical editors ceased to consider manuscripts which came in over the transom and dealt only with agents. The *Saturday Evening Post,* for example, paid a weekly call to Paul Revere Reynolds to pick up the material by his authors that *he* thought might interest them.

Authors were also quick to recognize the advantages of employing a literary agent. The agent, who often had some training in law and accounting, could examine publishers' contracts and royalty statements for hidden clauses or mathematical errors. Agents were indispensable in dealing with the bureaucracy and inefficiency of large trade publishing firms. The agent was usually a stronger and less emotional negotiator than the author, and he had a better notion of the monetary value of a manuscript. If the agent handled the work of other famous authors he could bargain from a stronger position, using the promise of a submission from a popular client to encourage purchase of a manuscript by a lesser-known writer. And the agent was invaluable when he could cause houses to bid against one another for an author's work—or even auction the manuscript to the highest bidder. These are slightly unethical practices for an author but perfectly acceptable for an agent. The agent could function as the author's banker, taking his royalty and magazine receipts, paying off his creditors, doling out funds from a reserve account, and advancing money on unwritten or unsold work. It is not surprising, therefore, that many authors came to feel more loyalty toward their agents than toward their editors or publishers. Especially today, when an editor's job is apt to depend on the profits shown by the books he brings in, the author is inclined to ally himself more closely to his agent. The agent, one presumes, will always be there; the editor may be gone tomorrow if the books by his authors have not been selling well.

The agent also serves a useful psychological purpose. He can rid the author-publisher relationship of the taint of business, leaving the author and editor free to discuss artistic and aesthetic matters without a residue of ill feeling from prior contract negotiations. Put more bluntly, the agent is someone on whom both the author and the publisher can blame their greed. If the contract negotiations have been difficult and the publisher has had to concede more than he wished to, the author can explain that the agent was to blame for the holdout. The publisher may in fact have been parsimonious in his original offer, and the agent may only have forced him to agree to reasonable terms, but the publisher, too, can conveniently blame the delay on the agent. The publisher and the author understand, of course, that the agent was simply reflecting greed (or niggardliness) on both sides, but neither one need admit that fact. The editing, production, and selling of the book can proceed without rancor. On the question of literary agents, one must learn that there is a great difference between what people say and what they really believe. The agent must simply learn to accept this shifting of blame as one of the drawbacks of his "profession."

If one is to understand the literary career of a serious public writer, one must study his relationship with his literary agent. We need a great many more books like Kennedy's edition of this correspondence, and we need studies of individual relationships between particular writers and agents. There is a good edition of F. Scott Fitzgerald's correspondence with his agent Harold

Ober, but beyond that, very little has been published.[7] The Stephen Vincent Benét-Carl Brandt partnership is a promising one for study, as are the relationships between Upton Sinclair and Bertha Klausner, Ida Tarbell and Paul Revere Reynolds, John Steinbeck and Annie Laurie Williams, and Flannery O'Connor and Elizabeth McKee.

Beyond Love and Loyalty appears to have been a pleasant labor for Kennedy, who knew Nowell and was aided by her early in his own career.[8] Kennedy has done an excellent job of presenting and annotating these letters, and the University of North Carolina Press has produced a handsome, well designed book. Two small cavils: the textual emendations policy is vague, and the letter from Wolfe to Vardis Fisher on pages 25-26 might better have been worked into the introduction. Kennedy has scrupulously included the full texts of all letters, however, even when they deal with such mundanities as typing fees and German royalties. That is the kind of information from which one kind of literary history is made, and this is the kind of book that scholars in the field of modern American literature should welcome.

Notes

1. On the "Wolfegate" controversy, see John Halberstadt, "The Making of Thomas Wolfe's Posthumous Novels," *Yale Review*, 70 (Autumn 1980), 79-94; Kennedy, "The 'Wolfegate' Affair," *Harvard Magazine*, Sept.-Oct. 1981, pp. 48-62; Halberstadt, "The 'Creative Editing' of Thomas Wolfe," *Harvard Magazine*, Jan.-Feb. 1982, pp. 41-46; and Kennedy, "Editorial Influence and Authorial Intention: A Manuscript Exhibition," in *Thomas Wolfe: A Harvard Perspective* (Athens, Ohio: Croissant, 1983).

2. Sometimes the negotiations, concessions, and rewritings damage the literary artifact. A good example is Wolfe's story "No More Rivers," which he wrote in 1936 and which Nowell attempted to sell without success until 1939. Wolfe had worked too closely to his sources, and some of the objects of his satire were recognizable. Also (and as usual) the story was too long. With Nowell's help Wolfe cut the manuscript from sixty-three to thirty-four pages and rewrote to disguise his prototypes, but the narrative suffered. His hero's character does not cohere, and the piece is still overwritten. Kennedy includes "No More Rivers" as an appendix to this volume, and it is a welcome addition, for it includes some of Wolfe's fine, emotional writing about trains and cities, but one wonders why Kennedy printed the cut-down and rewritten version. Is

the original version no longer extant? It would be the more valuable document, one would think, though perhaps Kennedy wanted to include the version Nowell had a hand in making.

3. Thomas L. McHaney, "An Early 19th Century Literary Agent: James Lawson of New York," *PBSA*, 64 (Second Quarter 1970), 177-92.

4. Lillian B. Gilkes, "Park Benjamin: Literary Agent, *et cetera*," *Proof*, 1 (1971), 87.

5. See "Agency in America," chapter 6 of James Hepburn, *The Author's Empty Purse and the Rise of the Literary Agent* (New York: Oxford Univ. Press, 1968).

6. Frederick Lewis Allen, *Paul Revere Reynolds* (New York: privately published, 1944).

7. *As Ever, Scott Fitz—Letters between F. Scott Fitzgerald and His Literary Agent Harold Ober, 1919-1940*, ed. Matthew J. Bruccoli and Jennifer McCabe Atkinson (Philadelphia: Lippincott, 1972).

8. Kennedy has apparently been working on this project for several years. Portions of the introduction were published earlier in his article "Thomas Wolfe and Elizabeth Nowell: A Unique Relationship," *South Atlantic Quarterly*, 81 (1982), 202-13.

Retouching Mark Twain's Portrait

Guy Cardwell

Horst H. Kruse. *Mark Twain and* Life on the Mississippi. Amherst: University of Massachusetts Press, 1981. xxiii, 183 pp.

James L. Johnson. *Mark Twain and the Limits of Power: Emerson's God in Ruins*. Knoxville: University of Tennessee Press, 1982. x, 206 pp.

Susan K. Harris. *Mark Twain's Escape from Time: A Study of Patterns and Images*. Columbia: University of Missouri Press, 1982. xii, 169 pp.

When we are under the duress of compelling evidence or logic, we have a proclivity to make limited conceptual changes but to resist making related changes in our patterns of thought that would appear to be necessitated by the same evidence or logic. As the body may produce antibodies in defense against a virus, so the mind rallies its champions to preserve the old order and ensure that established patterns are kept as nearly undisturbed as possible. And, as has been observed, whereas large revisions in ideas may seem to come suddenly, they in fact possess histories, are more processes than events.

In the small world of literary history and literary criticism, such general observations are applicable to attitudes toward Mark Twain as man and writer. Scholars have noted—though piecemeal or parenthetically and with hesitant recessions—his pessimism, determinism, and political élitism, his ethnic arrogance, his delighted ascension to bourgeois gentility, his timidity in the face of public opinion, and his many neurotic manifestations, such as exhibitionism, compulsive speculating, fear of mature sex, and, especially during the final decade of his life, his almost surely unconsummated paedophilia. It has been recognized that he felt himself to be an outsider in any society, a transcendent stranger, the object, finally, of a malign God's particular hatred.

Despite these observations, the scholarship persists in maintaining overall quite different traditional suppositions— patterns of ideas grounded in a cult of personality which was in turn based on the legend that Mark Twain was a healthily robust, optimistic Westerner, sanely humorous, ideally humanitarian, the deviser of a new democratic ethos rooted in the life and character of the folk. Little exception has been taken to typical assertions like that by Dixon Wecter in the *Literary History of the United States* (1948): "In the activities of the external man as well as in character and temperament, Mark Twain was a representative American" (p. 917). By this still surprisingly intact view, Twain remains, more than any other writer, the heroically second self of each of us. Glaciers and scholarship move slowly.

When one examines new books on Twain, it is interesting to see whether they are intended to effect changes in image and legend or to revise critical attitudes toward the works which were shaped to conform to image and legend. The volumes reviewed here vary widely in the extent to which they break out of the accustomed problematic.

Mark Twain and Life on the Mississippi is in a way true to its type: it has most of the virtues and some of the defects that British and American scholars regularly suppose to be characteristic of German dissertations. Professor Kruse's book was first accepted as a *Habilitationsschrift* at the University of Kiel and was later published in German.[1] The English version is expanded and updated from the German and is in every way superior to it. This first full-length book on *Life on the Mississippi* is primarily a genetic study that attempts to trace Clemens's initial intentions and their actualization between 1866, when he first mentioned wishing to write a "Mississippi book," and 1883, when the volume was published. Some of the details that Kruse has assembled are new, and it is helpful to have all the data, old and new, brought together. The author credits Henry Nash Smith, dean of living Twainians, and

Everett Emerson, then a professor at the University of Massachusetts, with support that made possible the publication of this translation and amplification.

The outstanding virtue of the volume is the thoroughness with which Kruse has searched out both printed and manuscript materials that provide information bearing on composition. He adds a good deal to our knowledge of Clemens's use of literary and extra-literary sources. Questions arise, however, with respect to the interpretation of evidence and the conclusions that may be drawn from the study.

One of Professor Kruse's primary theses is that by printing two rather misleading letters by Twain, Albert Bigelow Paine, Clemens's official biographer, gave false clues to critics who in turn failed to grasp Clemens's intentions and misjudged *Life on the Mississippi*, considering it incoherent. These critics have assumed that the demands of the subscription book trade for a large volume when added to the need to submit a manuscript within a limited time—and here Kruse shows that they are only in part correct—forced Clemens to incorporate hastily selected, unintegrated borrowings from travel books and therefore to be disappointed in his finished volume. *Life on the Mississippi* is, by this view, neither the book Twain meant to write nor so good as it should have been.

In challenging these suppositions, Kruse devotes a great deal of attention to proving that in 1871, when Clemens said that he intended to write a "standard" book on the Mississippi, the word "standard" denoted in his lexicon a volume with a general structure sufficiently loose to accommodate a wide variety of incongruous yet appropriately integrated materials. A "standard" work would, Kruse thinks, rest primarily on observation, experience during a field trip, and the use of relevant source materials. Clemens intended his digressions; his appendices were not afterthoughts.

Important though the meaning of the term "standard" is to the study, Kruse is not entirely convincing in his efforts to define what Clemens meant by it at what seems to have been the only time that he used it, nor does Kruse indicate that the meaning of the term, if Clemens ever thought of it again, must have changed in time. He envisions, I believe, a more precise and stable idea of a standard travel book than Clemens ever had any notion of. In this instance, either Clemens did not have a fixed plan in mind or he abandoned it. As Kruse observes on page 12, the "Old Times on the Mississippi" chapters (which appeared first in the *Atlantic Monthly* in 1875) had nothing to do with the earlier conceptions of the "Mississippi book." Neither, he could have added, did they bear any relationship to Clemens's use of the word "standard."

While entering a few caveats (e.g., pp. 62-69; 106 ff.), especially with respect to chapters 51-56, Kruse repeatedly defends the literary merits and formal integrity of *Life on the Mississippi* on the grounds that Clemens succeeded in doing what he set out to do: he never intended the conventionally unified work that adverse critics have hypothesized for him. One simple way to combat the fallacy that Clemens's adherence to something like a long-standing plan makes his book a good one is to point out that the most significantly extraneous material— the "Old Times" chapters—is the best part of the volume. Even if one were to agree that the "Old Times" chapters are well assimilated and that Clemens fulfilled a long-standing, carefully elaborated plan, the grounds as stated are not sufficient for making an aesthetic judgment.

A corollary to Kruse's chief argument will seem unacceptably paradoxical to those who take a mechanistic view of overall structure as well as a mechanistic (or traditionally logical) view of the proper relationships among internal details. In essence Kruse holds that *Life on the Mississippi* is coherent because Clemens planned its incoherence. This conception calls for brief consideration of a set of ideas about form as they relate, closely or distantly, to Clemens's travel books.

Kruse alludes repeatedly to Clemens's two congeneric predecessors to *Life on the Mississippi—The Innocents Abroad* and *Roughing It*—and thinks Clemens made significant structural advances in the later book, yet he never exposes formal relationships among the three with any completeness. He opposes the idea, but I think it probable that Clemens would have thought *The Innocents Abroad* and *Roughing It* to be "standard" works; and the same might be true if Clemens had actually used an emissary's notes as a basis for writing a volume on the South African diamond fields. He was less planner than improviser. Whatever he had in mind when he wrote to his wife on 27 November 1871, "I bet you I will make a standard work," went through one major change (the inclusion of the "Old Times" chapters) and many minor ones. No plan need have demanded the use of long passages that critics have rightly pointed to as superfluous, tedious, and stuffed lumpishly in. In opposition to these critics, Kruse holds that Clemens's assimilation of borrowings always shows ingenious and successful artistry and that he obviously "maintained a high critical standard in his selection of materials throughout the writing" (pp. 82, 99-100). In any case critics must apply criteria for judging the merits of a book, including its structural merits, other than its conformity or nonconformity to an author's plans.

Clemens's plans tended to be highly indefinite when he originated them and to break down and be reconstituted during the course of composition. He regularly became bored, fretful, and exhausted as he drove himself through the later stages of writing, revision, and proofreading; and in consequence there were times when relevance and integration were slighted and nearly anything went, plan or no plan. *Life on the Mississippi* shows this. Clemens's borrowings were, of course, not always dull or badly assimilated; some of his more challenging ideas and successful passages are to a usually unrecognized extent pastiches. Kruse demonstrates this well, for example, in discussing sources for Clemens's treatment of Walter Scott, burial customs, decorative art, and architecture (pp. 69-82).

The major point made by Kruse—that structurally *Life on the Mississippi* is much the book that Clemens intended—has, for reasons different from his, been taken for granted by some readers and critics, especially by those who have taken into account Clemens's career in journalism, his literary models, and his view of his books as products for the market. With these considerations in mind, for one to "prove" that Twain had an inclusive scheme in mind does not demonstrate that he was careful with respect to internal structural relationships or that he labored with vigilance to bring some exigently conceived aesthetic artifact into existence. To come to so firm a conclusion would be as inappropriate as it would be to think that he desired to play the role of the disappearing author and to keep his personality out of his semi-autobiographical travel books. His general intentions were nevertheless much along the lines indicated by Kruse: he would put together a travel volume suitable for subscription publishing, leaving ample room for improvisation and borrowings, and would then enrich the whole with infusions of his pseudonymous persona.

If *The Innocents Abroad* and *Roughing It* served as precursors and models for Clemens, so in a less immediate way did any number of the travel books that he knew. Contemptuous though he was of their naiveté, sentimentality, and hyperbole, when he prepared his *Quaker City* letters he learned from books like Samuel Irenaeus Prime, *Travels in Europe and the East*; William C. Prime, *Tent Life in the Holy Lands*; Lamartine, *A Pilgrimage to the Holy Land*; and Charles Wyllys Elliott, *Remarkable Characters and Memorable Places of the Holy Land*. Guide books, if we may in this context distinguish them from travel books, could also be considered influential, for they too could be *omnia gathera* of facts, opinions, shreds of history, legends, descriptive flights, and quotations in verse and prose; nor did they exclude the ludic. Clemens made extensive use of such books as Harper's *Handbook for Travelers in Europe and the East*, Galignani's *New Paris Guide*, and Murray's *Handbook for Travellers in Northern Italy*.

The eclectic form that Clemens elected to use had in addition remote and distinguished antecedents that a critic might take into account in forming his judgments. Northrop Frye, Joan Webber, and others have speculated on the epic as an encyclopaedic genre, one that accompanies the myths of a culture, probes the boundaries of Heaven and Hell, and is comprehensive in space, time, and philosophy. It has been said of Homer's poems that they were "sources of romance, satire, hymns, orations, epigrams, and histories"; because of Homer, subsequent poets consciously adopted inclusiveness as a technique.[2] What, then, might a historically minded critic of structure properly claim for those romantic, epic-like American narratives, *The Innocents Abroad, Roughing It,* and most particularly *Life on the Mississippi?*

Also behind Clemens's travel books were loosely organized genres that came later than the Greek epics, heterogeneous forms such as were common in the Middle Ages and, closer at hand, among the Romantics. J. G. von Herder emphasized the need for naturalness and spontaneity, for the display of nationalistic emotions drawn from the soil. Jean Paul Richter believed his *The Invisible Lodge,* a Menippean satire, to be— like Schiller's *Ghostseer* and Goethe's *Faust*—both complete and a work in progress, a ruin at birth, unfinished in a way that mirrors the incompleteness of life. Richter's novels exhibit the intrusive author who self-reflexively scrutinizes his own work. (Not totally dissimilar are some of the short, hybrid sketches by newspaper humorists whom Clemens enjoyed and imitated.) *Don Quixote* and other novels admired by Clemens were loosely inclusive, and *Life on the Mississippi* has often been characterized as a blend of materials that ends by being a kind of autobiographical fiction.

In assuming that Clemens's Mississippi book would have been greatly superior artistically to the book he actually wrote if only the writer had not been diverted from some hypothecated, tightly organized model, critics are both neglecting the volume's antecedents and tacitly attempting to categorize the writer as akin to Henry James or Gustave Flaubert. Kruse, facing the question of artistry, argues that because Clemens wrote the kind of book he meant to write and was satisfied with it, *Life on the Mississippi* must be considered an artistic success. But this is only to substitute a positive way of defending Clemens for the negative one that circumstances were adverse to authorial scrupulosity. In their different fashions, both Kruse and the critics with whom he disagrees are in the camp of Gladys Bellamy and the numerous Twainians who have been eager to show that although Clemens sometimes nodded, he was a highly self-conscious, exacting artist. The greater part of the body of Mark Twain criticism has, in fact, been muddied by large, exaggeratedly partisan assumptions concerning such things as the profundity of Clemens's social thought and the intensity of his artistic vision. To qualify partisan optimism, it is necessary to hold in mind that Clemens was a humorist and a long-term newspaperman with, as he saw it, a constant, pressing need for cash; he wrote for a wide audience, not for the Jamesians.

Although to discredit excessively aggrandizing assumptions is not the purpose of Kruse's limited demonstrations and assembled materials, this is what they tend to do. Only at a distance was *Life on the Mississippi* cast against elevated models; Clemens elaborated and acted on no theory of literary encyclopaedism; except for the "Old Times" chapters and a few subsequent chapters in a similar vein, his book was more constructed—cobbled together—than written. Most of Clemens's contemporary readers saw no great cause for complaint, however, in the rambling nature of his travel books. They knew comparable types; they recognized some sort of adequately encyclopaedic unity supported by the binding influence of a strong, already much admired, narrative persona. Moreover, defenses both simple and sophisticated have been marshalled, or may be.

Howells was well aware that problems with respect to structure were posed by Clemens's travel books but satisfied himself and those who accepted his then distinguished authority with a series of vindicatory explanations. Reviewing *Roughing It* in the *Atlantic Monthly* for June 1872, he declared that although an encyclopaedia probably could not be constructed from the book, excursions and digressions were the very woof of it, and the resulting complex was a triumphant harmony of colors. In the *North American Review* for February 1901, his explanations were more detailed and various. One was semi-joking: Clemens possibly owed "his literary method to the colloquial style of some far ancestress who was more concerned in getting there, and in amusing herself on the way, than in ordering her steps." Clemens's "personal" books, he added for theoretical good measure, "have not only the charm of the essay's inconsequent and desultory method . . . but they are of an immediate and most informal hospitality which admits you at once to the author's confidence, and makes you frankly welcome not only to his thought but to his way of thinking." (This explanation that the author's desultory way of thinking parallels and exonerates looseness of structure is echoed by Kruse on page 39 when he writes that the presence in *Life on the Mississippi* of an author-narrator with a discursive intelligence to a degree justifies lack of unity.) Howells praised, too, the "naturalness" of Clemens's prose, his setting down whatever came into his mind, his instinct for "something chaotic, ironic, empiric in the order of experience." Disorder is a kind of natural order. Formlessness in literature is, one gathers, an aspect of organicism: it corresponds to the shapelessness, discontinuities, and indeterminateness of life. Formlessness becomes a necessary attribute of realism, of literature adapted to and representative of the best of all epochs, the best of all nations.

The kind of justification for disorder to be found in Howells is, of course, a cliché: it is to be discovered scattered widely in nineteenth- and twentieth-century literature. Simone de Beauvoir speaks of a draft of a novel that she was working on: "Les intrigues trop bien bâties m'agaçaient par leur artifice; j'avais voulu imiter le désordre, l'indécision, la contingence de la vie; j'avais laissé filer dans tous les sens les personnages et les événements."[3]

A more intricate treatment of the matter bringing in the idea of contemplative reflexivity plays a role in *La Prisonnière* (1923), where Proust, an inveterate penetrant of emotional-literary subtleties and velleities, offers what may serve as a gloss on the rhetorical drift of Clemens's unifying epigraph (to be considered below). Musing on Wagner's music and on the painting of Elstir (Monet?), Marcel notes the power of art to help him plunge down into himself and understand the sensations of another. The works of Wagner so operate as to participate in the character of being "toujours incomplètes, qui est le caractère de toutes les grandes oeuvres du xixe siècle; du xixe siècle dont les plus grands écrivains ont manqué leurs livres, mais, se regardant travailler comme s'ils étaient à la fois l'ouvrier et le juge, ont tiré de cette auto-contemplation une beauté nouvelle extérieure et supérieure à l'oeuvre, lui imposant rétroactivement une unité, une grandeur qu'elle n'a pas." Although Clemens could not have perceived the thematic bearings of his book with complete retrospective suddenness— they are too obvious for that—his selection of an epigraph may well have been an impromptu stroke of genius. The passage chosen lends, certainly, the air of a "Unité ultérieure, non factice." Although not so intricately and mechanically made as the type to which Proust refers, without the epigraph, the book, "fût tombée en poussière comme tant de systématisations d'écrivains médiocres qui, à grand renfort de titres et de sous-titres, se donnent l'apparence d'avoir poursuivi un seul et transcendant dessein." Howells's analysis parallels Proust's praise of a "Unité qui s'ignorait, donc vitale et non logique, qui n'a pas proscrit la variété, refroidi l'exécution."[4]

In some ways Kruse does not press as hard as he might his defense of the purposiveness of Clemens's open structure. When he states (pp. 106, 109) that Chapters 53-56 uncharacteristically deviate from the plan for a standard work and violate structure, he is taking too absolutely *his* hypothecated notion of a "standard" work and scanting various integrating forces, including that of the narrator's personality. As he says, these chapters are valuable for biographical information, for "finely sensed psychological analysis," dramatic liveliness, and truth. Do they, then, deviate "from the plan for the standard work" and "clearly violate the structure"? If so, what of the "Old Times" chapters? It is not enough to say, as Kruse does (pp. 129-30), that Clemens was so successful in designing the rest of the book as a complement to the "Old Times" section that the two parts taken together form a standard work. The "Old Times" chapters remain, in truth, almost violently extraneous. Did Clemens at any point feel that he had departed from his plan, bring himself up short, and snub himself back to his plan by reverting to the connectedness of a journey and to the integrating themes of material progress, democracy, and moral improvement? Probably not. Probably Clemens's schema becomes in Professor Kruse's mind more strict than it ever was in that of the author.

One example from many of Kruse's attempts to make Clemens into a consistent planner may serve to illustrate the questionable nature of the enterprise. Editors and critics have debated whether the "raftsmen" episode taken from what was to become *Huckleberry Finn* and used in Chapter 3 of *Life on the Mississippi* should be returned to *Huckleberry Finn*. Kruse asserts that Clemens pointedly took the episode with him from Elmira to Quarry Farm and that the documentary and historical value of the passage, emphasized by the author in its new context, rather than its value as copy, must have determined its inclusion. One need not disagree flatly with this interpretation to consider it speculative and its implications doubtful. The transfer of the passage could have taken place for reasons of the moment: publication of *Life on the Mississippi* was approaching; more good copy was always needed; the passage was highly readable and would add interest to the work at hand. Its value as "document" in *Life on the Mississippi* seems not to have prevented Clemens from contemplating returning it to a later edition of *Huckleberry Finn*. That he did not do so could lead one to believe, with some reason, that in this instance he was not the considered artist, that inertia probably operated. We know, at any rate, that for no very cogent literary reasons he repeatedly inserted or attempted to insert anecdotes, sketches, tales, diatribes, and descriptive passages into books for which they were neither originally intended nor particularly well suited.

The extent to which *Life on the Mississippi* is suffused with ideas of progress and the not quite opposed idea of nostalgia (Walter Benjamin would link the two) will impress nearly any reader. Professor Kruse takes up—though rather unsystematically—the roles played by these ideas, especially with respect to structure. It is his conviction that Clemens had programmatic purposes fixedly in mind (apparently from the beginning), that his "standard" work was "intended to function like Cervantes's *Don Quixote* and would serve as an instrument of social as well as political change" (p. 124). It is almost impossible for me to believe that Clemens had any such intention when he first conceived a book on the Mississippi, and it is difficult for me to believe that his social purposes were carefully plotted; on the other hand, to see that he struck thematic attitudes—ones he had struck earlier and would later—is unavoidable.

Clemens contrasts past and present, barbarism and civilization, social stasis and industrial progress. These were natural, popular oppositions. They flooded the magazines in Britain and in America, were prominent in the English travel books about America that Clemens read and borrowed from, were suggested by the life he observed in the course of his actual return to the Mississippi, and almost necessarily found their places in the book during composition. As Kruse intimates on pages 123-24, few comments on *Life on the Mississippi* have been less perceptive than that by Edward Wagenknecht, who asked, "Did any book ever begin less invitingly? And was there ever a less beguiling epigraph than 'The Body of the Nation'?" In fact the epigraph (which begins, *"But the basin of the Mississippi is the BODY OF THE NATION"*) struck a pervasively national chord—the Mississippi Valley as symbolic of the country's unity, as the heartland—that still reverberates. It was derived from *Harper's New Monthly Magazine* for February 1863 and drew for its language on Lincoln's Annual Message to Congress of 1 December 1862. I interpret it as more general and less topically political than does Kruse. I doubt that Clemens was insisting on the rightness "of the Republican Party and its Reconstruction policy" and was stressing that his book was an instrument for raising the South from "maudlin Romanticism" and civilizational backwardness (p. 124). The epigraph was, however, as inevitable as an epigraph may be, was indicative of the self-reflective, self-contemplative organization of the book which followed, and foreshadowed the themes of progress, stasis, and nostalgia.

Kruse attempts, I think completely unnecessarily, to explain what he takes to be the incongruity of social commentary in a "standard" travel book. He also supposes that removal of certain criticisms of the present indicates that Clemens was overtly a consistent devotee of progress (p. 54 ff). In fact, Clemens was accustomed to entering social commentary in his writings, the magazines were filled with it, Howells not only praised it but wrote it, and it was stock-in-trade for English travel writers. Like Clemens, both English and American travelers often identified New England and the upper Mississippi with progress and the present, the South, particularly the lower South, with stasis or regress and the past. Certainly Clemens tended to eliminate obvious contradictions, but minor revisions in the manuscript of *Life on the Mississippi* intended to remove doubts about progress (if that were indeed their purpose) can be only supplementary to more general considerations. Clemens was never a consistent thinker (whence spring urgent disagreements about, say, *Huckleberry Finn* and *A Connecticut Yankee*). His oscillation between nostalgia and praise of progress was, furthermore, characteristic of *mentalité* among Americans. Throughout his writings one finds sentimentality, nostalgia, pessimism, and reportorial cynicism side by side with anti-sentimentality, rationalism, and an enthusiastically optimistic view of technology and industrial capitalism. Like others, he clung to and idealized a simpler past that had been a matrix for heroism and found disturbing some of the effects of a generally beneficial technology and industry, of the perilous great shift from *Gemeinschaft* to *Gesellschaft*. Change, including political and commercial corruption, threatened the comfortably democratic society (once slavery was gone) that industrial progress had made possible in the northern and western states.

Treatment by Kruse of Clemens's social criticism in *Life on the Mississippi* seems particularly questionable on the key issue of his attitudes toward the South. A countervailing strain of nostalgia remains very strong despite dominantly hostile attitudes toward the Old South, the lower not-so-New South, and, wherever he found it, the atmosphere of dreamy sentimentality that he categorized and castigated as Walter Scottism. In fact, as others have recognized, his attacks on the South whether in the manuscript or in the published book were not so sharp as those by some of the English writers that he riffled through or as those made and implied in *Huckleberry Finn, Pudd'nhead Wilson*, and the notebooks. Nor does a belief in spiritualism represent "another peculiarly Southern sham"

(p. 104); as Clemens writes, the medium sent his bogus letters from the spirit world "all over this country" to his satisfied clients. The two chapters that Twain omitted were not directed specifically against the South, although they have been said to be.

Clemens's inconsistencies in thought may be matched by carelessness in revising. Nor was he so meticulous or ingenious about integrating borrowed or extraneous materials into his work as Kruse believes. If evidences of his artistry in this respect "are to be found throughout his writings," so are evidences of his negligence and inattention, and not least in *Life on the Mississippi*. For the incoherence that Kruse himself finds toward the end of the book, he accepts Clemens's explanation of "broken continuity" as the chief problem (pp. 100; 106-9). (Clemens lays responsibility for the broken continuity at the door of James Osgood because of his suggestions for excisions and revisions.) Difficulties arise with this as with a number of other instances of Kruse's interpretation of evidence. Osgood's deletions and suggested changes were relatively minor; and the loose structure of the volume accommodated many breaks in logical continuity. Furthermore, ambiguity exists with respect to the meaning of *broken continuity*; for Kruse it seems to include interruptions occasioned by social and business activities. Hindering social activities are very different things from literary discontinuities resulting from revisions. In any case, Clemens frequently groaned and despaired toward the end of a fatiguing task, and it is not uncharacteristic that he assign the blame for his plight to others.

One of Professor Kruse's most initially plausible efforts to disentangle logical conflict and, incidentally, to defend Clemens as a thinker betrayed into inconsistency by his unconscious is in the end unconvincing. Kruse argues on page 112 that Clemens presents an "unholy train" (disrupting the tranquillity of the upper River with its "devil's war-whoop" instead of appearing as a symbol of Midwestern progress) because he needs a transition from a purple passage describing scenery to a passage of colloquial dialogue illustrative of the passing of steamboating, the boats having been made redundant by railroads. The image is indeed apt for effecting a transition; but decidedly less apt is the further explanation that this "momentary reversal of the earlier overt system of values can only be explained by the existence of a subconscious uneasiness about the forces transforming life on and along the Mississippi" (p. 113).

It is not necessary to call upon the "subconscious"; other, simpler explanations may be adduced. The implied reversal of values may not represent a reversal at all. Images of the locomotive as satanic were common in the prose and poetry of Romanticism, and Clemens could have been remembering and mimicking. We need not believe that he was unconsciously opposing progress and then consciously removing evidence of his doubts. The spirit of the "Old Times" chapters, particularly, is one of nostalgia, and the enchantingly palatial steamboat — celebrated in these chapters—was itself in the then recent past an instrument of progress. Who more fittingly than the memorialist of the river boat could view its successor, the devouring locomotive, with its blazing firebox and screaming whistle, as a kind of Beelzebub? Not that the regretted paddle-wheelers escaped opprobrium in all contexts. The steamer, too, may be a mechanical monster, as in *Life on the Mississippi* in the chapters on the "fatal voyage" of the *Pennsylvania* when its boilers blew up and, more imagistically, in *Huckleberry Finn* when a side-wheeler bore murderously down on the raft of Huck and Jim, two children of nature. *Mentalité* may deny ideology; ideas and images may be at variance; contexts exert their special demands; and Clemens was not rigorously logical.

In a comparable analysis (pp. 101-2), Kruse treats the inconsistency in statement and imagery in a passage in which a parrot, identified with "a vulgar little tugboat" on which he is a pet, destroys romance and sentiment with his "discordant, ear-splitting, metallic laugh . . . a machine-made laugh, a Frankenstein laugh, with the soul left out of it." Does this sound like an emanation from the unconscious? I cannot believe that Clemens made a conscious identification of himself with "the antisentimental parrot" and technological advances and then unconsciously expressed doubts about progress by way of repellent imagery (p. 105).

James L. Johnson indicates at the beginning of his study on Mark Twain and the limits of power that his purpose is to modify portraits of Twain that emphasize his late skepticism, bitterness, and determinism; he intends to show how the writings always rely profoundly on a conception of a free empowered self that, like Emerson's, can create and control the human environment. Against the background of a critical synopsis of Emerson's shifting conceptions of the Self, Johnson pursues his thesis through novels (with incidental examinations of short pieces) from Twain's early, middle, and late years. In the process of scrutinizing these works for parallels to Emerson, Johnson records, he believes, "the fate of a romantic idea passing from one mind to another, from one era to another" (p. vii) by relating Twain's "fascination with power figures" to Emerson's absorption in "the Man-God" (p. 192). Emerson displayed this absorption particularly in those early essays in which he perceives man as able to achieve the right axis of being and thus to master the world of time and circumstance.

Stimulating though Mr. Johnson's study sometimes is, his linking of the "embittered determinist" and the "optimistic sage" in this way may, as he admits, seem "spurious at the outset." To me, I am sorry to say, it continues to seem fundamentally spurious to the end. Others have noted Clemens's fascination by power and his, I think lesser, absorption in moral issues raised by the possession and exercise of power. His concern with power, it has been suggested, may be explained by reference to the American culture, especially to tales and biographies of Western heroes. This could be the beginning of a reasonable explanation, although one would also need to take into account important personal psychological factors.

To claim basic parallels between Emerson and Clemens, two men radically different in outlook, is another matter. They were men of their times and puzzled, quite naturally, over such questions as freedom and necessity, unity and multiplicity, appearance and reality; and they modified or changed their opinions over the years. Each pondered the nature of the Self, the relationship of the individual to the community, and the clash of the empirical and the spiritual. But their conceptions and attitudes showed little similarity. In the midst of his early agonizings, Emerson already saw himself as insignificant among men but significant through God; he accepted the idea of a moral sense. He lived a comfortably Concordian life, but he placed his faith in what, following Coleridge, he called Reason. The frail, mortal self, he decided early, encases an immortal mind. That mind, that soul, is God: and the pressing claims of materiality may not invalidate this certainty. He could have remarked with Goethe, Et ego in Arcadia—Auch ich war in Arkadia geboren. His thought was insistently moral: the divine inflates and deifies the Self—potentially all Selves. Divinity working through man gives man power over the phenomenal. His egoism was a Transcendental egoism; his empiricist strain did not rule out Spirit.

Unlike Goethe, Samuel Clemens was not born an idealist; it is questionable whether he ever seriously became one. His personal life was flamboyantly extravagant and fleshly. He entertained no Transcendental ideas. To him the "external evidences" of Christianity were a subject for ridicule. He believed in general improvement of society as a consequence of technological progress; but except at a very few uncharacteristic moments he never seems to have envisioned spiritually ennobled possibilities for man. More and more he thought man to be, by and large, contemptible. He wallowed in self-guilt and self-disesteem; alternatively he exhibited an *amour propre* so hypertrophied that it resembled a secular antinomianism. In his imperial moods he soared above ordinary humanity. At his least narcissistic his was never a divine Selfhood available to all who partook of the nectar and ambrosia set before them by a preacher-Platonist; his Self combined the autonomy that Freud discovered in the infant with the hubris of the Romantic artist. Rousseau, Davy Crockett, Thomas Edison, Bob Ingersoll, and Diamond Jim Brady seem likelier cognates than does Emerson. A benevolently progressive moral order, with man occupying a high, harmonious place in a spiritualized, evolutionary plenum, was no more a part of his thinking than it was of that of Henry H. Rogers, the Standard Oil magnate whom he liked and admired more than he did any other man.

An effort at the closing of the synoptic chapter on Emerson to establish likenesses in the attitudes taken by Clemens and Emerson toward "power figures" is no more successful than is the attempt to find close similarities in their conceptions of the Self. Johnson points out that in *The Innocents Abroad* (1869) Clemens made temporary heroes of Czar Alexander II and Emperor Napoleon III and relates this heroizing to Emerson's treatment of Napoleon I. Emerson's view of Napoleon was, of course, shifting and equivocal; moreover, the passage cited from Emerson to attest a correspondence actually invalidates it. Emerson observes that the joyful loyalty with which men suffer the important man to "represent the law in his person, was the hieroglyphic by which they obscurely signified the conscious-ness of their own right and comeliness, the right of every man" (p. 37). This hint of the representativeness of great men, of the divinity in each of us that they foreshadow finds no counterpart in the awed wonderment of Clemens, the traveling journalist, at the worldly authority and significance of Czar and Emperor. When Emerson was most bemused with dreams of heroic activists, he could not have put on the naiveté of Clemens; he could not have made Henry Rogers his most admired man.

When Johnson applies his thesis to *The Adventures of Tom Sawyer, Adventures of Huckleberry Finn, A Connecticut Yankee,* and *The Mysterious Stranger* he finds those novels presenting not triumphantly liberated, spiritualized Selves but materially empowered Selves on slippery slopes, baffled by moral dilemmas, or, as Johnson puts it, reflecting Twain's problems in saving the free but continually threatened Self. Thus out of Emerson comes the subtitle, "Emerson's God in Ruins." Emerson, too, had to recognize man's limitations.

Johnson's analyses determine that Clemens could not work out satisfactorily in either aesthetic or moral terms the operations of "power figures" in the real world; in the end he "found himself in near despair over the implications he discovered" as his characters drift or are drawn into cruelty, tyranny, and egocentricity (p. 9). That Clemens could not work out his problems is clear. What I question is his understanding of and anguish at the moral failures attributed by Johnson to Tom, Huck, Hank, and "Number 44." I am not persuaded that hypothetically heavy emotional investment in the ideal Self explains his bitterness at his supposed discovery that the ideal Self cannot function in the real world. It is true, of course, that he was bitter. In his later years he exerted himself not to achieving an Emersonian, a moral domination of the real world but to despising it and imagining it out of existence.

Clemens's fantasies frequently revolved around ideas of identity, doubles, vengeance, heroism, and transcendence. His narratives are peppered with images of escape from social responsibility and counter patterns of bourgeois acceptances—the combination a compelling reason in all probability for his accessibility and popularity. Neo-Platonic essences, limitlessly imperial Selves appeal to a restricted class of writers and readers. The dream self that Clemens claimed as his "other self" (p. 80) seems to have been a good deal like his ordinary self "freed from clogging flesh," a very different thing from the "rays of organization" thrown out by the exploring soul "to conform"—here Emerson cited Bacon—"the shows of things to the desires of the mind."[5] With reference to Clemens's dream selves and dualities, Johnson himself speculates, I think correctly, that "Twain is at some level flirting with psychic beatification on the one hand and psychic suicide on the other—expressions of a man tangled in an infinite self-love and an infinite self-contempt" (p. 80). Except that Emerson, too, suffered from abulia and gave consideration to Berkleian metaphysics, an Emersonian parallel may hardly be found in this.

A good many of Johnson's incidental reflections, though provocative, involve what I take to be over-readings. One of their virtues is that they often bring at least covertly into question traditional images of Mark Twain. There is a not particularly original Freudian echo in the opinion (pp. 88-89) that Tom erotizes death in *Tom Sawyer* and that Huck, desiring to retreat from the adult world and the reality principle, does the same in *Huckleberry Finn*. To believe that by searching for an identity, and discarding several temporary identities, Huck is expressing father-like powers of generation and the Emersonian Self is less easy to accept. I doubt that Clemens recognized

Huck's inability to establish a sense of self without reference to
the past and without adopting a convincing social role; nor do I
find it probable that when Pap in a delirium calls his son the
"Angel of Death" he is intimating that Huck's dreams of
freedom are more diabolic than holy.

Another illustrative over-reading asserts that in Pap "resides
the authority of reality itself"; and that the struggle between Pap
and Huck is "to determine who will prevail, the world, which
demands of its sons accommodation to the Not Me, or Huck,
with his desire to escape from these limitations" (p. 90). A critic
may not avoid modernizing, but, if any normative influences
exist, by my understanding of Clemens and his texts,
interpretations of the kind cited are overly subtle moderniza-
tions; and the mingling of Freudian and Emersonian Selves does
not help.

Johnson makes plain that Clemens was inconsistent in
thought and ambivalent in attitudes. One would assume that
this adds to the usual difficulties encountered in explicating
texts; Johnson's explications are usually presented, nevertheless,
very firmly, with no hints of the possibility of Fishian
multiplicities. A large-scale problem with the entire volume
seems to me to beset the critic as he seeks confirmation of
Emersonian parallels, moving from life to text and from text to
life. Clemens's writings are strikingly autobiographical, and
circularity in interpretation may not always be avoided; but it is
notoriously questionable to suppose that a speculative reading
may be used to support an uncertain interpretation of the life, or
worse, that a speculative reading confirmed by reference to the
life may then be used to ratify the speculative view of the life that
has corroborated the reading.

Such fictions, such almost fairy tales as the novels by Twain
that Johnson analyzes, are not mathematical propositions; they
are open, inconclusive, and subject to multiple readings.
Nevertheless the hypothesis that Clemens's heroes are divided
between creativeness and destructiveness because doubts evolved
in Clemens about something resembling the Emersonian Self as
he attempted in his fictions to exhibit it at work in the world
suffers from inherent difficulties—the Emersonian Self is so
thoroughly un-Twainian. To my mind problems are

compounded when it is assumed that what may be chiefly technical snarls, as in plotting, generate changes in the author's mind. Nor are the relationships between author and text such that inconsistencies in an author's thinking would explain in all instances either inconsistencies in character development or what seem to be flaws in technique. Characters and technical details possess their own exigencies, exercise their own constraints. Carelessness, too, is a distinct possibility.

Johnson is right, I think, in saying that Hank Morgan is to a great degree a projection of Clemens's own personality. To believe this does not necessarily lead, however, to the conviction that Morgan's inability to sustain his role as a benevolent power figure who modernizes medieval Britain moves Clemens to question the capacity of the Emersonian Self to function in the real world. A less dubious explanation of novelist and novel presents itself. As Johnson knows, Clemens had an irrational, destructive side—witnessed to by his rages, diatribes, and capacity to frighten his own children. Heterogeneous emotions warred within him: sympathy for the victimized, a craving for the security of love, a lust for power and acclaim, a hatred for mankind, and a devotion to technological devices. A mélange of such feelings appears in *A Connecticut Yankee*, mainly because Clemens was writing for himself, partly because he was writing for, among others, Livy and the children. The sentimental love story and overt humanitarianism were to the taste of Clemens and Livy; the cataclysmic finale—almost necessitated by history—suited Clemens's novelistic purposes and his affection for Grand-Guignolism and the portentously theatrical. Too, it may have struck pleasurable terror to the hearts of Susy, Clara, and Jean.

Hank was indeed "the picture of his creator," neither all creativity nor all destructiveness (p. 141). He was another version of Huck Finn, another version of Tom Sawyer. Clemens put him in a sympathetic but not unreasonably good light when he wrote to Clara of an attempted dramatization by Howard Taylor, an old Western friend, that Taylor had captured but one side of the Yankee's character, "his rude animal side, his circus side; the good heart & high intent are left out . . . . I told Taylor he had degraded a natural gentleman to a low-down blackguard."[6]

In his chapter on *The Connecticut Yankee* and in his following chapter on *The Mysterious Stranger*, Johnson speculates on several large topics important to students of Twain—technology, the Moral Sense, dreams, subjective idealism, philosophical nihilism—relating them to Emerson's empowered Self and its disastrous "encroachment on divine prerogatives" (p. 121). Unhappily, he attempts nothing like a systematic account of any of these topics; his comments do little to shore up his analogies to Emerson and are too desultory to be otherwise useful.

Clemens fretted at a limiting world, aspired to wealth, power, and position, and felt both ebullient optimism and intense pessimism about man and society. He lived in an America in the process of being phantasmagorically transformed by industrial capitalism—technology and republicanism had not created a utopia. His early pleasure in his own success was increasingly vitiated by money and family problems; and as close readings of his works in anything like chronological order amply testify, his initial tendencies toward indecision and generalized *Angst* intensified over the years. Like such a modern master of whispered indeterminacies, advances, retreats, and balancings as Italo Calvino, he exhibited a wonderfully irresolute complexity of dualities, aggressions, cowardices, dogmatisms, and equivocations. He interested himself in pseudo-sciences—the activity itself an avoidance of the burdens of reality and hard thought—and dreamed of better worlds and better books, both to be constructed with little existential anguish through the mediation of a second, immaterialized Self. He was very "modern" in temperament.

As a young man, before he made his Grand Tour on the *Quaker City* in 1867, Clemens was unhappy in routine work. He was ambitious, restless, uncertain of his identity, and psychically distressed by pressures to conform to the social norms to which he consciously committed himself. On board the *Quaker City* he met head-on what he conceived of as an American Establishment and for the most part he despised its members. Yet he felt an almost intolerable Romantic *Sehnsucht* which focused on winning membership in the Establishment, and he paid desperate court to Olivia Langdon and to her newly wealthy, solid, commonplace family. Marriage did not relieve anxieties for long; tensions fluctuated, but he was almost endlessly escapist.

A number of Johnson's analyses of the writings—like those of "The Facts Concerning the Recent Carnival of Crime in Connecticut" and of *The Prince and the Pauper* (pp. 71-79)—confirm the view that Clemens was a writer compulsively in flight from social responsibility, promptings of conscience, and even from the reality principle. Nearly any attentive reader will have observed that one way in which his escapism manifests itself is through images. Susan K. Harris, using as a guide Gaston Bachelard's ideas about "preferred images" from his existentialist-phenomenological *The Poetics of Reverie* (1971), elects to explore the implications of several such related images, viewing them as a third instrument (though surely less conscious and of a different order?), supplementary to his early humor and late satire, for coping with moral frustration. "Preferred images" of water, space, childhood, and women helped unify his imaginative world, relieved loneliness, and alleviated despair. These images, generally embedded in lyrical passages, are to current taste frequently sentimental and resonate with the "peace," "tranquillity," and "contentment" that Twain and those of his characters (usually narrators) who reflect his sense of moral alienation could not find in ordinary life. The most common characteristic causing alienation is, Harris indicates, sensitivity to suffering: these characters "cannot harden themselves to the inevitability of human pain" (p. 5).

As a background for her discussions of the images themselves, Harris shows how they operate to provide respite when first-person narrators are deeply disturbed. The sieur Louis de Conte, August Feldner, Hank Morgan, and Huck Finn are all sensitive, all spiritually alienated. Alienation creates problems: in rejecting their communities, the narrators lose the security of shared values and suffer extreme tensions. Images permit temporary release from conflicts: flux and tension are transmuted into immutability and tranquillity. Harris believes that the patterns of alienation and resolution of conflicts that develop anticipate the "philosophy of mind" that Clemens evolved in his later years as a way of escaping from a determinist universe.

Common as analyses of imagery in literature have been, they are rare in the criticism of Twain. Harris's discussions of the four characters whom she selects in order to throw the light of their narratives on images of escape therefore have the added interest of novelty. Her general conclusions, however, are sensibly conventional: Clemens himself, as revealed through his narrators, moved from a position of relative optimism about man, man's perfectibility, and the possibility of a desirable life in society to a complete loss of faith; he decided that freedom may be experienced only in the world of the mind. Very briefly and incidentally but helpfully (chiefly in notes) Harris reviews recent critical attitudes toward the narrators discussed. As in Johnson's analyses, an underlying sympathy for community and a questioning of the capacity of alienated heroes to avoid egocentricity and to maintain unalloyed virtue seems to inform these critiques. Most readers might without prompting take a position of this sort with respect to Hank Morgan, but anything faintly resembling the hostile attitude of the Concord Library Committee toward Huck Finn has not heretofore been common. Is Romantic individualism in nineteenth-century American literature passsing out of critical favor?

Having set the scene with her discussions of alienated narrators, Harris turns to her images. Atemporality and ecstasy are at the heart of "preferred images" of water and space, childhood, and (good) women. Because an extensive general literature now exists on Victorian conceptions of women and children and because there are a few useful studies on Clemens's women and children, one anticipates much of what Harris has to say about them. She notes that Twain represents one kind of childhood that justifies the process of teaching the child to become a member of the community, a second whereby the child escapes the community's confines. The escaping child makes us (and Clemens) aware of the possibility of a life in nature; he experiences an intuitive moment when he feels his kinship with the organic world. Descriptive passages reveal that through nature the child achieves the release of atemporality. Often, as in *Huckleberry Finn*, the manipulation of tenses to obliterate grammatical distinctions between past, present, and future reinforces the effect of freedom from time, freedom from a cause-and-effect universe.

Even more conventionally, good women are sympathetic monitors for boys, provide peace and contentment to men, make the home a sacred refuge, reassure men as to the reality of the experiential world and reconcile them to it, and are agents of spiritual redemption. Older unmarried women are guardians of conscience; younger unmarried ones are moral exemplars; married women are homemakers and creators of stability. So far as Clemens himself was concerned, his ideal woman would permit him to be conventionally rebellious, and in the late autobiographical writings wives guard the sanity of their husbands, tug them back from dream worlds and solipsistic fantasies.

Images of water and space, particularly images of outer space, are probably the least well understood of Clemens's major images; and they lead Harris to some of her less readily predictable conclusions. These images may release Clemens and his narrators from social constraints or from all human limitations. From about 1866 to 1886, their emphasis is on psychological transcendence; later they function more as philosophical resolutions of the bondage of human history and determinism: through imagery a Self is set free from time and the human condition. In much of the late fiction, Clemens's alienated narrators—trapped in nightmares or microscopic worlds—explore the connections between "dream" and "reality" and suggest the possibility of alternative realities. This suggestion relates to Clemens's decision that his sluggish material Self is matched by a dream Self or a spiritualized Self— unrestricted by time and space—which escapes necessity, floats in infinitude, and is capable of creating.

For more than forty years Clemens was fascinated by a series of fashionable, often extra-empirical, fads and fancies. He devoted himself to health foods, mind cure, faith healing, phrenology, spiritualism, and telepathy. Such interests are not unrelated to the still relatively unknown late writings—most of which were never brought to literarily satisfactory conclusions—in which he puzzled over determinism and indeterminism, sterile waking selves and creative dream selves, and, like Chuang-tzu̯, whether dream worlds are real and the real world a dream. We know that he took these things seriously, but it is not always possible to say how seriously. Belief operates at various levels: to an extent he was playing parlor games; yet the writings have high biographical-psychological significance—they not only served to pass the time and to abstract him from the world, they also reduced guilt and assuaged sickness of heart. Although it is difficult to treat these late writings very seriously as literature or philosophy, it is easy to find them absorbing as defensive self-gratification and as quasi-intellectual diddling appropriate to the period.

In a final chapter, Harris takes up several aspects of Clemens's late thought. "My Platonic Sweetheart," for example, presses belief in an alternate, immortal Self and in an optimistically conceived creative solipsism to oppose the materialist determinism that Clemens expressed most fully in *What Is Man?* The dream artist creates; like the dream artist, the waking artist can, by means of language, create worlds from thought. Images convey intimations of "thought visions." Clemens believed, it seems, that in the "real" world he had transcended time and space and communicated with others by means of telepathy. By means of dreams he communicated with his spiritualized Self.

In keeping with these beliefs, Clemens came to regard writing "as an experience of an altered state of consciousness," and "by a logical regression" came to believe that the writer can live in the "stately temples" he creates. Unfortunately, as Harris notes, Clemens's dream creations were not particularly stately, and Clemens, in "The Mysterious Stranger," finds that "the dreamer himself is intrinsically flawed," that is, unable to dream better dreams, better realities. And although Harris's presentation of Clemens's belief in transcendence is carefully argued, she may be too absolute in her conclusions about it. At any rate, I prefer to suppose that Clemens was never so inclined as was Emerson to think of himself as a conduit for Spirit nor so hopelessly out of his everyday mind about the source and constitutive virtue of his creations as was Harriet Beecher Stowe.

There are, indeed, in Harris's more interesting chapters many small points at which one would like to raise questions. One example will have to suffice. Clemens's water and space images often involve flying or sensations of flying. To Harris this means in essence atemporality and freedom. Would Freudian interpretations have any bearing? None are mentioned, not even to reject them. Nor are cliché aspects of the imagery and their attached sentiments given as much attention as I should like. Tranquillity and remoteness are felt and valued by balloonists, wind surfers, hang gliders, and pilots of small aircraft. This community of feeling may have cultural importance; it may help to explain the sympathetic attitude of readers.

Although Harris's study remains in the end, as she says, "predominantly traditional in approach" (p. 12), she deserves praise for bringing ideas from recent European critics into the usually hermetic Twain scholarship. Nevertheless, a number of her references to authority seem inapplicable; and her dependence on Bachelard, in particular, impresses me as being at least as harmful as it is helpful. No matter how poetically seductive, Bachelard is a kind of philosopher for flower children, an enthusiastic irrationalist, and perhaps most so in *La Poétique de la rêverie,* one of his weaker books. He exhibits a disinclination for the historical treatment of ideas and for close analysis of the images he cites. That the categories Harris borrows from him are useful may be doubted. The images that she examines are clichés of the culture; close readings of the New Critical sort could have placed them in their literary contexts and have facilitated decisions about the degree to which Clemens made stereotypical images his own.

Harris defines some of her major terms but, like Bachelard, leaves us to guess at the meanings of others. Highly Romantic notions concerning Self, Nature, and society dominate criticism of Twain, and Harris does not depart from the norm. She seems to accept what we divine from Bachelard, that the true Self is a tranquil entity afloat in reverie, a cosmicized and paradoxically a cosmicizing *I*. This Self appears to be an etherealized version of the Romantic Self, which when uncorrupted by society is natural and good. Society, especially genteel society, is artificial and bad. Nature is, of course, good. The natural Self must reform oppressive society, submit to it, or reject it. (Harris, incidentally, uses *community* regularly where most writers after Tönnies would use *society*.)

Contrary views may be opposed to these Romantic formulations. To Marxists, for example, the individual is an ensemble of human relationships, and so are community and society. Self and society are not, then, necessarily hostile, not necessarily good or bad. But definitions in this vein would not content Bachelard. Presumably any political or sociological definition of the Self would impress him as being exterior and superficial: the dreamer's *cogito* diffuses into the world; the dreamer dreams the world. Bachelard would probably have been sympathetic to—and Harris approves—Richard Poirier's suggestion in an estimably provocative essay that in *Huckleberry Finn* Twain creates by means of the narrator's style a metaphorical definition of society as no more than a fabrication of art and artifice: both Twain and the reader recognize society as being what Emerson called a conspiracy "against the manhood of every one of its members." But Emerson's Transcendentally solipsistic definition is inconsistent with Twain's life and thought; Huck's use of colloquial speech does not carry with it that kind of solipsism. Neither Twain's ideas nor Huck's metaphors reflect, as Harris thinks they do, "the influence of Emerson's image of nature as the resting place for the self-reliant soul" (p. 67).

Emerson implies a radical opposition between spirit and matter, and I cannot believe that Clemens, in his visions of infinitude and paradise, was philosophical in this way. Huck's repudiations of society are not equivalent to that empowered life of the soul that Emerson opposed to the Understanding. I question, furthermore, that Clemens ever found himself a part of the Bachelardian plenum of nature. His tendency was to evade, not to transcend, to escape into self-communion and fantasy. Pictorial images are a prevalent, studied form in Twain, not instant pre-cognitive apprehensions of the world inspired by the *anima.* Apparent affinities between Emerson's bright Reason or Bachelard's cosmic reveries and Clemens's daydreams disappear if Clemens's images are inspected closely. The best of the passages in which Huck immerses himself in nature are set-pieces of a kind that Clemens practiced assiduously, often with ill-success. Theatricality and convention are noticeably present. Knowing their origins, we must classify these passages as more products of the *animus* than of the *anima.*

The question of the relationship between Twain's autobiographical heroes and genteel society is one of the most controverted matters in Twain scholarship. The argument usually focuses on Huck's separation from and dependence on a society which Clemens sometimes defended but more often than not pictured as ignorantly religious, violent on principle, tyrannical, and sentimentally banal, existing by illusions and absurd rituals; but *Huckleberry Finn* is only the centerpiece. Images expressive of escape from society run throughout Twain's mature work, escapist activities throughout his life. Reveries free him, as they do all of us, from time and history; but Clemens hardly achieves restorative cosmicity through reverie— which Bachelard would have the dreamer do—as a prelude to making a mythic reentry into life. Clemens resented the responsibilities that attend maturing in society; he mourned the loss of the child's assumption of autonomy. Huckleberry Finn is usually credited with achieving moral responsibility at least temporarily by rejecting the values of his society, and appreciation of Huck often spills over onto Clemens. But Huck and Clemens are not identical: Huck's opposition is to society in one of its worser aspects; although Clemens like Huck is ambivalent, he at times is inclusive, extending his animus to American and European societies at their best and to community as well.

Each of the volumes reviewed here has its merits and points of local interest. The first is much the most thorough, the most scholarly in its depth and coverage, and most mindful about such not altogether unimportant matters as using the best available texts, giving acceptably full bibliographical information, supplying a useful index, and weeding out typographical errors. Yet Kruse's use of evidence is hardly conservative: often when he writes "clearly" or "certainly" or "evidently" his determinations are subject to debate. More important, I find myself in substantial disagreement with the central propositions: that Clemens knew years in advance almost exactly what kind of book he was going to write about the Mississippi, and that because he wrote the book he had in mind it is therefore a good book. It was once conventional to think of Mark Twain as what he sometimes pretended to be—an original, an untutored genius. Observations on his borrowings, his wide readings—for he did read widely, if not particularly well—and his revisions led to the correction, and over-correction, of this aspect of the image. The overall bearings of Kruse's study operate to validate a now conventional but I think partly inaccurate conception of Clemens: Kruse would have him be an attentive planner, vigilant in excluding irrelevant matter, and, in general, a meticulous artist.

The second two volumes reviewed are exceptionally heuristic, leaving questions and promptings in their wake. Both treat the identity of the Self and the relationship of the individual to society, issues that were even more urgent to nineteenth-century American writers suffering from one or another form of anomie than was the grander question of national identity. Coming together as they preeminently do in Mark Twain, the issues furnish Johnson and Harris with well known but still dominating subjects. Johnson's exemplifications of the empowered Self fan out under such rubrics as the double, dream selves, autonomy, solipsism, social heroism, and metaphysical nihilism. And, as we have seen, no sooner is this imperial Self established and set in motion than it tends to corrupt, dehumanize, and assume undue authority. Important though the tracing out of this empowerment and corruption is, the ideas of the study are skewed and scumbled from the beginning by the choice of Emerson as an aid in defining Clemens's conception of the Self and in locating his thought in the culture.

In general the characterization of Clemens that emerges from Johnson's book is one to which I cannot subscribe. To conceive of Clemens as a prey to gnawing anxieties evoked by the recognition—forced on him repeatedly by his characters and their actions—that in practice the most spiritualized exercise of power is corrupted by materiality has to my mind the ill-advised effect of enshrining Mark Twain (though not Hank Morgan) as an etherealized saint of democracy and progress, though a disappointed saint. This is to blur reality, to obscure our understanding of the complicated, ambivalent, materialistic, bourgeois individual that Samuel Clemens was.

Harris limits herself to examining a few recurring images that testify to Clemens's desire to escape, whether from society, reality, or life. She might have gained by proceeding, at least in the beginning, more inductively and by examining early works more closely than she does to see whether they contain persistent images analogous to those she treats. Discussion of additional images could have relieved an effect of meagerness and might possibly have shown that the images chosen were not anomalously obsessional with Clemens but that he compulsively adjusted a multiplicity of images to his needs. Although Harris excludes images of fire from her study, an examination of images of the pipe would, among others, have been a welcome addition.

If Harris sometimes seems to make Clemens's thought and thought processes, especially in his late writings, to be more precise and meaningful than I think they were, she also remarks appropriately that his chief gifts to us are his language, figures of speech, sentence structures, narrative strategies, and experiments with dialect. When we subordinate attention to Clemens's obvious merits to the analysis of his "philosophical" writings, she adds, "all we discover is that Mark Twain was neither an original, a logical, nor even a very interesting thinker" (p. 13). Equally justly, she writes: "For all his philosophical pretensions, Twain's emotional quest was to escape anxiety, guilt, and loneliness rather than to explain them" (p. 157).

Exculpatory explanations of Clemens's alienation offered by Harris are too much in a dying tradition, too partisan. Like Johnson, she makes Clemens a flawed saint of the culture: his acute sensitivity separates him from his fellows; his fear that man is innately evil and not to be redeemed alienates him. This rationale omits a great deal, whether we are speaking of Clemens or of his fictional personae: the characters of his autobiographical heroes, the evidence of the notebooks, and much besides fail to bear it out. We find strange instances of violence and cruelty. Clemens expresses and exploits humane sentiments in his writings, but sentiment often melts into sentimentality and self-pity; the rhetoric often rings false. Much more solid are his intellectual antagonisms, as toward the Roman Catholic Church; his hostilities may derive as much from assumptions of intellectual superiority as from tenderness of heart. Perhaps Harris's explanation is a new way of refurbishing an old image. If so, it is not because she fails to recognize that a new image is in the making; it may be because an old, well-established image is not dismantled all at once.

The appearance of a new image of Mark Twain is attributed by Harris to the death on 19 November 1962 of Clemens's surviving daughter, Clara, and to the publication in 1973 by Hamlin Hill of *Mark Twain: God's Fool*, a biographical study of the last ten years of Clemens's life. She thinks the traditional image is no longer possible: "We now see an explosive, paranoid old man who saw slights where they may not have existed, railed at cruelty and injustice, turned on himself in a bathos of guilt when family and friends suffered, and manifested his frustrations in a series of scatological attacks on God, the universe, and the human race" (p. 14). Clemens's alienation was not limited, she recognizes, to his old age.

Although dissenting voices protested the traditional image of Mark Twain well before 1962 or 1973, the more complete opening of the Mark Twain Papers followed by the still ongoing publication of previously unpublished writings have forced reconsideration of established beliefs and have made it increasingly difficult for scholars to hold fixedly to untenable positions. By examining what they perceive to be the relationship of Mark Twain to society, the Johnson and Harris studies have the effect of chipping away at the image.

Up to this point, the traditional image of Mark Twain as

American hero has absorbed and neutralized or benefited from the fact of his alienation and the alienation of his characters. Tom Sawyer was only childishly in revolt against society; he was undergoing a rite of passage. Huckleberry Finn rises above his society; but his was a slaveholding society to which all of us are superior. Or, Huck is protesting any unreasonable restriction of individual freedom. Similar explanations take care of other autobiographical characters. Henry Nash Smith resolves the paradox that Tom, Huck, Hank, and others stand apart from society, seek freedom from it, and deny its values. Risking the distortions attendant on synopsis, one may say that in *Mark Twain: The Development of a Writer*, Smith's resolution—a more variously argued version of what most Twainians have said or implied—instructs us that Clemens is not really in revolt against society, because there are *two* American societies. He is in revolt against the genteel and false society; he allies himself with a natural, moral, free, democratic society—with what Smith calls, I think vaguely, "the vernacular."

It is against any such conventional resolution that the studies by Johnson and Harris militate. Their Mark Twain is not a hearty Western humorist, the representatively free, heroic American. Johnson indicates that Clemens's lonely auto-biographical heroes stand above community but are not the better for it; they find no redemption. Although Harris's thesis is not identical, it is consonant. Clemens and his heroes are unhappy outsiders, morally alienated, psychologically dependent, inveterately escapist. Whether either Johnson or Harris quite realizes it, their studies contribute to the subversion of one of the best established, most widely accepted, and most powerful of American images. Among other and more beneficial consequences, the *Faschingsschwankmeister* appears to be becoming, too exclusively, I fear, the *romantischer Tragödiendichter*.

Notes

1. *Mark Twains* Life on the Mississippi: *Eine entstehungs-und-quellengeschichtliche Untersuchung zu Mark Twains "Standard Work"* (Neumünster: Karl Wachholtz Verlag, 1970).

2. Joan Mallory Webber, *Milton and His Epic Tradition* (Seattle: Univ. of Washington Press, 1979), p. 4; and Northrop Frye, *Anatomy of Criticism* (Princeton: Princeton Univ. Press, 1957), pp. 55-58 and *passim*.

3. *La Force des choses* (Paris: Editions Gallimard, 1963), p. 268.

4. Marcel Proust, *A la recherche du temps perdu*, 3 vols. Bibliothèque de la Pléiade (Paris: Editions Gallimard, 1954), III, 160-61.

5. Stephen E. Whicher, *Freedom and Fate* (Philadelphia: Univ. of Pennsylvania Press, 1955), p. vii.

6. *The Love Letters of Mark Twain*, ed. Dixon Wecter (New York: Harper and Bros., 1949), pp. 257-58.

Richard Steele and His Periodicals

Calhoun Winton

The Guardian, ed. John Calhoun Stephens. Lexington: University Press of Kentucky, 1982. iv, 825 pp.

Richard Dammers. *Richard Steele*. Boston: Twayne Publishers, 1982. xii, 160 pp.

Fritz Rau. *Zur Verbreitung und Nachahmung des* Tatler *und* Spectator. Heidelberg: Carl Winter, 1980. 449 pp.

In March 1709 Richard Steele was an unlikely candidate for the literary immortality which was, quite suddenly, about to come his way. Years before he had left Oxford without taking a degree, to join the army. He had left the army in 1705, selling his captain's commission after a career of little distinction—to do what? To shuffle around London, cadging preferment where he could, and to write. He had picked up some minor preferment here and there by 1709, and he was the working editor of *The London Gazette*, official newspaper of the government. His written work was a mixture, too miscellaneous to permit any final judgment at the time. None of the verse he had done rose more than a notch or two above doggerel. Two of his stage comedies, it is true, had achieved some initial success: *The Funeral* (1701) and *The Tender Husband* (1705). These two were working themselves into the repertory of the London theater companies where they would remain for a long time. And his religio-political tract, *The Christian Hero*, had attracted considerable attention when it appeared in 1701, partly no doubt because of the novelty of a Coldstream Guards officer's writing a work which according to its subtitle sought to prove "that no Principles but those of Religion are sufficient to make a Great Man." Still, in 1709, at age thirty-seven, Richard Steele scarcely resembled one of life's winners, much less a literary immortal. But whatever he resembled he was about to have greatness thrust upon him.

It was, of course, *The Tatler* which did it, and *The Tatler* was Steele's creation. One of Richard Dammers's principal concerns in *Richard Steele* has been to disentangle Steele's achievement from that of his friend and collaborator Addison. Steele's contribution has been decidedly under the shadow of Addison in recent years, as Louis Milic observed some time ago.[1] *The Tatler's* success, and that of *Spectator* and *Guardian* after it, have obscured what an original piece of work it was. Success often seems in retrospect inevitable but in this case there was nothing inevitable about it. Steele recognized the dynamism of London print culture, recently freed from the trammels of the Licensing Act, and the flexibility of the halfsheet periodical, which could diminish the distance between author and reader in a way the book never could. He also evidently recognized that with proper editorial control a periodical could possess its own tone and yet print the work of a number of contributors; that the tone would in effect *attract* contributors. This was an insight of some profundity and every periodical of any quality since has benefitted from it: tone comes first. *The New Yorker's* anniversary cover of the dandy inspecting a butterfly through his monocle is a visual reminder of this journalistic truism.

Nothing that Steele did in *The Tatler* was enrirely new; everything that he tried had been tried before, in some periodical or another, during those turbulent years of Queen Anne journalism. Yet it is still remarkable how thoroughly *The Tatler* and its lineal successors *Spectator* and *Guardian* combed the possibilities: in something over four-and-a-half-years' time Steele's and Addison's periodicals had introduced almost every category included in literary or general-interest periodicals today: foreign and domestic news, political commentary and propaganda, letters to the editor and advice to the lovelorn, literary theory and literary criticism, dramatic criticism and theatrical reporting, poetry and fiction.

Because Addison was in Ireland on government business during the first several months of *The Tatler's* publication, Steele must be given credit for its early success. Addison's return signaled the beginning of the great collaboration, though Steele continued to be regarded as the principal author and editor of *The Tatler* and probably was so in fact. With *Spectator* and *Guardian* Addison and Steele, comfortably in harness now, were able to shift responsibility for running the paper back and forth between them, to suit the convenience of their private lives. It is a harmless exercise to pronounce on the comparative merits of the three papers; Dammers awards the palm to *The Spectator*, calling it "perhaps the outstanding periodical of its kind in English literary history" (p. 84), whereas I have always preferred *The Tatler*, with its variety and somewhat lighter tone.

No matter. As all the world knows, they were good things and they were enormously popular and influential. And rewarding, in material terms, to their authors. I have elsewhere calculated that *The Spectator* alone must have brought its authors greater direct financial rewards than any other enterprise in literary history to that time. As for literary influence, where does one begin? Many of us no doubt have looked with stunned fascination at those long bibliographical lists in G. A. Aitken's *Life of Richard Steele*, where Aitken put down every possible imitation of these periodicals that he had ever heard of, whether or not he had seen a copy of the imitation: *The Hawaiian Spectator*, for example, or *Den Danske Spectator*. Fritz Rau, in *Zur Verbreitung und Nachahmung des* Tatler *und* Spectator, has undertaken to run to earth as many of those imitations as possible, to read and comment on them, and furthermore to read and comment on the secondary books and articles about the imitations. This is a heroic undertaking and we are in debt to Dr. Rau for, if nothing else, bringing together in his eighty-nine page bibliography the results of what must have amounted to half a lifetime's sifting and searching.

His book is one which induces scholarly humility. We Anglicists may have some hazy notion of Marivaux's *Spectateur*, but when Dr. Rau says of *Der Leipziger Spectateur* (copies of which he locates in the Leipzig University Library), "Die Verbindung zum Amsterdamer *Spectateur* oder gar zum originalen *Spectator* ist in dieser periodischen Narrensatire kaum erkennbar" (p. 187), most of us are, I dare say, inclined to take his word for it. It may not be generally known—this reviewer certainly did not know it—that there were Polish imitations, one of which, the *Monitor Warszawski*, ran for 2,164 numbers in the later eighteenth century. This printed, we learn, the satirical essays of Bishop Ignacy Krasicki, which were consciously patterned on the *Spectator's* example. It is an appealing thought, a bishop writing satirical essays. There is similar material on *Tatler/Spectator* offspring in Scandinavia (including *Den Danske Spectator*), Italy, France, and so on.

Art being long, as the poet says, and time fleeting, Rau has perforce relied on the scholarship of others, though his footnotes tell us that he has himself spent many hours in libraries all over Europe. Relying on others in this way occasionally produces some distortion, in that he has more to say about periodicals which have been studied than those which have not. An example is the first chapter of Section III ("Rezeption und Nachwirkung in Amerika"): "Benjamin Franklin und andere Nachahmer." The chapter title conveys the impression that Franklin was a dominant *literary* influence in the colonial American periodical press. Franklin was arguably the best prose writer in colonial America but his Silence Dogood essays—gems though they are—did not as such exert much literary influence when they appeared in 1722. Influence at that time was coming directly from England, from Steele and Addison's periodicals. Franklin has received more attention from scholars than other essayists, so he is granted more space here, perhaps more than he deserves. A good, comprehensive book on early American periodicals is still to be written, but Rau raises significant questions which that book will have to address. In summary, *Zur Verbreitung und Nachahmung des* Tatler *und* Spectator is an important work which deserves a place in every research library. It would be a great pity if it were overlooked because of our Anglophone centricity.

It may be that Rau limited his discussion to *Tatler* and *Spectator* because no adequate edition of *The Guardian* was available when he was doing his research and writing. No annotated edition has existed, in fact, since that of John Nichols, published in 1789, and it was not up to Nichols's usual scholarship. The omission has now been remedied with the appearance of the edition by John C. Stephens, edited to the high standards set by Donald F. Bond in his *Spectator* and produced in a sumptuous volume by the University Press of Kentucky. If we are faced, as we are constantly told we *are* faced, with the demise of letterpress editions and a scholarly career of microfiche and CRT screens, then at least we and our successors have *The Guardian* before us on acid-free paper. This is a good edition to hold and to look at: sturdy blue binding, generous margins, the text leaded for legibility and printed in a handsome modern Roman. For the dwindling band of bibliophiles among us, this edition is an aesthetic pleasure. And very reasonably priced, too, in today's market.

Quite apart from its aesthetic appeal, of course, is the question of the edition's quality as a scholarly undertaking. Here again, as indicated earlier, the judgment must be very favorable. For copy-text Stephens sensibly uses a set of original folio halfsheets at Harvard, introducing emendations which he judges to be those of the authors from the first collected octavo and duodecimo editions of 1713. His practice is generally conservative, but if anyone wishes to quarrel with his decisions the evidence is before him in the form of an appendix which lists textual emendations (separately of substantives and accidentals) and substantive variant readings from the collected editions which the editor has rejected. As Fredson Bowers used to say, the cards are on the table.

In the introduction Stephens surveys what is known about the circumstances of *The Guardian's* publication, drawing on the scholarship of the last two centuries and especially that of the last fifty years. The most important part of any edition's introduction must be that on authorship, if there is any doubt about authorship. As is well known, in the case of *The Guardian* there is plenty of doubt. Given the assiduity which Stephens has devoted to this work, it is surprising how little it advances our knowledge about authorship. Sometimes he even seems to be pressing his evidence in order to provide something new. For example, Nos. 9 and 52, which concern the retired city merchant, Mr. Charwell, and which Stephens assigns to Henry

Martyn. Martyn wrote Whig propaganda on economic matters and he had been a contributor to *The Spectator,* but there is, I believe, no contemporary evidence that he wrote for *The Guardian.* The homespun mercantilism of No. 9, which describes how Charwell turned a broken-down country estate into a going concern, and the thinly disguised Whig propaganda of No. 52 are topics Steele liked to treat, too, in his political writings and elsewhere. They "sound" more like Steele than Martyn to me, though No. 76, which Stephens also assigns to Martyn, does "sound" like his prose. The quotation marks around "sounds" point to the problem: control of tone, as remarked earlier, is one of the aspects of *The Guardian's* greatness (and that of *Tatler* and *Spectator*), but it makes identification of authorship by internal evidence very difficult.

For example: Gnatho, the "mad doctor" who writes to the *Guardian* in No. 11, telling of the cures he effects by administering his Grand Elixir. One dose "corrects and extracts all that is painful in the Knowledge of a Man's Self" (p. 74). A cure for the month of February he performed on a playwright:

'*George Spondee,* Esq; Poet, and Inmate of the Parish of St. *Paul's Convent-Garden,* fell into violent Fits of the Spleen upon a thin Third Night. He had been frighted into a Vertigo by the Sound of Catcalls on the First Day; and the frequent Hissings on the Second made him unable to endure the bare Pronunciation of the Letter S. I searched into the Causes of his Distemper; and by the Prescription of a Dose of my *Obsequium,* prepared *secundum Artem,* recovered him to his Natural State of Madness. I cast in at proper Intervals the Words, *Ill Taste of the Town, Envy of Criticks, Bad Performance of the Actors,* and the like. He is so perfectly cured, that he has promised to bring another Play upon the Stage next Winter. [p. 74]

Who wrote this? Addison? Steele? Stephens, using external evidence, assigns it as a joint undertaking to Gay and Pope. Any one of the four could have done it.

In spite of Stephens's strenuous efforts, then, we are left with many problems in determining who wrote what. This is the more frustrating because Steele was drawing on a remarkable staff of contributors, not to mention his own work. Addison was writing at the very top of his form. George Berkeley, just over from Ireland, probably contributed at least ten numbers. Thomas Tickell, though disastrously worsted by Pope in No.

40, presumably wrote the series of *Guardians* which presented the naturalistic theory of pastoral poetry as well as it has been presented. Furthermore, although party controversies were brewing up and although Steele and Swift had reached by 1713 a final parting of the ways, the Scriblerians Pope, Gay and Parnell sent in good material.

Keeping the contributors happy would have been a problem. The editors had in their gift, of course, the immense prestige of publishing in the successor to *Tatler* and *Spectator*. Even so, when Pope sent up Thomas Tickell, Ambrose Philips and their theory of the pastoral in the famous *Guardian* No. 40, he must have set Addison and Steele hard at work to allay the injured feelings all around. That they were successful is demonstrated by the paper itself: the contributors continued to contribute. Tickell sent in a poem for No. 125, and Pope certainly wrote the letter in No. 132 and probably had a hand in writing all or part of several other numbers.

The Guardian was popular in its own day, as references to and quotations from it attest. For example, a number of years ago Walter Edgar surveyed the libraries of colonial South Carolina by using probate records and found *The Spectator* to be the book most frequently collected (excluding Bibles) followed by *The Guardian* in fourth and *The Tatler* in fifth place.[2] It is a periodical remarkably lively and varied in content; one that deserves rediscovery. Now, with this splendid new edition there is no excuse for its remaining so little known. I recommend that everyone interested in the eighteenth century order at least two copies for their college or university library; that way they will be sure to find it when they want to use it. As they will.

Steele probably wound up *The Guardian* because as the Whigs' leading propagandist he knew that he would be spending his energies during the winter of 1713-1714 on political writing. Much of the rest of his life he was writing about politics, and this accounts for the fact that Richard Dammers devotes most of his analysis to those of Steele's works written before 1715. This is proper for a Twayne volume designed for students of literature, but it does somewhat warp the story from a point of view purely biographical. Steele himself would certainly not have thought his political writings such as *The Crisis* were of secondary importance in his canon.

Dammers examines Steele's literary works from an interesting perspective: they were written, he argues, in support of the rational Christianity which Steele had first enunciated in his early tract, *The Christian Hero*. The first chapter of Dammers's book is an analysis of that tract, with an account of its reception. Two chapters on Steele's dramatic works follow, then a chapter each on *Tatler* and *Spectator* and a final chapter on all the later periodicals: *Guardian*, both series of *Englishman, Lover* and so on. There may be a certain risk in this arrangement as far as the putative student is concerned, because Chapter 3 advances us as far as 1722, while Chapter 4 recalls the reader to 1709 and the beginning of *The Tatler*. Dammers, however, provides a biographical chronology following the preface, for the guidance of the reader. He also supplies a good index and a most useful, annotated selected bibliography.

Not much is here that will be new to scholars in the field; the book is by design a synthesis of relevant scholarship and criticism. Dammers has mastered his sources and he writes in a clear, straightforward prose, without flowers of rhetoric. The book may safely be put into the hands of a student new to eighteenth-century studies, perhaps with the remark that it does present a thesis—the importance of *The Christian Hero* to Steele's later work—which other scholars will debate. Within the restricted format of a Twayne volume Dammers has a great deal to say and says it well.

Many years ago, during a threatened nationwide steel strike, I reported to George Sherburn at an MLA meeting that my biographical research was going well. With straight face and twinkle in eye he responded, "I'm glad to hear that the Steele industry is reviving." There is no danger of scholarship on Addison and Steele becoming a growth industry, but the three books under review offer encouraging evidence that the field is not moribund. We still need books on *Spectator* and *Guardian* comparable to that by Richmond P. Bond on *Tatler*.[3] We sorely need an edition of Addison's works other than his contributions to periodicals. And of course we are all looking forward to Donald F. Bond's edition of *The Tatler* now that we have his *Spectator* and Stephens's *Guardian* in hand. Scholars are being provided for. Dare we pedagogues hope for a paperbound selection from the writings of these authors, which could be used as a classroom text?

Notes

1. Louis T. Milic, "Tone in Steele's *Tatler*," in *Newsletters to Newspapers: Eighteenth-Century Journalism*, ed. Donovan H. Bond and Reynolds McLeod (Morgantown: School of Journalism, West Virginia University, 1977), pp. 33-45.

2. Walter B. Edgar, "Some Popular Books in Colonial South Carolina," *The South Carolina Historical Magazine*, 72 (1971), 174-78.

3. Richmond P. Bond, *The Tatler: The Making of a Literary Journal* (Cambridge: Harvard Univ. Press, 1971).

"No Harm Trying": More Approaches to Fitzgerald

Veronica A. Makowsky

André Le Vot. *F. Scott Fitzgerald: A Biography.* Trans. from the French by William Byron. Garden City, N.Y.: Doubleday and Company, Inc., 1983. xiv, 393 pp.

Scott Donaldson. *Fool for Love: F. Scott Fitzgerald.* New York: Congdon and Weed, Inc., 1983. xii, 262 pp.

Jackson R. Bryer, ed. *The Short Stories of F. Scott Fitzgerald: New Approaches in Criticism.* Madison: University of Wisconsin Press, 1982. xx, 392 pp.

"There never was a good biography of a good novelist. There couldn't be. He is too many people if he's any good," commented F. Scott Fitzgerald in his notebook.[1] Perhaps Fitzgerald had not considered the possibility that a separate book might be devoted to each one of those "many people," leaving the reader to assemble a composite portrait. Consider the versions of Fitzgerald presented since his death in comparative obscurity in 1940: Arthur Mizener's groundbreaking *The Far Side of Paradise* (1951); Andrew Turnbull's more intimate and admiring *Scott Fitzgerald* (1962); Henry Dan Piper's study of Fitzgerald's "life as a writer," *F. Scott Fitzgerald* (1965); Nancy Milford's *Zelda* (1970), which illuminates Fitzgerald as much as his wife; and most recently, Matthew Bruccoli's lengthy and factually dense biography, *Some Sort of Epic Grandeur* (1981). Various collections of Fitzgerald's letters provide primary sources for those who prefer their artist uninterpreted.[2] If, as Henry James claimed, the writer's essential life is discovered in his work, the figure in the carpet, the countless critical studies of Fitzgerald's fiction may have picked the carpet threadbare. In confronting three new books on Fitzgerald, one inevitably wonders if there is anything left to be said. Can these books contribute anything new?

Coming so hard on the heels of Bruccoli's substantial biography, Le Vot's *F. Scott Fitzgerald* might appear redundant. In terms of important facts about Fitzgerald's life, nothing is really new. LeVot's work, however, does make a solid contribution to Fitzgerald studies, for LeVot is a masterful and sensitive interpreter of Fitzgerald's life and works. The Fitzgerald fan jaded by too much information about what happened is reinvigorated by LeVot's theories about why.

To some extent, LeVot's fresh perspective may be explained by his status as an expert on American culture who is not an American. He is Professor of American Literature at the Sorbonne and Director of its Center for Research on Contemporary American Literature. Since the book was originally intended for a French audience, LeVot deems it necessary to provide lengthy explanations of some phenomena of American culture. These discussions also turn out to be valuable to the American reader for whom a phrase such as "the Jazz Age" has been reiterated into meaninglessness. LeVot places the "Roaring Twenties" in their political and social context before providing a montage of the Fitzgeralds' notorious exploits during the era. He ends with a meditation upon the Hearst newspaper portrait of the couple in 1923 as a sort of icon for the period's love of youth and beauty allied with the vulgarity and materialism evoked by the Hearst name.

Equally illuminating to an American reader is LeVot's portrait of American education in his discussion of Fitzgerald's Princeton years. He meticulously explains the club system to his French readers, drawing the moral that social status, not intellectual development, was the reason for a Princeton education in those days. In this context, Fitzgerald's academic failure becomes representative of the lackadaisical mainstream, not the act of a superior iconoclast. LeVot suggests that the real rebels were intellectuals such as John Peale Bishop, Edmund Wilson, and Christian Gauss. His description of Gauss, then a professor of Romance Languages, is telling: "In that atmosphere of absorption in struggles for prestige, in which all that seemed to matter were the tumultuous glories of the stadium, the frippery of the Triangle's operettas and the smug vanity of the big men on campus, this retiring little man quietly affirmed the unarguable superiority of the life of the mind, ushering the best of those young men into a higher culture and igniting their literary ambitions" (p. 37).

LeVot astutely points out that this social struggle took place under a beautiful facade of neo-Gothic buildings with all their evocations of the great European centers of learning. He does, however, emphasize the "neo" of their Gothic in this discussion of the buildings Fitzgerald so lyrically describes in *This Side of Paradise*. "We see that of the twelve buildings cited, only one, West, dates from before the Civil War; one of the two towers whose spires symbolize the poetry of his campus had been standing for three years at the time of Amory/Fitzgerald's song to them, the other only a few months" (p. 32). This is not European derision for the American parvenu. LeVot, rather, is stressing that a struggle for a visible status, as opposed to intellectual achievement, is an inevitable part of a relatively new culture.

LeVot also emphasizes Princeton's paradoxical status as an "aristocratic" enclave in an ostensibly egalitarian society, and the price its undergraduates had to pay upon facing the very different world beyond its arches: "In a closed society the importance—indeed, the necessity—of clubs is obvious, as are the importance and necessity of those great group rituals, football games . . . . Equally understandable is the in-surmountable nostalgia that stalked them when they left the magic circle to face, alone, the material and psychological realities of a world that had been fashioned without them" (p. 44). Though LeVot occasionally sounds like an anthropologist zealously stalking the primitive tribe, his account of Fitzgerald's Princeton reveals that Fitzgerald as the perpetual parvenu may have been uncomfortably representative of his university at the time. That, of course, would explain its failure to recognize his merits until well into the 1960s.

Occasionally, however, LeVot's French perspective skews

some of the evidence a bit. Despite his description of Princeton as a social club, he weighs Fitzgerald's failure to attain a diploma as heavily as a European's failing his baccalaureate (p. ix). In his introduction, undue importance is given to Fitzgerald's infrequent socialistic or Marxist comments by listing them in a discussion of Fitzgerald's closeness to the European point of view. In his lengthier treatment of Fitzgerald's politics during the thirties, he does conclude that "Fitzgerald's new convictions remained theoretical, however, fitting into the logic of his criticism of the American system and the power of money; they did not encroach on his hedonistic notion of life" (p. 270). I would speculate that Fitzgerald, the chameleon who always wanted to "fit in," from Princeton to the Riviera, considered leftist views an additional piece of protective coloration, as in this letter to his daughter at college: "You are in the midst of a communist dominated student movement at Vassar which you do nothing about. The movement will go both up and down in the next few years . . . . It would be foolish ever to make enemies of those girls. Silly and fanatical as they seem now some of them are going to be forces in the future of that section."[3] Fitzgerald's "leftist" views conform to the general "do-what-I-say-not-as-I-did" tone of his letters to his daughter, comfortably leaving hard work, austerity, and egalitarianism for the next generation.

Since I have not seen the original French, I cannot judge the quality of William Byron's translation of LeVot. Sometimes a sentence sounds stilted: "Oh, yes, Paris in 1925 was a ball for American expatriates" (p. 187). Syntax is occasionally rather snarled: "Newly emerged from a harsh period in his life, a particularly vulnerable Fitzgerald, thanks to Sigourney Fay, acquired the balance and self-confidence he had lost as a small child" (p. 28). "Wolsheim" (p. 68) and "The Camel's Pack" (p. 77) indicate the need for more careful proofreading. In general, however, the prose, though somewhat dense, is quite readable.

The volume has no pictures but really needs none since the images of the Fitzgeralds are graven onto everyone's consciousness by now. A geneological chart is provided to clarify LeVot's perceptive treatment of Fitzgerald's background.

The index is useful, but a bit quirky. For example, under Fitzgerald's "personal characteristics" are listed: "boozing, boozing becomes alcoholism, brawls, chauvinism and prejudice, escapades, ideal of masculine perfection, must write only about self and Zelda, philosophy of life, shame over feet, sports, suicidal risk-taking, talking in sleep." Truth really is stranger than fiction, *n'est-ce pas?*

The true strength of LeVot's work, though, does not stem from his French perspective, his translator, or the apparatus to his volume, but from his ability to analyze character within the dynamics of a relationship. He is particularly interesting on what might by now seem exceedingly well-trodden ground, Fitzgerald's relationships with Ernest Hemingway and Gerald Murphy. Hemingway "was the very image of the man he would have wished to be" because "Hemingway had succeeded where he, Fitzgerald, had failed in combining the man of letters with the man of action" (p. 220). The Murphys were "examples of the only possible alternatives" since they "incarnated the grace, the optimum fulfillment of a civilized state based on culture, leisure and money, but also on elegance and generosity" (p. 221). There may be nothing new here, but LeVot proceeds to place Fitzgerald's relationships with both men in the context of the Murphy-Hemingway friendship:

> To the Murphys the writer who was full of promise, the really modern innovator, apparently was Hemingway . . . . Fitzgerald made an obscure and predictable decision: without admitting it to himself or those close to him, he opted for the easy way, for . . . a life of aristocratic leisure negligently financed by a few shallow, effortless stories written to amuse the *Post*'s three million readers. To Hemingway, younger, tougher, sure of himself, more naive, too, was left the ungrateful, never satisfying daily chore of writing for his peers, with no other reward but their approval—or their spite. [pp. 221-22]

Fitzgerald apparently chose to compete with the gentleman of leisure because he was too afraid of defeat in what really mattered to him, his work, his art.

Of course, as LeVot points out, Fitzgerald did redeem himself by finishing *Tender Is the Night* and sobering up to start *The Last Tycoon*. LeVot's biography is essentially a drama of redemption, as the penultimate section, "Salvage and

Salvation," indicates. For LeVot, Fitzgerald's life is a tale of modern greatness in which the hero, without any clear values higher than materialism, and without either a considered intellectual perspective or the consolations of faith, still strives, however stumblingly, to make his life meaningful. He writes that Fitzgerald's experience was a "testimony to the limitations of a man who, after long years of mundane frivolity, struggled and sacrificed without the help of faith to achieve self-renunciation. And who acceded in the process to the supreme dignity of those who acknowledge defeat but go on fighting" (p. 354-55). Not only did Fitzgerald bear defeat with dignity, but he actually needed it to achieve: "Progress was a series of falls transformed into forward motion" (p. xii).

This "felix culpa" theory of Fitzgerald's life, shared by Scott Donaldson, is summarized in his introduction:

Fool For Love, F. Scott Fitzgerald attempts to seek out what Leon Edel calls the figure under the carpet, the special set of mind that made Fitzgerald the kind of man and writer he was. The book's thesis is that F. Scott Fitzgerald was driven to please other people, especially rich and prominent people . . . . He was not very good at pleasing men, who thought he talked too much or tried too hard. He was more successful with women, who liked his looks, his way of flattering them, and his gift for nuance . . . . He needed their approval, which meant their love and adoration . . . . Fitzgerald despised himself for his persistent and demeaning compulsion to attract the attention and admiration of others . . . . Purgation came hard, but to Fitzgerald's credit it finally did come. [p. x]

"So what's new?" the weary Fitzgerald devotée asks. Everyone knows Fitzgerald was permanently warped by spending his childhood, as he put it, "In a house below the average, of a street above the average."[4] After all, could a book with a title reminiscent of the supermarket's hottest Gothic romance reveal the "figure under the carpet" to be anything more serious than the Playmate of the Month?

Much to my surprise, after being put off by the title and the introduction, I must report that Donaldson's book is not only a serious contribution to Fitzgerald studies, but provides the best psychological portrait of Fitzgerald I have encountered. Donaldson believes that Fitzgerald's pattern of dealing with others was formed by his mother, who spoiled him terribly.

Since Fitzgerald found both of his parents embarassing and considered their adoration worthless, he sought validation from the approval of those he believed in some way "better." With men, his charm failed. He was considered the "freshest boy" at prep school. As Donaldson notes in his description of Fitzgerald's relationship with Princeton, masculine rejection insured the continued need for approval: "Like an over-eager swain, Fitzgerald repeatedly made a hash of his courtship of his Alma Mater. Had she succumbed to his blandishments, he might have modified the idealized picture of Princeton he carried in his heart. But the university kept its distance and so remained a hallowed place for him" (p. 40). Although I think Donaldson clouds the issue by using a feminine personification for an institution run by and for men, Fitzgerald's relation to Princeton fits Donaldson's theory that "Fitzgerald suffered a series of repudiations from men. For consolation, for validation of his very worth as a person, he turned to women" (p. 42).

Not only did Fitzgerald turn to women, but he wanted the woman who would supply the most status and so compensate for his failures in the eyes of men. Donaldson rightly believes that Ginevra King, not Zelda Sayre, set the pattern for Fitzgerald's pursuit of rich, upper-class women. Ginevra was extremely wealthy and one of the "Big Four" debutantes on Ivy League campuses. Fitzgerald was reaching as high as any young man could, and the magnitude of his sense of loss was proportionally great: "The hurt of losing her never left him, and thinking about it invariably brought tears to his eyes. Furthermore, his rejection by Ginevra motivated much of his fiction . . . . Ginevra sat for most of Daisy Buchanan in *The Great Gatsby* and for much of Nicole Diver in *Tender Is the Night*. She modeled for Josephine Perry in his Josephine stories" (p. 51). Ginevra King, as Donaldson points out, was the golden girl, "the *Kings'* daughter" (p. 109) who set the standard for all others.

This upscaling of Ginevra King's place in Fitzgerald's life and fiction necessitates the devaluation of Zelda Sayre's role. This adjustment of values is where I believe Donaldson makes his greatest contribution because his account of the Fitzgeralds' marriage explains the bitter failure which never seemed to fit the glowing legend of their youthful courtship and the early years of their marriage. Like LeVot and Bruccoli, Donaldson scotches the tale of love at first sight. Fitzgerald's ledger states that he did not fall in love with Zelda until two months after he met her and that he linked her name with that of another girl, May Steiner, in his notes. Since Fitzgerald always wanted what he could not have, his seduction of Zelda meant that she lost value in his eyes when he did possess her physically, as her letter about the abortion pills and other documents show he did (pp. 61-65).

Zelda, however, turned the tables on Fitzgerald by showing him that a physical act did not mean he owned her. Like Gatsby after his seduction of Daisy, Fitzgerald now felt married to Zelda, but she did not reciprocate. As Donaldson states, "Zelda understood that her attractiveness to other men mattered a good deal to Fitzgerald and repeatedly let him know of her adventures" (p. 63) with other young men. Through this elusive behavior, she kept the value of the unattainable in Fitzgerald's eyes, but lost some of it by her conditions for marrying him. Donaldson seems to suggest that Zelda was selling herself to the highest bidder because she would not marry Fitzgerald until his writing started to earn a great deal of money: "Such behavior smacked of calculation, and the romantic side of Fitzgerald objected. By the time she said *yes*, some of the magic had dissipated" (p. 65). The tarnish spread when Zelda's family also reversed themselves. The Sayres had objected to Fitzgerald on moral grounds as an unstable artist who drank, "but all the Sayres capitulated when the movie studios began buying film rights to Fitzgerald stories for four-figure sums" (p. 66).

Zelda shared Fitzgerald's view of the relation between the sexes as a competition. What did she have to keep her advantage once she had married him? Unfortunately, only more of the same; she continued to play on Fitzgerald's jealousy which, as Donaldson notes, "was at the root of the trouble" (p. 67). She flirted, apparently harmlessly, with Fitzgerald's friends from Princeton and with critic George Jean Nathan in the early New York and Westport years of their marriage. When she felt herself most neglected, with Fitzgerald lost in the manuscript of

Gatsby, she had a more serious affair on the Riviera with Edouard Jozan, a French aviator. Although we still do not know how mutual the romance was, it apparently backfired for Zelda. Perhaps Jozan did not want her, or perhaps she was afraid to leave Fitzgerald. Whatever the case, the affair left emotional scars on Zelda, and she stopped using sexual jealousy as a means of proving her worth.

Instead she tried some more mature gambits. She decided to attempt to have another child and even had a minor operation to this end, but was not successful. As Donaldson indicates, she began to want a house and some roots, but "in all his life Scott Fitzgerald never owned a house or settled in one spot for longer than a year or two" (p. 96). She tried dancing, painting, and writing, in all three of which she "achieved the level of the inspired amateur . . . . It was this point that her husband made to her, over and over, often with a brutality and tactlessness that betrayed his own insecurity" (p. 79). She became obsessed with other women, including her ballet teacher Egorova, again trying to prove her worth through others.

Unfortunately for Zelda, her propensity for mental illness which, as Donaldson notes, ran in her family, caused her to lose the competition for mastery to Fitzgerald. Donaldson writes of a conversation Fitzgerald had with one of Zelda's psychiatrists in 1931: "Only then did he begin to grasp the power he held over her. In fifteen minutes of 'well-planned conversation,' he told Dr. Thomas A. C. Rennie, he could bring on her insanity again. 'I would only need intimate that I was interested in some other woman.' For whatever it was worth, he had won their battle for sexual supremacy" (p. 72). Zelda realized she had lost. Donaldson emphasizes her "tone of humility toward Scott" after 1931 and the fact that "Forty-six of the more than 300 letters she wrote him begin with 'Thanks' or 'Thank you.' Often the thanks were for money. She was the supplicant, he the provider" (p. 94).

Fitzgerald may have won the battle with Zelda, but he had not won what Donaldson calls his "War Between the Sexes" (p. 116). Obviously, Fitzgerald's personality could never get enough admiration, so he constantly looked for women, before, during, and after Zelda, as Donaldson's chapters "I Love You, Miss X" and "Running Amuck" demonstrate: "Through the years there was almost always someone besides Zelda . . . . Just how significant these encounters were is difficult to determine . . ." (p. 53). Donaldson does attempt to make that determination, though, as he explores a lengthy list of women with whom Fitzgerald attempted to feed an insatiable need for approval. Donaldson posits that Fitzgerald fits psychologist Avodah K. Offit's description of the "histrionic personality":

Drama is the essence of life to such people, Offit points out. They covet attention and become actors to get it. Their "primary art" is seduction, but since some resist seduction, the histrionic often "turns to less artful but more direct maneuvers for attention," such as bemoaning cruel fate. Often the histrionic personality plays the role Samuel Johnson's dictionary defined as that of a "seeksorrow," one who is certain that no one else has ever suffered so much and determined that others should realize this. No amount of sympathy or attention or love is ever enough to satisfy such a person. [p. 188]

Perhaps Fitzgerald was simply worn out when he settled down with Sheilah Graham at the end of his life and stopped seeking approval. I think Donaldson is correct, though, in suggesting that in Graham, "At last Fitzgerald found a beautiful woman who loved him, no matter what" (p. 205), and in linking her with Fitzgerald's original source of limitless love, his mother: "Perhaps most of all, Sheilah and Mollie were alike in loving Fitzgerald enough to overlook his failings" (p. 204).

Although I find Donaldson's interpretation of Fitzgerald's relations with others most persuasive, I would give more emphasis to a strain in Fitzgerald's character mentioned by both LeVot and Donaldson, his need for punishment. LeVot writes that "Fitzgerald liked being whipsawed. He needed floggings more than praise, provided the strokes were well placed. He was grateful to whoever uncovered his weak points and hammered at them" (p. 41). Donaldson also alludes to this need when he discusses Fitzgerald's drinking: "Drunk, Fitzgerald was a terror. Yet always just below the surface lay an accusing voice that said 'Christ, how can you stand me?' or 'I'm really no good'" (p. 161). In other words, Fitzgerald had such a low opinion of himself that he respected only those who "saw through" him and punished him; those who admired him were obviously deluded and therefore were less highly esteemed by him.

This need for punishment holds true for Fitzgerald's dealings with both men and women. His relationship with Hemingway in which, as he puts it, he would "half bait, half truckle to him" is a good example.[5] During Hemingway's boxing match with Morley Callaghan, Fitzgerald inadvertently forgot to watch the clock, causing Hemingway to lose. He humbly apologized and accepted Hemingway's excessive wrath and scorn over such a small matter. Even Hemingway's crack about "poor Scott Fitzgerald" and his "romantic awe" of the rich in "The Snows of Kilimanjaro" did not provoke the repudiation of Hemingway such a low blow would merit. Fitzgerald, I think, was always afraid Hemingway was right. One could also interpret his relationship with the masculine world of Princeton in the same way. Donaldson calls Fitzgerald an "ardent suitor" (p. 36) of his alma mater, but would a suitor who really wants to succeed get embarassingly drunk on a number of public social occasions, insult one of the university's principal benefactors, and call it a country club in his first novel? Rather than seeking Princeton's affection, Fitzgerald seemed to work very hard at convincing the university of his unworthiness and the mistake they made in taking him. This way, he continued to respect Princeton and remain devoted to it up to his final hour, dying while making notes on an article about Princeton football.

His relations with women follow a similar pattern. His mother's love was worthless because she loved him despite his faults. Ginevra King had the good sense to reject him, so she remained an ideal in life and fiction. As long as Zelda Sayre refused to commit herself to him, which was really not until the debacle of her affair with Jozan, she remained desirable. Once she took on a tone of humility and dependency after her breakdown, calling Fitzgerald her "Sun-god,"[6] she was now, like his mother, a foolish person of little perspicuity from whom he should begin to detach himself. He repeatedly insulted Sheilah Graham in his drunkenness, calling her his "paramour" in front of guests, and sending a fur he had given her to his daughter. Only when she had reached her limit and refused to see him did he apologize and settle down with her in a more civilized way. Whether one calls Fitzgerald a romantic who only wants the unattainable or a spoiled child who cries for what is forbidden, neglecting the plethora of toys around him, this was his pattern, to his lasting unhappiness.

LeVot and Donaldson try to relate Fitzgerald's fiction to their observations about his psyche. LeVot's forte is connecting patterns of images in Fitzgerald's life and works. In his *Ledger*, Fitzgerald notes that at age five he attended the Pan-American Exposition in Buffalo. According to LeVot, the inauguration of the Exposition was dominated by the assassination of President McKinley and the presence of a "Goddess of Light whose glow could be seen as far away as Niagara Falls" (p. 27). LeVot claims that although Fitzgerald noted neither the assassination nor the lights in his *Ledger*, the Exposition started an association of lights with beauty and disaster which was reinforced by another incident which Fitzgerald also records in his *Ledger*, as quoted by LeVot:

I ran away when I was seven on the Fourth of July. I spent the day with a friend in a pear orchard and the police were informed that I was missing and on my return my father thrashed me according to the customs of the nineties— on the bottom—and then let me come out and watch the night fireworks from the balcony with my pants still down and my behind smarting and knowing in my heart that he was absolutely right. Afterwards, seeing in his face his regret that it had to happen, I asked him to tell me a story. [p. 28]

LeVot associates this incident with Fitzgerald's story "Absolution":

The festival of lights follows the stern punishment little Rudolph receives from his father and is immediately followed by the death of another, spiritual father, the priest. The festival's brilliance is associated with the boy's rejection—in a sense the murder—of his father and remains a symbol of his resultant guilt. This Oedipal metaphor, this key to Fitzgerald's imaginative process of generalizing from particulars, may explain to us why Fitzgerald's role was so important in forming the sensibility of his time. It may signify the general refusal of daily constraints, the sense of radical liberation from the grip of the past that Americans manifested in the twenties. Fitzgerald identified himself with this rejection of tradition, gave it a voice, a style. He became his generation's spokesman, he raced passionately toward the mirage of festival lights; at the same time he felt remorse at having transgressed his limits, having violated quasi-divine laws—an orphan awaiting his punishment and accepting it. [p. 28]

This masterful movement from life to fiction back to life is characteristic of LeVot. I would only add two observations. The young Fitzgerald's Independence Day was not a successful break from the fatherland; it left him caught with his pants down. It also seems highly significant that Fitzgerald and his father seek refuge and reconciliation in a fiction, a story, a method the novelist would repeat through Dick Diver's tribute to his dead father in *Tender Is the Night*. He has broken away from his father and his country, but feels only loss, not liberation: "Dick had no more ties here now and did not believe he would come back . . . . 'Good-by, my father—good-by, all my fathers.'"[7]

Unfortunately, brilliant though a passage like this is, it brings LeVot's narrative to a halt. A biography is, after all, a story, and the reader, to Fitzgerald and LeVot's credit, is eager to know what happened next. LeVot completely stops the narrative at 1923 in order to insert two chapters devoted to Fitzgerald's imagery. In chapter 10, "The Colors in the Crest," LeVot posits that "the colors yellow and blue are the most significant" and "best reflect the fundamental duality of Fitzgerald's imaginary world" (p. 145). He proceeds to trace their permutations in the fiction from the thesis that "their conjunction seems to be the sign of a fleeting instant of harmony and beauty, whereas their dissociation suggests disorder or latent conflict" (p. 145). In "An American-Style God," Chapter Eleven, he extends this discussion to the eyes of Dr. T. J. Eckleburg in *The Great Gatsby* and to Fitzgerald's use of music. Both chapters are interesting and illuminating, but they seem more like journal articles inserted for wider exposure than an integral part of a biography.

Donaldson's narrative suffers a similar fate. After two chapters on Zelda Fitzgerald, he includes two chapters on love in Fitzgerald's fiction, "The Glittering Things" and "War Between the Sexes." Although perhaps more obvious than LeVot's brand of analysis, Donaldson's insights into the relations between Fitzgerald's fiction and life are still useful, particularly when clearly summarized in two chapters. He traces Fitzgerald's linkage of money and women from his early uncritical glamorizing to his "mature view" that money served to "facilitate corruption," as in the case of Dick Diver (p. 112). His conclusion about love in Fitzgerald's fiction could as easily be applied to Fitzgerald's life since he was unable to sustain an adult relationship with a woman: "The course of true love does not run smooth in Fitzgerald's fiction. In all his work he created no lovers whose attachment was honest, mutual, and permanent, no unions in which partners equally shared burdens and blessings" (p. 116). Although Donaldson's book is not a biography, he does consider Fitzgerald's women in chronological order so that the two chapters on the fiction interrupt the narrative flow.

As I have indicated, Donaldson and LeVot use the short stories to illustrate larger themes in their works. Donaldson says little about the quality of Fitzgerald's short fiction, but LeVot believes it declines after early achievement into a "few shallow, effortless stories written to amuse the *Post's* three million readers" (p. 221) and for money. Eventually Fitzgerald could not even please that audience so the "mass-circulation magazines . . . showed their reluctance to publish hastily written, badly constructed stories that perpetuated an obsolete formula" (p. 315). The refutation of this typical attitude toward Fitzgerald's short stories and their rescue from critical neglect are the purposes of *The Short Stories of F. Scott: New Approaches in Criticism*, edited by Jackson R. Bryer (p. xiv). In his introduction Bryer also states that "The single greatest need in Fitzgerald studies has long been for close attention to the style and artistry of the texts themselves" (p. xvi). To this end, Bryer solicited two kinds of essays, "overview essays which dealt with several stories, and close readings of individual stories" including "essays on the most popular and best stories . . . as well as essays on stories which have been unfairly neglected" (pp. xvii-xviii).

Admirable as these goals are, the whole is only as good as its different parts, making as varied an assortment as is usual in this type of collection. In the case of the essays which consider several stories, some are not particularly helpful. Scott Donaldson's "Money and Marriage in Fitzgerald's Stories" is a simplified version of Chapter Six of *Fool For Love*, so the reader would be better served by consulting the fuller treatment in that book. John Mancini, Jr.'s, "To Be Both Light and Dark: The Jungian Process of Individuation in Fitzgerald's Basil Duke Lee Stories" manages to reduce Fitzgerald's rich stories to a dreary pattern of maturation. Sometimes Mancini is even prescriptive: "Gatsby might well have avoided such a fate [murder by Wilson] if he had adequately resolved the Basil-like crises of his youth" (p. 109). That is like saying that *The Great Gatsby* is a plea for Jungian analysis. In "The Significance of Fantasy in Fitzgerald's Short Fiction," Lawrence Buell presents the intriguing thesis that Fitzgerald inserts "continual reminders, especially in the fantasies, that the work before us is an artifact, that the fictive world is something more or less than a representation of social reality or the expression of somebody's commitment or dream" (p. 26). Sadly, this interesting idea gets lost in an article which is hard to follow, moving from Fitzgerald's types of fantasy to "The Diamond as Big as the Ritz" to biographical sources to *The Great Gatsby*, ending with the suggestion that Fitzgerald predicts Donald Barthelme as fabulist as well as John O'Hara as recorder.

The two articles on the relation of Hollywood to Fitzgerald's short fiction are both informative. In "'Kissing, Shooting, and Sacrificing': F. Scott Fitzgerald and the Hollywood Market," Alan Margolies demonstrates the way Fitzgerald's misconceptions about Hollywood caused him to "write down" to what he considered its level, to the detriment of his early contributions to film and to the short stories he wrote in the hope that they would be bought for the movies. Robert A. Martin's "Hollywood in Fitzgerald: After Paradise" asserts that "the pattern that was to haunt Fitzgerald for the rest of his life— artistic failure, debt, and Hollywood—was firmly established within the relatively short period of five years after the publication of *This Side of Paradise*" (p. 128). Martin then illustrates the permutations of this sequence in the depiction of Hollywood and its representatives in Fitzgerald's fiction. I wish, though, that the contributors had read each other's work because Martin mentions that the movie *Grit* is based on an "unidentified" original story by Fitzgerald (p. 134), and Margolies quotes *Film Daily* to show that *Grit* was a "'Crook melodrama'" and then relates its plot (p. 70).

Richard Lehan, C. Hugh Holman, and Kenneth E. Eble consider Fitzgerald's view of time and place. In "The Romantic Self and the Uses of Place in the Stories of F. Scott Fitzgerald," Lehan provides a richly rewarding treatment of the romantic self in the novels as well as the short stories throughout Fitzgerald's career. Despite its title, Lehan's article is more concerned with the romantic notion of time rather than place in statements such as "Throughout Fitzgerald's fiction the past has a way of consuming the present" (p. 17). Holman's "Fitzgerald's Changes on the Southern Belle: The Tarleton Trilogy" arrives at a similar conclusion about the relation between past and present for Fitzgerald. Holman demonstrates that the belle "was wistful nostalgia made flesh" in the three stories set in the small town of Tarleton, Georgia: "The Ice Palace," "The Jelly-Bean," and "The Last of the Belles" (p. 64). Fiction not only reincarnates the past, but also predicts the future, as Kenneth E. Eble shows in "Touches of Disaster: Alcoholism and Mental Illness in Fitzgerald's Short Stories." Fitzgerald's early characters who are alcoholics or suffer from mental illness experience a loss of control or vitality long before their creator reached a similar nadir in the thirties. Eble emphasizes the value Fitzgerald placed on continuing to function despite this mysterious depletion of life-force, both in his life and in his fiction.

The most illuminationg of the articles on several stories, though, is Ruth Prigozy's "Fitzgerald's Short Stories and the Depression: An Artistic Crisis." Prigozy makes a genuine contribution to Fitzgerald studies by exploring the evolution of the radically different kind of story he was writing by the end of the thirties. She astutely and clearly traces his struggle to find plots to replace the love story and to develop a style that would suit those new subjects, "nuanced and elliptical" (p. 113). James L. W. West III most ably furthers this study of Fitzgerald's late style in his "Fitzgerald and *Esquire.*"

I found the section which treats individual stories rather disappointing. The essays usually fall into three categories. In the first, an excellent critic devotes much attention to a relatively slight story: Victor Doyno's "'No Americans Have Any Imagination': 'Rags Martin-Jones and the Pr-nce of W-les,'" Christiane Johnson's "Freedom, Contingency, and Ethics in 'The Adjuster,'" Milton J. Friedman's "'The Swimmers': Paris and Virginia Reconciled," and James J. Martine's "Rich Boys and Rich Men: 'The Bridal Party.'" George Monteiro's "Two Sets of Books, One Balance Sheet" posits that the slight "Financing Finnegan" is Fitzgerald's hidden response to Hemingway's insult in "The Snows of Kilimanjaro." The fine analyses, however, only convince me that these stories have been justly neglected since the critics look so good and the stories so overwhelmed.

The second group are the essays on well-known stories. These essays do not contribute much that is new, but are quite good close readings. John Kuehl's "Psychic Geography in 'The Ice Palace'" is an excellent and thorough tracing of the fairly obvious way Fitzgerald uses imagery of heat and cold to suggest the differences between northern and southern characters. Neil D. Isaacs considers Fitzgerald's use of sports imagery in "Winter Dreams" and the rest of his fiction as "a primary element in accounting for the persistence of his strong following among young contemporary audiences" in sportsminded America (p. 207). In "Faces in a Dream: Innocence Perpetuated in 'The Rich Boy,'" Peter Wolfe points out that Anson Hunter's "princely code rules out adult actions" and keeps him immature and unhappy (p. 242). Carlos Baker's "When the Story Ends" ably traces the imagery of freedom and imprisonment in "Babylon Revisited." In all these articles the lack of anything really new leaves me uncertain that well done means worth doing.

In several essays, the critic's ability, subject, and contributions did unite more successfully. In "'Absolution': Absolving Lies," Irving Malin concludes that "Fitzgerald has been offering 'alternatives' (light and dark, youth and maturity, earth and Heaven, lie and truth), suggesting thereby that daily life—as recounted here—is a *double-edged* source of uncertainty" (p. 216). Although Malin's prose is sometimes as labyrinthine as Fitzgerald's meaning, the essay is an interesting and suggestive approach to a story which is valuable in itself and in its status as a discarded piece of Gatsby's childhood. Sheldon Grebstein clearly explains the intricate relationship between structure and meaning in one of Fitzgerald's last great stories in "The Sane Method of 'Crazy Sunday.'" James W. Tuttleton's explication of "May Day," entitled "Seeing Slightly Red," uses an array of biographical, historical, and literary information to illuminate Fitzgerald's early interest in Socialism and the story's embryonic suggestions of the later Fitzgerald.

Although I cannot assert that anyone has discovered the figure under, in, or on Fitzgerald's carpet, LeVot, Donaldson, and Bryer have contributed a plethora of intriguing insights into that design. After so many books and articles about Fitzgerald and his fiction, the fact that more remains to be said is a tribute to the complexity of Fitzgerald's mind and art, as well as a spur to other critics. At the very least, I can conclude with Pat Hobby that there's "No Harm Trying." Indeed there is much to be gained.

Notes

1. *The Crack-Up*, ed. Edmund Wilson (New York: New Directions, 1956), p. 177.

2. *The Letters of F. Scott Fitzgerald*, ed. Andrew Turnbull (New York: Scribners, 1963); *As Ever, Scott Fitz—Letters Between F. Scott Fitzgerald and His Literary Agent Harold Ober, 1919-1940*, ed. Matthew J. Bruccoli with the assistance of Jennifer McCabe Atkinson (Philadelphia: Lippincott, 1972); *Dear Scott/Dear Max: The Fitzgerald-Perkins Correspondence*, ed. John Kuehl and Jackson R. Bryer (New York: Scribners, 1971); *Correspondence of F. Scott Fitzgerald*, eds. Matthew J. Bruccoli and Margaret M. Duggan with the assistance of Susan Walker (New York: Random House, 1980).

3. 26 February 1940, *Correspondence*, p. 583.

4. To Alida Bigelow, *Letters*, p. 456.

5. To Edmund Wilson [probably March 1933], *Letters*, p. 345.

6. From Zelda Fitzgerald to F. Scott Fitzgerald [after August 1931], *Correspondence*, p. 268.

7. *Tender Is the Night* (New York: Scribners, 1934), p. 267.

"Future Generations Will Read It with Admiration": The Collected Letters of Joseph Conrad

David Leon Higdon

Frederick R. Karl and Laurence Davies, eds. *The Collected Letters of Joseph Conrad*, Volume I, 1861-1897. Cambridge: Cambridge University Press, 1983. lxviii, 446 pp.

To a noticeable degree, Joseph Conrad scholarship has lagged behind scholarship on James Joyce, D. H. Lawrence, and Virginia Woolf, who, with Conrad, constitute the "Big Four" of English modernism. Where they had definitive biographies in 1955 (Harry T. Moore on Lawrence), 1959 (Richard Ellmann on Joyce) and 1972 (Clive Bell on Woolf), Conrad had to wait until Frederick R. Karl's *Joseph Conrad: The Three Lives* (1979) and Zdzislaw Najder's *Joseph Conrad: A Chronicle* (1983), even though it had long been recognized that G. Jean-Aubry's *Life and Letters* (1927) was riddled with flaws and that Jocelyn Baines's *Joseph Conrad: A Critical Biography* (1960) was inadequate for a number of reasons. Where Joyce, Lawrence, and Woolf were accorded primary bibliographies in 1953 (John Slocum and H. Cahoon on Joyce), 1957 (B. J. Kirkpatrick on Woolf), and 1963 (Warren Roberts on Lawrence), Conrad has yet to be treated in a primary bibliography, though William R. Cagle and Donald W. Rude have for some time been working respectively on a bibliography and a census of pre-publication materials.[1] Where Joyce, Lawrence, and Woolf have had scholarly editions of their works published or the full extent of the textual problems in their works aired in scholarly essays and books, Conrad's canon remains available to readers in faulty editions.[2] Conrad, moreover, seems never to have attracted the intense theorizing of Joyce scholarship and criticism, the social causes which have attached themselves to Woolf, or the notoriety of Lawrence's works. Still, Conrad endures. His works have a definite staying power, and his influence on later fiction in Europe, America, Africa, Asia, and South America is daily felt. When Francis Ford Coppola wished an adequate metaphor for interpreting America's Viet Nam experience, or Thion'o wa Ngugi a fictional pattern for *A Grain of Wheat*, or Michael Straight a philosophical backdrop for *After Long Silence*, they turned not to Joyce, Lawrence, or Woolf, but rather to Conrad.

A complete edition of Conrad's letters has long been missing from the scholarship which mediates between the canon and the readers. Jean-Aubry published a large selection of these letters in 1927, but as Karl points out, these suffer from "deletions," "haphazard transcriptions," "mispunctuation based on misreading of the original and misconceptions of the correction itself," "whimsical transpositions, misnumbered pages; extraneous comments," and "attempts at regularization of Conrad's French usage" (p. xli). Since 1927, individual volumes of letters to Edward Garnett, Richard Curle, Marguerite Poradowska, William Blackwood, R. B. Cunninghame Graham, and Francis Warrington Dawson have been published; however, these volumes stand as isolated works, as though one were reading one chapter from a larger novel or hearing one instrument from a major orchestral score. Attempts at synthesis have been made. Edward Said, for example, contemplating "an almost embarrassingly rich testimonial to the intensity and variety of [Conrad's] intellectual life" in the available letters found "an organic whole" in which the letters "fall naturally into groups that corresponded to stages in Conrad's developing sense of himself as a man and as a writer."[3] Joyce's letters were edited in 1957 and 1966; Virginia Woolf's letters were meticulously edited and lavishly annotated between 1975 and 1980, and D. H. Lawrence's letters began to appear in scholarly form in 1979. The gap in Conrad's scholarship is about to be filled, and filled handsomely, with the Frederick R. Karl and Laurence Davies edition of the *Collected Letters*, in eight volumes, being published by Cambridge University Press.

Physically, the first volume is elegant, a joy to hold in one's hands. From its attractive black, blue, and gold binding to its quality paper, to its legible and varied type faces, to its ample margins, this volume pleases both the physical and the mental eyes; moreover, it is freer from typographical errors than any volume I have ever reviewed. More to the point, the first volume, covering the years 1861 to 1897, offers 309 letters to forty-six correspondents (letters scattered through thirty different private and public, individual and institutional collections), a detailed chronology, two perceptive introductions, nineteen plates (only one, disappointingly, of a letter), helpful paragraph-length biographies of the correspondents, and two meticulously prepared indexes—the first of recipients, the second of names of people, places, ships, organizations, and publications. (One hopes that the final volume will also include a subject/topic index making access to the relevant letters even more efficient.) Sixty-three of the 309 letters, over twenty percent, are published here for the first time. Still, serious gaps, probably never to be filled, exist. Except for one brief note, no letter exists before Conrad's twenty-sixth year; no letters to his wife during courtship or the early years of their marriage exist; none of his letters to his uncle and guardian, Tadeusz Bobrowski, remains, and the extent of the loss can only be glimpsed by inferences from Bobrowski's own lengthy responses. For some years, correspondence is represented by only one recipient. With three exceptions, the correspondence for 1891, 1892, 1893, and the first half of 1894, the crucial years in which Conrad completed his first novel and recovered from his Congo experiences, is only with Marguerite Poradowska. The volume's letters range from a note written by the three-and-a-half year old Conrad to his father in 1861 to a New Year's greeting to Baroness Janina de Brunnow on the last day of 1897. In other words, the letters trace Conrad's journey from Polish infant to international sailor to recognized English author of three novels and one collection of short stories and leave him at the crucial turning point when he had found his mature stylistic, theoretical, and thematic voice, on the verge of greatness with *Heart of Darkness* and *Lord Jim* in the offing.

Although the letters are addressed to forty-six different recipients, most of them were received by Marguerite Poradowska (89), Edward Garnett (70), T. Fisher Unwin (37), and Edward Lancelot Sanderson (17). Since the Poradowska, Garnett, and most of the Sanderson letters have been published previously, there are few major surprises for Conradians in this volume—unlike the promises held out for the later volumes. Instead, there is a crisp newness. The Garnett letters have been checked against the originals wherever possible and corrected, providing a number of new readings, and the Poradowska letters have been freshly translated, offering much more idiomatic readings than the earlier John A. Gee and Paul J. Strum translations of 1940.

Although there is much to be said about the new facets of Conrad revealed in the unpublished letters and some adjustments to be made in light of his letters to T. Fisher Unwin, Jane Cobden Unwin, and H. G. Wells, attention should first be given to the contexts Karl and Davies establish in which readers may explore and understand the letters, to the textual principles assumed by the edition, and to the apparatus created for use in the volume.

Karl's "General Editor's Introduction" clearly establishes the nature of the task facing the editors and also provides a vantage point from which to view the letters. Extant Conrad letters total over 3,500—in Polish, French, and English—and some 1,500 of them have never been published. Karl briefly surveys the history of previous editions, generously conceding that "we should stress that [Jean-Aubry's] conception of an edition of letters was very different from our own" (p. xliii), rather than savaging *Life and Letters* as he rightly could. Jean-Aubry, Karl continues, "attempted to shape Conrad's image." Karl, too, attempts to shape our image of Conrad, not by manipulating letters as did Jean-Aubry, but rather by creating a perspective, an assumption about what the letters tell us. "No other medium," Karl argues, "can take us so intimately into both [a major author's] personal life and his way of working. Letters are more effective than journals, memoirs, or diaries, for these are conscious efforts, written out of what the author understands to be his intentions and motivations. Letters, however, provide patterns and schemes which move beyond conscious planning" (p. xxvii). One might argue that Conrad's letters are also "conscious efforts," particularly since Karl moves on to conclude that "like his creative work, his letters became for him the public shaping of the private imaginative act" (p. xxviii). Conrad's letters record a search for an audience, and the first volume shows Conrad moving from a narrowly prescribed private audience to an ever more public one demanding various voices and various masks. Karl suggests that "Conrad's letters help establish a network of Edwardian correspondence of a density hitherto unrealized" (p. xxxvi), but this will have to be borne out by the later volumes, as this one ends in the year of Victoria's Diamond Jubilee. Although no one will disagree with Karl's conclusion that the letters "compellingly mirror [Conrad's] intellectual growth" (p. xxviii), I remain unconvinced that they "reflect an author still learning English" (p. xxviii), and Karl's comment that "Conrad was not a self-conscious correspondent" (p. xxxiv) seems checked by Davies' conclusion that "to the extent that they mask or suppress one aspect or another of Conrad's self, the letters could be considered miniature fictions in themselves, and the early correspondence a series of rehearsals for his performance as a novelist" (p. lx), though Davies hesitates to follow up on the "could be" and settles for viewing them as "trials, explorations, a writer's attempts at understanding his medium and his circumstances" (p. lx). Since Conrad wrote Karol Zagórski, 22 May 1980, that "considering the distinguished personage who is penning this autograph, it ought to be a pleasure to you too. You can bequeath it to your children. Future generations will read it with admiration (and I hope with profit)" (pp. 52-53), the extent of the self-consciousness should not be underestimated.

The edition as a whole stands in the shadows of Gordon Sherman Haight's magistral multi-volume edition of the George Eliot letters in terms of format, theory, and methodology, though it could have profited from adopting features from later editions. For example, numbering the letters in the manner of the Lawrence and Woolf editions would have been helpful since on some days Conrad wrote several letters, and a fuller description of the search undertaken for the letters would have been welcomed.

Editing letters is perhaps the one time when W. W. Greg's rationale of copy-text can appropriately be applied without qualification, because the letter is simultaneously the manuscript and the intended form of "publication." Thus, one cannot fault the theory of copy-text that informs this volume. As Karl points out, "editing principles have been kept simple. The overall plan has been to transcribe Conrad's more than 3500 letters as they appear in the original holograph or typescript. The aim throughout is to provide a text representing what Conrad wrote and what his recipients read with a minimum of alteration or interference" (p. xlv). Karl and Davies faced two major problems in achieving this goal, and their solutions, however reasonable, will not please everyone.

The first problem involves choice of copy-text. Many of Conrad's letters no longer exist in manuscript. They have been destroyed or—worse—lost in one way or another. "About 250 letters at most" (p. xliv) out of the 3500 fall into this category. Karl states the editorial principles for treating such cases as follows: "When the original or photocopies of the original are unavailable, we print from books, magazines, other editions, including transcriptions which we know are not free from error" (pp. xliii-xliv). This is the only sensible solution, the solution editors of, say, "Karain" will have to reach since the manuscript of this particular short story sank with the *Titanic*. For example, the Polish original of the 12 June 1896 letter to Aniela Zagórska (p. 287) has disappeared. Karl and Davies print the Najder translation based "on a collation of French and English versions" (p. 287). In other instances, they accept Garnett's text, adopt copies from Emily Briquel's diary, and, in one instance, refuse to attempt to construct from mere fragments (p. 304). Regardless of the copy-text used, Karl and Davies provide translations of the Polish and French letters. Whether their decision to print the French originals but to exclude the Polish originals was wise or even economical is debatable and none too logical considering the relatively small body of Polish letters.

Just as in editing a short story, a poem, or a novel, editors must at times emend letters. As Karl points out, "Conrad's uncorrected errors of punctuation, accentuation, grammar, spelling, and idiom are . . . another question" (p. xlv), especially since Conrad was writing in his second and third languages. They decided, quite rightly, to "keep Conrad's erratic but lavish capitalization of personal pronouns" (p. xlvi) and to take "ease of reading as [the] criterion" (p. xlv) in bracketing missing letters, missing words, expanded contractions, and to mark "other peculiarities" with asterisks (p. xlvi). "Tacit correction of the letters," they argue with every justification, "would water down their characteristic flavour" (p. xlv). One misses in the discussion of editorial principles some description of the problems in transcribing Conrad's hand. His hand does present problems at times, though not to the extent that William Faulkner's, Virginia Woolf's, and Jean Rhys's do.[4] Many of his letters can be taken for either upper- or lower-case; his paragraph indicators are erratic; and his use of the dash remains ambiguous. In transcribing the "Author's Note" to *Almayer's Folly*, for example, John Quinn's secretary misread "huts" as "tents," an error which has stood for sixty-four years in Conrad texts.[5]

The good news for scholars, then, is that this volume is physically attractive, perceptively introduced, firmly grounded on solid editorial principles, and most useable. One cannot, in this day, even complain about the price. Translating these editorial goals into actual practice, however, left several problems which must be addressed and which, one hopes, will not affect the remaining volumes.

Of primary concern to the users are the accuracy, inclusiveness, and usefulness of the edition and its apparatus— qualities only fully assessed after extensive use of the volume. One can easily pass over the misdating of the completion of *Almayer's Folly* in the "Chronology" as 20 April 1984 (p. xxiv)—it was completed *24* April 1894 (see letter to Marguerite Poradowska, p. 153) — were it not that this error is symptomatic of recurrent problems affecting identification of the letters, annotation, and transcription.

Each letter, for instance, is identified by manuscript location and by its status as previously published or unpublished. The mid-October/mid-November letter to W. H. Chesson pasted in Chesson's copy of *Almayer's Folly* is rightly identified as having been published in Ugo Mursia's *The True 'Discoverer' of Joseph Conrad's Literary Talent* (p. 186), yet a second letter to Chesson, dated Wednesday, 1895, pasted in the same copy and twice published by Mursia, is listed as unpublished (p. 198).[6] Elsewhere, the 20 March 1896 letter to Jane Cobden Unwin (p. 267) is listed as unpublished, though it and its companions of 17 June 1895 and 3 July 1896 (pp. 229 and 289) were first published in Mario Curreli's "Four Unpublished Conrad Letters."[7] Curreli identified these three letters (the fourth belongs to 1898) as being in the West Sussex Record Office, County Hall, Chichester, MSS 972 and 988, but Karl and Davies place the 7 July 1896 letter in Leeds, while leaving the other two in Chichester. Also, Conrad's letter to T. Fisher Unwin, partially published in George T. Keating's *A Conrad Memorial Library*, is redated from 11 December 1897 to 8 November 1897 (p. 407), without explanation other than a note which dead-ends without enlightening the reader.[8]

The annotations also raise doubts and spectres. On 9 April 1896, Conrad wrote Garnett, concerning T. Fisher Unwin: "Is he very sick at the very thought of me? Or cocky? Or rampagious? Or fishyti icyty, dummy li indifferent?" (p. 272). The last phrase demands some annotation. Is it slang? Is it anglicized Polish, or Italian, or French? Is it a near-illegible crux in the original? Karl and Davies silently pass over the phrase. On 2 June 1897, Conrad wrote Garnett that "The *Nigger* is bought in the states by the Batchelor syndicate for serial and by Appleton for book" (p. 356), and Karl and Davies provide the annotation: "The Bachellor Syndicate did not succeed in serializing *The Nigger* in the United States." This is simply wrong. Joseph Katz identified, William Cagle confirmed, and Donald W. Rude, Kenneth W. Davis, and Marlene Salome discussed the serialization of this novel in the *Illustrated Buffalo Express* in six installments on consecutive Sundays between 8 August and 12 September 1897.[9] Although the serialization is not significant in the ways the serializations of *Lord Jim* in *Blackwood's*, *The Secret Agent* in *Ridgeway's*, or *Under Western Eyes* in *The English Review* are, it has a unique status, because, as the authors of "The American Serial Edition" point out: "Although it is greatly condensed the American serial text has a special significance for textual scholars interested in the work, for, where it preserves Conrad's text it preserves the substance of the novel in an early, intermediate form distinct from either the holograph manuscript or the other editions of the novel appearing in 1897."[10]

Other inaccuracies and inconsistencies surface. Hans van Marle's "unpublished researches in the Registry of Shipping and Seamen" (p. 13) were largely published in 1976;[11] the note, "Frequently, but by no means consistently, Conrad carried over into French (as well as English) the Polish convention of capitalizing *You* and *Your*" (p. 35) needs to appear on page 11 to explain the capitalization of "You" in a letter to Spiridion Kliszczewski; the heading, "My dear Maryleczka," to the Maria Bobrowska letter (p. 48) needs more helpful annotation explaining the Polish diminutive; "Russian calendar" might more properly be called "Julian calendar" (p. 148) throughout; the comment "Text from Garnett; Jean-Aubry's copy is remarkably similar" (p. 245) raises several unanswered questions while explaining nothing. Occasionally, the annotations simply mislead. For example, Karl and Davies note that "In all, Conrad spent five years on the manuscript, from 1889 to 1894" (p. 252), implying wrongly that the composition of *Almayer's Folly* was a continuous process. Conrad may have thought about the manuscript for five years, and over four-and-a-half years did elapse between the initial inspiration in the fall of 1889 and the completion, but the novel was written in fits and starts. Its first seven chapters were apparently completed between fall 1889 and 10 June 1890; then the novel seems to have remained untouched until chapter eight was completed in Switzerland between 21 May and 14 June 1891. Chapter nine had been completed by August 1893; chapter ten was added between 6 December 1893 and 17 January 1894; chapter eleven in late March and early April 1894; and the final chapter was written at a furious pace between 16 and 24 April 1894.[12] Another note suggests that the 1902 Hythe printing of the "Preface" to *The Nigger of the "Narcissus"* may be "a forgery by Thomas J. Wise, later a collector of Conrad's manuscripts and typescripts" (p. 375), even though clear evidence exists from Neill Joy and David Smith that such is not the case. Joy summarizes the evidence thus:

Smith, pp. 12-13, fleetingly (and uniquely) conjures up the specter of a Thomas J. Wise forgery of the Hythe "Preface"—only to dismiss it. The Henry E. Huntington Library communicates that it does not tentatively list the Hythe "Preface" as a possible Wise forgery. Conrad too often inscribed the Hythe publication to allow the charge. See Wise, p. 4; Keating, p. 46, item 13; Gordan, p. 240. In addition, at Colgate University is a signed presentation copy to Richard Curle, Conrad's biographer and friend, which reads: "The Suppressed Preface printed by / Henley as Afterword in his N. R. / to R. Curle—J. Conrad." Conrad again confounds the Hythe text with that of *The New Review*. Surely also Conrad refers to the Hythe "Preface" in a letter to Curle . . . . Additional unpublished letters to John Quinn, August 24, 1911 (New York Public Library, Manuscripts Division); to Pinker [1914] (Berg Collection); to Knopf, March 27, 1914 (University of Texas) outrightly or circumstantially validate the Hythe . . . . I multiply evidence to forestall any future suppositions of counterfeiting.[13]

Finally, whether or not the annotations are repetitious may involve individual taste. I found all references to "The Patron" and the "Enlightened Patron of Letters" (pp. 272, 301, 306, 311, 313, 316, 317, 366, and 406) rather needlessly glossed each time with a reference to T. Fisher Unwin, and I see no reason why "This 'Author's Note' was not used in the Unwin edition" (p. 197) needs repetition as "Although dated 1895, this 'Author's Note' was not published until the Collected Edition of 1921. By that time, the manuscript belonged to John Quinn, the collector of Conradiana" (p. 199). The "Author's Note," incidentally, was first published in the Sun-Dial Collected Edition of 1920, not in 1921.

A potentially serious problem is raised by the quality of the transcriptions. Collation of the forty 1895 and 1896 Garnett letters reveals twenty-six substantive and 254 accidental variants between Garnett's 1928 edition and the Karl and Davies edition. Where Garnett reads *hanging by, the spade, (mem), sunshiny,*

heard for, commission, turned to with, and *offering,* Karl and
Davies read *handle by, blue spade, (must), smashing, heard of
you for, communion, returned with,* and *offer.* Only the most
careful check against the original manuscripts will reveal which
reading is accurate—or most likely. Where Karl and Davies have
corrected previous misreadings and mistranscriptions of
Conrad's hand, they are to be commended. A collation of the
Henry James letter given in facsimile in Karl's *Joseph Conrad:
The Three Lives* and of two T. Fisher Unwin letters reveals
exacting, accurate transcriptions.[14] Comparison of the Karl and
Davies transcription against a Mursia transcription and a
facsimile, however, yields mixed results. Mursia transcribed the
16 January 1894 letter to W. H. Chesson thus:

> Wednesday
> 17 Gillingham St.
> S. W.
>
> Dear Mr. Chesson.
>
>   In reference to a paragraph (of 2 sentences) left out in the setting of Almayer
> I must own that the fault is mine entirely. The typescript is in error not the
> printer. If it can be rectified without too much trouble I would be very glad.
>
>   As to the literary notices of the publication, I understand that you were good
> enough to undertake their composition. I am quite content to be in your hands
> but it struck me that perhaps a suggestion from me would meet with your
> approval. Could you not say something about it being a "Civilized story in
> savage surroundings?" Something in that sense if not in these words.
>
>   As to that preface (which I have shown you) I trust it may be dispensed with,
> but if it must appear you are quite right—*Aversion from* not "aversion for" as
> I wrote—and stuck to like a lunatic. You will correct?
>
> Yours very faithfully
> J. Conrad
>
> Remember me to Mr. Garnett[15]

Karl and Davies differ five times from Mursia; more
importantly, their transcription differs eight times, perhaps
nine, from the facsimile. Specifically, there are no periods after
Mr in the salutation or the postscript, rather, *Mr* is connected by
ligature with the following word in each instance. *Your* in the
second sentence of the second paragraph is capitalized, as is
Civilized in the third sentence. Where Mursia paragraphs
between *words* and *As,* Karl and Davies do not. The original

letter seems to indicate a paragraph, because it reads *words.—* and provides a slight indentation on the next page before *As.* Where Mursia and the facsimile read—*Aversion,* Karl and Davies read —*"aversion,* and Karl and Davies omit the *it* in the third sentence of the second paragraph, quite wrongly. There is a faint possibility that *printer* in the first paragraph may be a mistranscription by both parties for *printers.*

Midway through his career as an author, Conrad wrote Garnett: "And so you've kept my letters! Have you! Ah my dear you'll never meet the man who wrote them again."[16] The Karl and Davies edition of the letters assures that we may indeed meet the man who wrote them again and again and with a fullness and a completeness denied Garnett since we will have access to Conrad's letters to his many other correspondents. The edition suffers from some obvious flaws, but these can easily be corrected in the forthcoming volumes if the editors scrupulously check their manuscript records and transcriptions, if they meticulously comb existing Conrad scholarship, and if they hew faithfully to the high standards already defined, if not fully realized, in this first volume of the letters.

Notes

1. Cagle's bibliography, intended for the Soho series, is nearing completion. Rude's findings have been published in various places, most recently as "A Supplementary Bibliography of Conrad Manuscripts in American Libraries," *Conradiana,* 8 (1976), 169-71; "An Annotated Checklist of the Works of Joseph Conrad in Author's Corrected Proofs," *AEB,* 2 (1978), 87-102; and "The Richard Gimbel Collection of Conrad's Manuscripts and Typescripts at the Philadelphia Free Library," *Conradiana,* 15 (1983), 231-36.

2. A critical edition of Conrad's works is currently in progress and will be published by Cambridge University Press. *Almayer's Folly* (1895), Conrad's first novel, has been completed, and editions of *Youth, The Secret Agent,* and *Notes on Life and Letters* are nearing completion. Cambridge will thus have both the letters and works of Conrad as well as the letters and works of D. H. Lawrence.

3. Said, *Joseph Conrad and the Fiction of Autobiography* (Cambridge: Harvard Univ. Press, 1966), p. vii.

4. *The Letters of Virginia Woolf,* Volume I: 1888-1912, ed. Nigel Nicolson and Joanne Trautman (New York: Harcourt, Brace, Jovanovich, 1975), p. x, contains a succinct pattern for such a statement.

5. See Higdon, "The Text and Context of Conrad's First Critical Essay," *Polish Review*, 20: 2-3 (1975), 99.

6. Mursia, "The True 'Discoverer' of Joseph Conrad's Literary Talent and Other Notes on Conradian Biography with Three Unpublished Letters," *Conradiana*, 4: 2 (1972), 5-22, also printed as a pamphlet (Barese, Italy, 1971).

7. Curreli, "Four Unpublished Conrad Letters," *Conradiana*, 8 (1976), 209-17.

8. See Edward Garnett, "Tales of Unrest," in *A Conrad Memorial Library: The Collection of George T. Keating* (Garden City, N.Y.: Doubleday, Doran, 1929), p. 58. Garnett seems to have confused the dates on two letters, because he dates both 11 December 1897. Since the letter is headed "Monday," it could not have been written on 11 December which was a Saturday. In any case, the reference to the Olivia Garnett letter of 4 November 1897 does not explain why this letter should be dated 8 November.

9. Rude, Davis, and Salome, "The American Serial Edition of *The Nigger of the 'Narcissus,'*" *Conradiana*, 9 (1977), 35-45.

10. Rude, Davis, and Salome, p. 35.

11. See Hans van Marle, "Plucked and Passed on Tower Hill: Conrad's Examination Ordeals," *Conradiana*, 8 (1976), 99-109.

12. This information, which combines material from *A Personal Record* (1912), letters, and manuscript notations, is taken from the unpublished introduction to the critical edition of *Almayer's Folly*, ed. David Leon Higdon and Floyd Eugene Eddleman.

13. Joy, "Conrad's 'Preface' to *The Nigger of the 'Narcissus':* The Lost Typescript Recovered," *Conradiana*, 9 (1977), 29-30.

14. These are the Henry James letters of 16 October 1896 (p. 307), reproduced in the illustrations following p. 412 in *Joseph Conrad: The Three Lives* (New York: Farrar, Straus, and Giroux, 1979), and T. Fisher Unwin letters of 3 January 1897 (pp. 329-30) and 2 July 1897 (p. 364), photocopies from the Brotherton Library, University of Leeds.

15. Mursia, pp. 9-10; the facsimile is reproduced on pp. 18-20.

16. Letter of 12 January 1911, in *Letters from Joseph Conrad 1895-1924* (Indianapolis: Bobbs-Merrill, 1928), p. 222.

In Wand'ring Mazes Found: Hardy's Poetic Texts

Robert C. Schweik

Samuel Hynes, ed. *The Complete Poetical Works of Thomas Hardy*, Vol. I. Oxford: Clarendon Press, 1983. 403 pp.

Despite the quirkiness and idiosyncratic quality of some of the best known of Thomas Hardy's nearly 950 poems, there has been a growing consensus that his poetry is not only an important part of one main line of development in British poetry but a powerful influence on its subsequent history. A roster of modern British (and to a much lesser extent American) poets who have explicitly acknowledged his influence, or whose poetry reflects that influence, or whose work at least falls within what Samuel Hynes has called "the Hardy tradition,"[1] would have to include Kingsley Amis, W. H. Auden, John Betjeman, Edmund Blunden, Walter de la Mare, Roy Fisher, Roger Frith, Robert Frost, Robert Graves, Geoffrey Grigson, Philip Larkin, D. H. Lawrence, C. Day Lewis, Philip Oakes, Ezra Pound, J. H. Prynne, John Crowe Ransom, James Reeves, Siegfried Sassoon, C. H. Sorley, Dylan Thomas, Edward Thomas, and Andrew Young. Perhaps only Hopkins, Yeats, or Eliot might plausibly be said to have had a stronger impact on modern poetry.

It is appropriate, then, that attention has finally been paid to the preparation of scholarly editions of Hardy's poetry. In 1978, Macmillan of London published James Gibson's *The Variorum Edition of the Complete Poems of Thomas Hardy*; for this edition Gibson took as his copy-text the 1928 printing of Hardy's *Collected Poems* which he emended to correct misprints and to incorporate late revisions. Gibson also attempted to record in the margins (his *Variorum Edition* is a large-paper issue of a more compact *The Complete Poems of Thomas Hardy* published in 1976) all known variant readings in the manuscripts and printed texts having any authority, though he made no claim to absolute completeness and was unable to obtain access to some fifteen manuscripts in private hands. Hence, splendid as this edition is—it even indicates variations in line indentation—Gibson made no pretense at attempting to satisfy the need for a full and complete critical edition of Hardy's poetry. Now, with the appearance of Samuel Hynes's *The Complete Poetical Works of Thomas Hardy*, that need will be met.

The volume under review here is the first of a projected three-volume critical edition in the Oxford English Texts series; it provides the texts of Hardy's three earliest published volumes of poetry—*Wessex Poems* (1898), *Poems of the Past and Present* (1901), and *Time's Laughingstocks* (1909). Apart from the main critical apparatus and explanatory notes, it includes three appendixes: a note on Hardy's *Wessex Poems* drawings, identifying the scenes and manuscript of Hardy's musical setting for "The Stranger's Song"; and the text of a bowdlerized version of "The Bride-Night Fire" so different from the final version as to make it confusing to attempt to record variants in the usual way in the textual notes.[2] It is particularly fortunate that Hynes has been able to include in this edition all of Hardy's drawings for *Wessex Poems* which were dropped from later editions and one drawing never before printed. These pictures were important to Hardy: he once told Edmund Gosse that drawing them so engaged his interest that he neglected revising the texts of *Wessex Poems* themselves! Oddly, on p. 361, Hynes states that these drawings are provided in an appendix; in fact, they appear precisely where they should be—accompanying the texts of the poems as Hardy intended.

But such matters as the recovery of Hardy's illustrations are peripheral to the central—and truly formidable—problem Hynes faced in establishing the texts of the actual poems themselves. Of the manifold difficulties editors must be prepared to confront in preparing scholarly editions of Hardy's writings, none, I think, are likely to be more daunting than those connected with the poetry. This special difficulty stems in part from Hardy's constitutional inability to refrain from revising at every opportunity—in the manuscripts, on the proof sheets, and at every occasion that the reprintings of his texts allowed. Even the lists of "corrections" Hardy sent to Macmillan from time to time were in fact more likely to contain revisions than corrections. Florence Hardy's comment about Hardy's "artistic inability to rest content with anything that he wrote until he had brought the expression as near to his thought as language would allow"[3] seems, given the evidence of the texts, almost an understatement; and one gets the impression that had Hardy lived another fifty years the revisions would have continued unabated.

Hardy exercised this penchant for constant revision on the texts of his fiction as well as his poetry, but an editor of the poems faces a more complex editorial problem because of the peculiar history of the transmission of those texts. The main course of that history involves, first, the printings of the eight separate volumes of Hardy's poetry, beginning with *Wessex Poems* in 1898. These individual volumes went through various revised reprintings in Hardy's lifetime (*Wessex Poems*, for example, was reprinted with revisions in 1903), but they were also incorporated in other collected editions such as the "Uniform" edition published by Osgood, McIlvaine, which text, in turn, with still further revisions, was the basis for the Pocket Edition of *Wessex Poems* and *Poems of the Past and the Present* issued in 1907. Then, in 1909, Hardy made revisions in both *Wessex Poems* and *Poems of the Past and the Present* for a proposed *Collected Poems*. After various delays, *Collected Poems* was finally published in 1919 and in 1920 went immediately into a second impression, which again included revisions, and, thereafter, into further revised printings in 1923 and 1928.

By itself, this relatively straight line of textual transmission would pose no special problems. But when in 1912 Hardy prepared printer's copy for the Wessex Edition texts of his poems, he did not use the revised texts he had prepared in 1909 for the yet unpublished *Collected Poems* nor did he use the revised text of the Pocket Edition; instead, he returned to the

Uniform Edition and made extensive, but often quite different, revisions. These Wessex Edition texts subsequently became the basis for a further revised printing in 1920 and were used as the printer's copy for the Mellstock Edition of the same year which incorporated additional revisions. The Wessex Edition texts were also used as the basis for the *Selected Poems* of 1916 in which Hardy made further revisions. Finally, just before he died, he revised *Selected Poems* for a new edition to be titled *Chosen Poems* which appeared posthumously.

In short, the textual history of Hardy's poetry was such that two distinct lines of development—that of the *Collected Poems* and that of the Wessex Edition—emerged; these influenced one another in various ways, but their divergences were never fully reconciled in Hardy's lifetime. To complicate matters further, the frequent lists of "corrections" Hardy sent to Macmillan would often be incorporated in one edition but not, sometimes for reasons of economy, in others; and Hardy made revisions in personal study copies of the Wessex Edition, of the *Collected Poems* of 1923, and of *Selected Poems* of 1916, sometimes more or less tentatively. Many of these revisions were never incorporated in any printed texts. It is this formidable textual maze that Hynes has undertaken to negotiate in establishing the text of *The Complete Poetical Works of Thomas Hardy*.

Certainly no editorial decision Hynes has made is more likely to be debated than his choice of first editions as copy-texts. Unquestionably Hardy was more careful with accidentals in the manuscripts of his poetry than he was in those of his fiction; nevertheless, the editors of the recent Clarendon Press critical editions of Hardy's fiction have chosen the manuscripts as copy-text, and Simon Gatrell has vigorously argued that Hardy's manuscript accidentals are grammatically satisfactory, aesthetically significant, and in every respect suitable as the basis for critical editions.[4] Because Gatrell's arguments apply, *ceteris paribus*, to the poetry as well (in fact, I would argue that they apply even more cogently to the poetry than to the fiction), some more detailed consideration of the appropriateness of Hynes's choice of copy-text is relevant here. Hynes argues the case for his choice as follows: "Hardy was not careful about punctuation in the holographs he prepared as printer's copies: clearly he was one of those writers who expected his copy to be corrected by the printer, and who would alter in proofs any corrections that displeased him. That he was a meticulous proof-reader the existing proofs make very clear; he not only made many substantive corrections, but he also caught faulty characters—even a lower-case *i* with the dot missing!—and numerous errors of punctuation. I have therefore taken the first editions of all the volumes except *Winter Words* as the best authority in punctuation, unless there is reason to think that later changes were authorial" (pp. xxiv-xxv). Hynes's argument that Hardy was not careful about his manuscript punctuation squares with my own observation. The point is not that much of a given Hardy manuscript may be punctuated in a way that is not obviously unsatisfactory; rather, it is that what is unsatisfactory may make dubious any assumption about Hardy's purposes in other places in the manuscript where it might be argued that some unconventional punctuation was deliberately intended to secure a special aesthetic effect. In the case of some of Hardy's novels this is especially true: some are pointed in such a slapdash way as to make it transparently clear that Hardy certainly did not intend his manuscript punctuation to be followed,[5] and it is something of a Hardyian irony that the punctuation system which editors have adopted in the Clarendon critical editions of Hardy's fiction may in fact be further from Hardy's final deliberate intention than the Wessex Edition punctuation itself.

Accordingly, I think Hynes is on solid ground in his choice of copy-texts for the poetry, and certainly that choice has important consequences. The variants in accidentals between Hynes's edition and the holograph of *Wessex Poems*, for example, amount to some 194 instances—nearly four variants for each poem—and surely so many differences would have, if nothing else, a powerful cumulative effect. Among other things, the general tendency in the manuscript punctuation is to have fewer exclamation and question marks—so that over all Hardy's holograph punctuation creates a somewhat more muted effect than does the printed version. Otherwise, it is sometimes decidedly queer, as, for example, Hardy's manuscript use of the semicolon in lines like these: "So; to-day I stand with a God-set brand . . ." or "'Twas in fealty. / Sir; I've nothing more to say . . ." (ll. 9-12).

But, although Hynes's decision to follow the punctuation of the first printed editions rather than that of the manuscripts makes sense generally, I think he does not always consider the claims of the manuscripts sufficiently. For example, Hardy had, as Hynes himself makes clear, a preference for capitalized personifications, and, when they appear in later printed texts, Hynes regularly adopts them on the assumption that they are likely to be Hardy's. In the reverse situation, however—where capitalized personifications appear in the manuscript but not in the first or subsequent printings—Hynes accepts the printed version even when it is clear that compositors have created strange inconsistencies which Hardy may have overlooked but which could scarcely represent his deliberate intention. Thus, in "A Sign Seeker," Hardy indulged his preference for capitalized personifications in stanzas such as the following: "I have seen the Lightning-blade, the leaping Star, / The cauldrons of the Sea in storm, / Have felt the Earthquake's lifting arm, / And trodden where abysmal Fires and Snow-cones are."

When "A Sign Seeker" first appeared in print, some eighteen of these capitalized personifications, including all those in the stanza quoted above, were reduced to lower case over the first thirty lines of the poem. But at that point, as the manuscript plainly shows, a new compositor took over who respected Hardy's unconventional capitals and retained them in such stanzas as this: "Or, when Earth's Frail lie bleeding of her Strong, / If some Recorder, as in Writ, Near to the weary scene should flit / And drop one plume as pledge that Heaven inscrolls / the wrong" (ll. 33-36). The result: printed versions all retain this strangely inconsistent capitalization which Hardy could scarcely have desired; in such cases, restoring Hardy's manuscript capitalization throughout would be a more satisfactory editorial solution than retaining the inconsistent treatment that resulted from a change in compositors. But such instances, I should stress, are rare and in no way invalidate the

general correctness of Hynes's preference for the accidentals of
the first printed editions where small punctuation changes,
certainly by Hardy, can have remarkably strong effects. In
"Ditty," for example, each of the first four stanzas ends with the
refrain "Where she dwells." So in the manuscript did the fifth
and last; but in the first printed edition of *Wessex Poems* Hardy
changed that last line to "—Where she dwells!" and the
combination of the initial hesitation created by the opening
dash and the emphasis in the final exclamation mark provides
the reader with clues necessary to know how Hardy wanted that
final line to be read.

In his treatment of Hardy's substantives, Hynes has of course
preferred Hardy's latest versions when these can be determined;
thus he naturally gives precedence to such late revisions as those
Hardy recorded up to 1927 in his copy of a 1917 volume of
Selected Poems which he was preparing for *Chosen Poems*. But
there are conflicting claims between readings in the divergent
lines of transmission that led on the one hand to the Wessex and
Mellstock editions and on the other to the successive printings of
Collected Poems in 1919, 1923, and 1928. Hardy is well known
to have regarded the Wessex Edition as the definitive
embodiment of his work, and in a 3 May 1913 letter to Frederick
Macmillan he specifically requested that "the corrections in the
Wessex edition . . . be incorporated into the other editions."[6]
At the time Hardy wrote that letter, however, plates made for the
first portion of the *Collected Poems*— i.e., *Wessex Poems* and
Poems of the Past and the Present—probably survived from a
setting made in 1909 for which Hardy had already read proofs,
and when the *Collected Poems* finally appeared in 1919, Hardy's
wish about incorporating the Wessex revisions in it was not
followed. Furthermore, although revised printings of *Collected
Poems* appeared in 1923 and again in 1928, when Hardy revised
for them, it was with the constraints of a text already set. All the
same, Hardy had a special regard for the *Collected Poems*: he
was certainly aware that it, rather than the Wessex Edition,
would be the form in which his poems would reach most
readers, and he was anxious to keep the price low enough to
make it available to a wide audience.

Hence both the revisions Hardy made for the Wessex Edition and those he made for the various printings of the *Collected Poems* have strong claims. Unlike James Gibson, who, in preparing his *Variorum Edition*, generally followed the versions in the *Collected Poems* printings of 1928 and 1930, Hynes has carefully threaded his way through the maze of Hardy's revisions to provide a far more eclectic text: the number of points of difference between the texts of *Wessex Poems, Poems of the Past and the Present,* and *Time's Laughingstocks* as they appear in Hynes's edition and in the Wessex Edition is a little more than 90, while the differences between Hynes's edition and the *Collected Poems* of 1923 is by my count 127—somewhat less than one variant per poem. But those variants can be clustered in such a way as to occasion very appreciable differences between Hynes's text and that of Gibson's. Thus a stanza from "The Supplanter" which in Hynes's text reads

> A year: and he is travelling back
> To one who wastes in clay;
> From dawn till eventide he fares
> Along the wintry way,
> From dawn till eventide he bears
> A wreath of blooms and bay.
>   [ll. 67-72]

reads in Gibson's edition

> A year beholds him wend again
> To her who wastes in clay;
> From day-dawn until eve he fares
> Along the wintry way,
> From day-dawn until eve repairs
> Towards her mound to pray.
>   [ll. 67-72]

Such marked differences reveal the extent to which the Wessex Edition line of development, which Hynes takes carefully into account, can vary from that which led to the *Collected Poems* and on to Gibson's *Variorum Edition*. In a recent review of Hynes's edition, Gibson characterizes its text as "very close" to that of his own *Variorum Edition* based on the 1930 *Collected Poems*: "In a random check of thirty poems, twenty-seven were identical in text, while of the other three Professor Hynes's text was different in a total of five words, one of these being his choice of 'beshorn of wings' in 1. 29 of 'The Impercipient,' on the authority of a written revision in Hardy's copy of the Wessex Edition and its inclusion in the 1920 Wessex and Mellstock Editions, in preference to 'deprived of wings' which is found in the 1923 *Collected Poems*. As on the 28 October 1922 Hardy sent Macmillan a list of the corrections he made to the 1919 *Collected Poems*, we must assume either that he forgot the 'beshorn' revision or had decided against it as it does not feature in that list, or, if it did, Macmillan omitted it."[7] I find Gibson's observations in two respects possibly misleading: not only are the differences between the Gibson and Hynes editions considerably greater than his random check revealed, but Hynes's choices, such as his preference for *beshorn* over *deprived*, are not simply between two equally likely possibilities but, rather, are choices based on the general principle that Hardy's last revision, not his last opportunity for revision, is in most cases the more telling witness. Of course in many places it is the *Collected Poems* version to which Hynes's principle applies. Thus, for line 64 of *"The Bridge at Lodi,"* the manuscript and first printed edition read, "Are but viewing crime aright? . . ." That reading persisted unchanged into the Wessex Edition, but for the *Collected Poems* Hardy revised *crime* to *war*, and it is this latest revised reading that Hynes provides. All things considered, I think the editorial principle Hynes has applied in such cases is the one most likely to yield a final eclectic text which Hardy would have preferred.

Moreover, Hynes's is a text edited to the highest standards of scholarly accuracy. Although I have made an extensive effort to check and recheck his text against the manuscripts and selected printed versions of Hardy's poems, I have found not a single typographical error and only one case of a failure to report a variant—a dash which appears in the manuscript and in five printed versions at the end of the fourth line of "Leipzig." I have also collated Hynes's text against extensive selections from Gibson's *Variorum Edition* and also against some of the citations of texual variants reported in Kenneth Marsden's *The Poems of Thomas Hardy* (London: The Athlone Press, 1969);

with the one exception noted above, whenever I found a difference—I noted five in all—it was Hynes's edition which proved to be correct. In short, I think that Hynes has provided the texts and variants of Hardy's poems with exceptional accuracy and in versions which in every respect conform more closely to Hardy's evident intention than any edition previously available. *The Complete Poetical Works of Thomas Hardy* is now unquestionably the preferred text for scholarly citation and, indeed, for use wherever soundness of editorial policy and accuracy of text are important.

But, although I have found Hynes's editing all but impeccable in most respects, his choice of what information to provide in the textual apparatus is sometimes less satisfactory. Hynes's concern to avoid cluttering the bottom of the page with redundant textual notes is commendable, and his economies in this direction—e.g., citing manuscript and proof readings only if they differ from the first printing—help greatly to avoid a cluttered text. But he went much further than this. As he notes, "In the case of printed texts I have reported variant accidentals only when (*a*) a corroborating correction in Hardy's hand exists, in a manuscript or a revised proof, or in one of Hardy's own books; or (*b*) a change of sense is involved . . ." (p. xxvi). The principle behind this procedure is clear enough: Hynes wishes to avoid congesting his textual notes with variants which presumably have no authority and do not alter meaning. Here, I think, Hynes presumes too much. For example, at the end of the first line of "The Temporary the All," both *Wessex Poems* (the first printed version) and *Complete Poems* have a comma whose presence is nowhere recorded in Hynes's edition on the ground that because the comma was absent in the manuscript and was later deleted in the Wessex Edition and in *Selected Poems*, it must have been an unauthorized compositor's addition. But Hynes can't have it both ways: if, as he has already argued in support of his copy-text choice, Hardy punctuated his manuscripts carelessly and carefully read proof where he would reject any punctuation he did not want, then there is good reason to assume that Hardy deliberately passed that comma in proofreading and only later changed his mind about it. I should emphasize here that Hynes's decision to leave such changes unrecorded is no small matter—it involves hundreds of variants whose existence will nowhere be recorded in Hynes's edition on the dubious assumption that they have no authority. Certainly, in such cases a concern for economy should have yielded to the requisite of a comprehensive record of all variants which, by Hynes's own argument in support of his choice of copy-text, have strong claims to be considered witnesses of Hardy's intentions. It is paradoxical that Gibson's *Variorum Edition*, while making no pretense to be a full critical edition, provides in this respect more information on variants than does Hynes's.

There are also some less serious problems with Hynes's textual notes—e.g., an ambiguity which could confuse readers not familiar with Hardy's invariable use of double quotation marks which printers regularly altered to single quotation marks in conformity with standard British practice. In his introduction Hynes nowhere mentions Hardy's customary use of double quotation marks, but in recording manuscript variants he scrupulously gives Hardy's double marks in notes like that in which he cites a variant in line 13 of "The Casterbridge Captains" which reads —'Who saves his life shall lose it, friends!' Hynes's textual note reads as follows: 13 — 'Who] "Who *Hol.* In such cases, a reader unfamiliar with Hardy's use of quotation marks in his manuscripts could well take the note to mean that Hardy himself had not only added the dash but had changed an inadvertent double quotation mark into a single one. And one final point about the textual notes: I think that Hynes has unwisely relegated Hardy's tentative revisions in his study copies and manuscripts to the explanatory notes at the end of the volume. Tentative changes and erased revisions should, of course, be differentiated from other elements of the textual history of a poem; but it would be far more convenient to have notes on such revisions clearly segregated but at the bottom of the appropriate page so that they would still stand with the other textual notes with which they certainly belong.

Hynes's explanatory notes are, as what I have said above implies, a mixture of special textual notes and other material. Hynes's own comment on what his explanatory notes were intended to include is unfortunately all too brief: "An asterisk following the title of a poem indicates an explanatory note at the back of the volume. Hardy's own explanatory notes are placed with the others, but are marked with an (H). His glossarial notes have been incorporated into the Glossary (Appendix F of Volume Three) and are also marked (H)" (p. xxvi). In fact, Hynes's notes provide a wealth of additional information: excellent brief histories of the composition and publication of each of the volumes of poetry and further explanatory notes ranging from glosses on individual words and allusions to careful documentation of the sources and publication history of individual poems. Most of these explanatory notes are in the form of extensive quotation from and citation of Hardy's letters, the correspondence of his contemporaries and contemporary writings—e.g., Hermann Lea's *Thomas Hardy's Wessex* (1913). Notable as these materials are for their range and fullness, however, there is much they do not contain and nowhere does Hynes make clear what principle of selection he has followed: explanations are given in inconsistent ways—or, at least, ways whose consistency is nowhere straightforwardly explained. Thus, the epigraphs from the Vulgate to the "In Tenebris" poems are translated by preference to the Authorized Version of the Bible, and a biblical allusion to *Revelation* in line 18 of "In Tenebris III" is identified; but, in other poems in which there are biblical allusions—e.g., "The Respectable Burgher on 'The Higher Criticism,'" which contains many—no explanations at all are provided. Explanatory notes almost invariably contain some indication of the source of the information they provide; but, again, this practice is not followed with complete consistency, and one can run into a note such as that for "Middle-Age Enthusiasms," whose dedicatory "To M. H." is simply glossed "M. H. is Hardy's sister, Mary (1841-1915)," with no further documentation. In other cases, however, Hynes appears to give explanatory glosses when there is some contemporary documentation to support them while ignoring other points in the same poem where such documentation is also available. Thus, for "The Well-Beloved," Hynes cites Lea's note on its setting at Jordan Hill and makes a further general reference to James Dyer's *Southern England: An Archaeological Guide,* but Hardy's other references to the Ikling Way and a pagan temple are not explained at all. Furthermore, although Hynes's note does indicate that the location at Jordan Hill applies to the Wessex Edition, one would have to refer to the textual notes to learn that in some other texts the location had been not Jordan but Hardy's "Kingsbere," which would, of course, make "the ancient hill" in the second stanza a reference to Woodbury Hill near Bere Regis. None of this information is provided in Hynes's note.

In short, in spite of the wealth of information Hynes's explanatory notes contain, they seem to me to be the least satisfactory part of *The Complete Poetical Works of Thomas Hardy.* They provide information in ways that sometimes appears oddly inconsistent or, at least, based upon an obscure principle of selection never explicitly stated. There are, as well, other kinds of inconsistencies. In spite of Hynes's concern for economy, many of the explanatory notes contain information (e.g., on Hardy's dating of his poems) which will again be supplied in an appendix to Volume Three. On the other hand, Hynes can sometimes be far too economical: an explanation of Hardy's picture of a broken key accompanying the poem "Nature's Questioning" could easily be given in a single sentence, but Hynes's note in Appendix A supplies no explanation—rather, it obliges the reader to consult a passage in *Far from the Madding Crowd* to obtain one.

But to assert that Hynes's explanatory notes are relatively unsatisfactory is to judge them against the exceptionally high standard set by the edition as a whole. In fact, the few gaps, inconsistencies, and unsatisfactory arrangements in Hynes's notes are easily compensated for by reference to F. B. Pinion's *A Commentary on the Poems of Thomas Hardy* supplemented by J. O. Bailey's extensive but somewhat less reliable *The Poetry of Thomas Hardy.* And, it should be emphasized, Hynes's notes extensively supplement both of those sources. Above all, what is most important about *The Complete Poetical Works of Thomas Hardy* is the text it provides, and here there can be no serious disagreement: Hynes has provided us with the most authoritative text of Hardy's poetry available and one which will surely remain the standard scholarly edition for a very long time.

Notes

1. Samuel Hynes, "The Hardy Tradition in Modern English Poetry," in Norman Page, ed., *Thomas Hardy: The Writer and His Background* (New York: St. Martin's Press, 1980), pp. 173-191. See also, Donald Davie, *Thomas Hardy and British Poetry* (New York: Oxford Univ. Press, 1973).

2. The succeeding two volumes will contain ten more appendixes, some of which will provide other versions of individual poems whose variations are so great as to make this method of presenting them preferable, while others will supply such material as glossaries of place names and of dialect, archaic, and obscure words; a chronological list of dated poems; a catalogue of revised texts and lists of revisions in the Dorset County Museum; and Hardy's notes locating the scenes of some of the poems.

3. Florence Emily Hardy, *The Later Years of Thomas Hardy* (London: Macmillan, 1930), p. 272.

4. See Gatrell's "Hardy, House-Style, and the Aesthetics of Punctuation" in *The Novels of Thomas Hardy*, ed. Anne Smith (Edinburgh: Vision Press, 1978).

5. See Robert C. Schweik and Michael Piret's "Editing Hardy" in *Browning Institute Studies: An Annual of Victorian Literary and Cultural History*, vol. 9, ed. N. John Hall (New York: The Browning Institute, Inc., 1981), 30-41. In his recent critical edition of *Tess of the d'Urbervilles* (Oxford: Clarendon Press, 1983), Simon Gatrell has defended his choice of the manuscript as copytext by arguing that Hardy's close scrutiny of his first edition proofs did not extend to accidentals because he was so occupied with substantive revision that it is "impossible to suppose that he was able to pay detailed attention to the punctuation, or indeed that he considered it important in comparison with the problems he was facing at the time" (pp. 78-80). Hardy's situation in regard to the proofreading of the first editions of his poetry was, of course, quite different. Furthermore, I think that Gatrell tends to minimize the evidences in Hardy's manuscripts that there, too, he paid far less attention to punctuation than to substantives. What Hardy's manuscripts reveal is that he tended to be preoccupied with substantive revision, so much so that substantive revisions are often made in ways which obscure or confuse the punctuation. Hardy's manuscripts reveal very little concern with revision of the punctuation. My point, then, is that the evidence I have seen indicates that Hardy's manuscripts are not as reliable witnesses to subtleties of intended rhetorical effects in punctuation as has sometimes been supposed; this holds

true, I think, even more strongly for Hardy's fiction than for his poetry, though it should be emphasized that the manuscripts of the novels differ very considerably in this respect.

6. British Library Additional Manuscript No. 54924.

7. The Thomas Hardy Society Ltd. *Newsletter* No. 54 (March 1983), 6-7.

Blake's Poetry: In Its Own Right

Pamela Dunbar

Nelson Hilton. *Literal Imagination: Blake's Vision of Words.* Berkeley and Los Angeles: University of California Press, 1983. xvii, 319 pp.

Robert F. Gleckner. *Blake's Prelude: "Poetical Sketches."* Baltimore: Johns Hopkins University Press, 1982. 202 pp.

Many commentators on Blake's poetry take refuge from its complexities by invoking its general cultural context. Others who do focus on the poems themselves tend to offer mere paraphrases—limited, "one-dimensional" explications—of particular terms and passages. Nelson Hilton's *Literal Imagination* proceeds through textual analysis to school us in ways—its ways—of reading Blake: this is its great strength. It emphasizes the "pattern of words" that lies behind all poetry's "pattern of images." Professor Hilton devotes himself to what he called "key-words": "certain words . . . seized by Blake . . . that induce questions about the structure of perception and the nature of reality" (p. 237). Typically— because of the interrelatedness, to Blake and presumably also to Hilton, of all aspects of reality—these key-words are "polysemous" (that is, they evoke multiple meanings). When they also happen to be homonyms (*Mourning/Morning, Veil/Vale, Son/Sun,* etc.) they have a particular attraction.

Literal Imagination presents a crisp, in-depth analysis of key-words and key word-clusters. An important credo of the book is that there is an intrinsic close relationship between the true life and the life of the language, even though some of the examples used, e.g., the two meanings of the word *Grave,* burial place and (en)grave, work against the spirit of the argument. Hilton's book owes its inspiration to recent linguistic and psychoanalytical trends in literary criticism. It has the main virtue of this school, a capacity for inspired close reading of texts, but also a few of its weaknesses—a touch of preciosity, a revelling in the obscure reverberations of its own terminology, and a lack of concern for the authenticity—in the text, in the nature of the language, or in the mind of either reader or author—of some of the word associations that it makes. What for instance of the relationship between *Babylon* and *Baby London*, or that between *veil* and *live* or *evil*? And when Hilton asserts that "enchanted" is "another term for enchainment, as in Milton's *Comus* 659-60" (p. 56), he is taking a liberty which not all readers may feel is justified.

These points aside, the book will be of lasting value. It emphasizes the magic of Blake's language; it shows us how to become better, more alert readers; and it is splendidly alive to the history of words, and to contemporary intellectual issues and conditions of life. It stands proudly as a member of a recently established school of criticism. As a member of that school it has done what more traditional Blake criticism has on the whole failed to do—pay due tribute to the sparkling "verbal surface" of its poetry. The fact that traditional criticism also has the tools to undertake this makes its failure to do so all the more (to use a key-word of Blake's) lamentable. The book is very attractively produced, with appropriate scholarly aids and many illustrations within the body of the text itself.

Blake's first volume of poetry was his *Poetical Sketches* (1783). Earlier criticism of it has concentrated either on the poems' indebtedness to others or on tracing the origin of Blake's "mature" works in them. In *Blake's Prelude* Robert F. Gleckner claims that the volume is fine enough to be studied for its own sake, and on its own terms. In this he is surely right: the lightness of touch in the best of *Sketches*, their challenging absence of a definite location of attitude, the depth of Blake's response in them both to the natural world and to the literary— all show the hand of the master.

Professor Gleckner explores the relationship of the poems to each other, and to their models. When he considers their relationship to each other, he tends to see them as antithetical pairs whose significance lies in the element of contrast between the poems in each pair—between "To the Evening Star" and "To Morning," for instance, or between "Contemplation" and "The Couch of Death." This method can be illuminating although it does impose limitations on our responses to the poems.

The author is at his most persuasive when he argues for the independent relationship that individual *Sketches* establish with their models (principally Milton, Spenser, Shakespeare, James Thomson, and the Bible):

> It is quite wrong . . . to regard the prose poems of *Poetical Sketches* as merely imitative in the conventional sense, Blake simply "trying his hand" at a currently popular mode. On the contrary, he is intent on rescuing the Poetic Genius from the trammels of derivativeness and adaptation in the same way that he will later deliver Milton's vision from the imprisoning clouds of theological dogma and familial adversity.[p. 138]

Gleckner argues that Blake has put familiar styles to new, and often broader, purposes. If he had applied this argument more widely, he would have been able to include in his revaluation even inferior poems like "Fair Elenor," a ballad in Walpolean Gothic which contains traces of aspiration that—however "mechanized" they may be—are well outside the range of Horace Walpole.

Most of Gleckner's textual criticism is astute, though his adherence to his own interpretations sometimes leads him to underplay certain details: he feels for instance that the conclusion of "To Winter" marks a break in what would otherwise be the cycle of Blake's four seasons poems. In fact, however, the conclusion with its reference to the expulsion of the dreaded monster Winter might well be seen as paving the way for Spring's return: "heaven smiles, and the monster / Is driven yelling to his caves beneath Mount Hecla" (ll. 15-16). As well as its literary criticism *Blake's Prelude* is rich in scholarly detail and in the perspectives it offers on critical issues related to its main thesis—though these sometimes distract from the main argument. Gleckner's range of vocabulary is finely expressive though some syntactical convolutions—especially in the earlier part of the book—make his argument difficult at times to follow.

Blake's Prelude shows intellectual rigor and a sensitive appreciation of Blake's poetry. It fully justifies its own claim that *Poetical Sketches* is worth studying in its own right. It shows a respect for tradition that is, in the manner of *Poetical Sketches* itself, salted with audacity. The volume itself is well produced with a clear type-face although the omission of an index and a bibliography will be frustrating to many readers.

Bad Guys Wear Business Suits

Wayne W. Westbrook

Emily Stipes Watts. *The Businessman in American Literature*. Athens: University of Georgia Press, 1982. x, 160 pp.

A feature article not long ago in *The Wall Street Journal* told about a student who copped the highest grade in his Competitive Decision Making course at Harvard Business School because, as he put it, "I was willing to lie to get a better score." The ethical issue, the student averred, is irrelevant. To fix on a goal and go after it, truth-telling aside, is an apparent lesson of this course, never mind the implied commentary about contemporary life. In literature, business and its moral conditions are a master theme, and have been since late in the nineteenth century when writers began analyzing the nature of business and chronicling the careers of scores of businessmen. But morality is only one of a wide spectrum of themes in American literature about business and the businessman, a subject sufficiently rich to yield, besides the ethical or moral bankruptcy theme, the theme of failure, the ideals of success, wealth, and materialism, the romance of poverty, the evils of money making, the motives of profit, power, position, and authority, and the dangers as well as rewards of the "system."

No historical survey or work of literary criticism has yet presented even the strictest chronology or the barest summary of American business literature. Though numerous studies exist, they are confined to historical periods or specific themes and aspects of the subject. An indispensable starting point is Lisle Rose Abbot's unpublished dissertation, "A Descriptive Catalogue of Economic and Politico-Economic Fiction in the United States, 1902-9" (University of Chicago, 1936). The most compendious study is Walter Fuller Taylor's *The Economic Novel in America*, a pioneering work that covers economic

literature from the post-Civil War period up to the turn of the
century. To date, the most valuable survey of the businessman in
American literature is Michael Millgate's *American Social
Fiction: James to Cozzens.*[1]

The central thesis of Emily Stipes Watts's *The Businessman
in American Literature* is that writers with anticapitalistic
biases have tarred all businessmen with the same brush, thereby
creating a negative image of this figure in American literature
that only since the Second World War has been replaced by a
more sympathetic portrayal. Watts's contention is excessively
generalized and formulaic. And her tracing of the image of the
businessman as it developed is certainly not new. Millgate's
approach, for example, was to trace "the development of the
image of the businessman through both its 'epic' and its
'obscure' phases . . . watching its gradual supersession by the
image of the individual in his relation to the ever-increasing
institutionalism of modern American society."[2] Furthermore,
what is promised by Watts's title disappoints since so much
important literature about businessmen is neglected while many
of those works included for discussion bear only a tenuous
relationship to the subject. Regarding those works, the author
disregards the historical context in which they were written,
insisting that the conception of the businessman was purely
intellectual. Evidence now abounds that many businessmen and
capitalists in American literature, as well as events, were copied
from real life. Nor is any attention given to the biographical
influences on writers who deal with business subjects. A number
of American writers knew business first hand, by being involved
in business themselves, by having come from business families,
or by having closely studied and researched business. Chief
among this book's defects then are the numerous errors of fact,
precarious judgments, and baneful generalities that call the
writer's treatment of the subject into doubt.

Chapter One, "Capitalism is God's Way for Fallen Man,"
traces the antibusiness bias characteristic of American writers
back to the Puritans. Contrary to Max Weber's theory in *The
Protestant Ethic and the Spirit of Capitalism* that Luther's
concept of the "calling" became the Puritan's justification for

private ownership and private enterprise, Watts provides evidence to show that capitalism and the accumulation of wealth were regarded as deviations from strict religious principles. From her examination of John Winthrop's *Journal*, the diaries of various Puritan businessmen, and Michael Wigglesworth's "The Day of Doom," Watts determines that rather than a sign of election, property and riches were more often indicative of damnation. She notes that Vernon Parrington, R. H. Tawney, and Richard Hofstadter perpetuated Weber's theory of the alliance between Puritanism and capitalism, an argument that only recently has been overturned. In *The Puritan Origins of the American Self*, Sacvan Bercovitch contends that Calvinistic Puritanism emphasized other-worldliness and salvation of the soul rather than espoused secular achievement as proof of God's grace.[3] Watts agrees with Bercovitch's conclusion that, as she puts it, "American Puritanism was antithetical to capitalism and that, even from the nation's beginnings, the businessman has been deingrated" (p. 20).

A fundamental premise in Watts's study is that 1945 is the year of the Great Divide in American business literature. She conveniently categorizes the figure of the businessman into two groups—pre-World War II businessmen and capitalists who are depicted as corrupt and post-World War II small businessmen and corporate employees who are portrayed more sympathetically and, thus, presumably retain a degree of goodness that commerce cannot defile. This premise she stolidly reiterates:

After *The American*, a rush of books appeared with the negative image of the businessman enlarged. Throughout the next eighty years, that is, generally until 1945 [note: eighty years after the publication of *The American* in 1877 would bring us up to 1957], American artists developed the image in a variety of ways. [p. 55]

As the depression became World War II, the communist movement among the literati lost momentum. Odet's play [*Waiting for Lefty*] and other works by the proletarian writers of the 1930s represent, it now appears, nearly the end of the vicious, one-sided attacks on the American capitalist. [p. 80]

In the post-World War II period, other writers began to distinguish more carefully between the private capitalist, often a small businessman, and the

corporate capitalist, in contrast to pre-1945 writers, who generally grouped all
businessmen together. [p. 105]

A statement made in the opening chapter—"I have
found . . . a growing tendency among our recent writers to
treat the businessman with compassion, understanding, and
even admiration" (p. 5)—is, however, directly at variance with
one set forth in the final chapter—"Most businessmen depicted
in post-1945 television and serious literature are still
characterized as greedy, unethical, and immoral (or amoral),
whether they are JR of William Gaddis's *JR: A Novel* or J. R. of
'Dallas'" (p. 150).

No reader will deny that the image of the businessman in
American literature is basically negative. The reasons for this
broad antibusiness bias on the part of writers have varied from
period to period as the repetitive boom-and-bust cycle of
economic activity has occasioned social change, and from writer
to writer as each has dealt with his socio-economic milieu in
different ways. Henry James, for example, who wrote fiction
while merchant princes and captains of industry were making
millions, felt himself impelled, as Michael Millgate points out,
to write about American businessmen of epic stature largely for
the purposes of cultural definition. Watts, citing Christopher
Newman in *The American* (1877), rightly indicates that not all
businessmen and capitalists in James's fiction are negative
characterizations. But those qualities of innocence and morality
that surround Newman do turn considerably darker by the time
the novelist applies his finishing touches to the portrait of the
businessman, a fact Watts does not mention. Mr. Ruck in "The
Pension Beaurepas" (1879) represents the sickness and moral
decay of a businessman who commits himself to a life of buying
and selling and "knows how to do nothing else." The
commission merchant, Morris Townsend, in *Washington
Square* (1881) ambiguously suggests the demonism and evil
James later associated with moneymaking, a depiction that
evolved into more satanically grotesque figures such as the
spectral capitalist in evening dress that Spencer Brydon
encounters in "The Jolly Corner" (1909)—a symbol of Brydon's
own end had he not renounced the deadly business world years

earlier—and the capitalists Frank Betterman and Abel Gaw in the unfinished *The Ivory Tower* (1916).

Trivialities, misstatements of fact, and errors of interpretation, here as well as elsewhere, impede Watts's discussion. That the name Christopher Newman "suggests an explorer—a Christopher Columbus—as well as a 'new man'" (p. 51) has, by now, I should think, been sufficiently explicated. And the notion that Newman has "an amazingly successful career on the stock market" is dubious. Newman made his money as a *businessman* in leather, washtubs, copper, and railroads, not as a speculator in stocks, as Watts says. (Part of the problem is that she freely mixes the terms "businessman," "speculator," and "capitalist" without properly distinguishing the differences among them.) Why would Newman travel a long distance to New York to conduct a vendetta over $60,000 that he had been done out of in a "business affair," and then once there feel such qualms about this undertaking, if high finance and speculation (and presumably Wall Street) were his natural habitude? Furthermore, Watts says that Newman becomes cultured when he gives up "money getting" and that when this occurs "the cultured American businessman is no longer a businessman" (p. 54). Is it not James's point that Newman challenges the European aristocracy precisely because he is a businessman *still*, though a moral one, since he seeks a wife in Europe who is the "best article on the market"? And doesn't he remain a businessman and cut short his losses with the Bellegarde family because, as Leon Edel reminds us, "A good American, a shrewd businessman does not indulge in waste effort"?[4]

In her analysis of Howells's *The Rise of Silas Lapham* (1885), Watts fails to build support for her thesis that after *The American* the negative image of the businessman enlarged. *Silas Lapham* is a moral history that traces the path of a good man who stumbles, is catapulted toward ruin by renouncing an evil act that would have saved him financially but destroyed others, and who, though bankrupt, rises in moral triumph. The depth to which Silas falls into economic ruin and despair is a measure of his ethical rise. Again, factual errors subvert Watts's analysis. She says that Silas "lacks the qualities of 'natural aristocracy' inherent in Henry James's Christopher Newman" (p. 57), when Newman, an American self-made millionaire who rises from nothing and comes to the city from the boondocks, is precisely the same parvenue breed. Further, Watts wrongly asserts that *Silas Lapham* "was soon followed by a flood of similar novels" (p. 58), when in fact Howells's novel was part of the deluge that began a decade earlier with John W. DeForest's *Honest John Vane* (1875) and Josiah G. Holland's long-time best seller *Sevenoaks* (1875). In her discussion of Dreiser's Cowperwood trilogy, the slipups continue. Watts states that in *The Financier* (1912), Frank Cowperwood borrows monies from the city of Philadelphia to "invest in Chicago" (p. 59). Actually, Cowperwood (modeled after street-car king Charles T. Yerkes) invests in railway stocks in Philadelphia, owning majority interest in the local Seventeenth and Nineteenth Street line. He doesn't make any investments in Chicago until he moves there in *The Titan* (1914), the next novel in the trilogy. The Chicago Fire of 1871 does trim Cowperwood's financial sails, not because he has holdings there, as Watts assumes, but because the Philadelphia banks that retain his collateral began calling in loans during the panic that spreads nationwide, forcing the financier to embezzle additional funds from that city. Watts refers to Cowperwood's "seemingly endless variety of wives and mistresses" (p. 59), when in fact he has many mistresses but only two wives. The assertion, finally, that Dreiser's trilogy introduces to the crooked-money novel the idea that the public is greedy, selfish, and foolish overlooks the appearance of this theme in DeForest and Holland's novels in 1875.

In Chapter Six, "The Generation Trap," Watts reveals that the suffering experienced by wealthy old-line families founded by millionaires is a further indication of the indictment of the businessman in American literature. Watts considers Dreiser's *An American Tragedy* and O'Neill's *The Hairy Ape*, yet makes no mention of the Patch family in Fitzgerald's *The Beautiful and Damned*. In the same place she treats the Boston Brahmin George Apley in Marquand's *The Late George Apley*, Watts discusses Thomas Sutpen's family in Faulkner's *Absalom, Absalom!*—hardly *vieux riche*. Upton Sinclair's *The Jungle* is given large space in the next chapter, though Watts admits "capitalists do not really appear," while other novels by Sinclair in which capitalists abound—*The Captain of Industry* (1906), *The Metropolis* (1908), *The Moneychangers* (1908), as well as the "Lanny Budd" novels—are not examined. In Chapter Nine, "Is Money Money or Isn't Money Money"—an especially weak chapter—Watts lists Jack London among the proletarian writers of the 1930s. London's most important work was published in the early 1900s, and he died in 1916.

Ernest Hemingway is mentioned passim; seven Hemingway works are included in the bibliography against only one by Sinclair, one by James, none by Edith Wharton, none by David Graham Phillips, none by Winston Churchill, none by Booth Tarkington, none by Nathanael West, none by Louis Auchincloss. *The Hairy Ape* is selected for its portrayal of third-generation money in favor of *The Great God Brown* or *Marco Millions*, plays in which businessmen appear. And Watts mentions Updike's *Rabbit, Run* for the incident of Rabbit's daughter's drowning (all children in American literature, not just those of the rich, "had problems no matter who their parents were" [p. 127], Watts concludes), yet on the subject of Rabbit Angstrom as Toyota dealer in *Rabbit is Rich* (1981), she is mute. Watts repeatedly pushes Hemingway into the breach, but none of the uses to which he is put contribute to her argument. Hemingway's place in any study of the businessman is at best tenuous, and Watts is more concerned with the writer Richard Gorton than with the Chicago grain broker who is on board his yacht at Key West in *To Have and Have Not*. Nonetheless, she compares this broker's sexual-financial prolixity to Frank Cowperwood's, missing the essential difference that Hemingway's character is shattered by remorse over being charged for income-tax evasion, while Dreiser's Cowperwood never feels the slightest twinge of conscience.

Watts does break new ground by discussing recent novelists such as James Dickey, Stanley Elkin, and Ken Kesey who have written about the American businessman. The heroes of Dickey's *Deliverance* (1970), Elkin's *A Bad Man* (1967) and *The Franchiser* (1976), and Kesey's *Sometimes a Great Notion* (1965) are four "sympathetic protagonists" who represent a shift in perspective away from the negative stereotype. But even here the ground is shaky. Watts devotes six pages to *Deliverance* (*Silas Lapham* and *The Great Gatsby* rate only two pages each) that offer little more than plot summary. About Elkin, Watts makes the bold claim that "of all our authors, [he] has perhaps wrestled most directly with the problems of capitalism and the businessman" (p. 142). Actually, Ben Flesh in *The Franchiser*, for all the corporate logotypes he has a finger in, suggests the on-the-road theme more than the business theme (the narrator informs us in the novel that Ben "knew nothing of business, that he was no businessman but only another consumer"). Like Jack McGriff, Larry McMurtry's colorful "businessman-hero" in his most recent novel *Cadillac Jack* (1982), Flesh is a Sal Paradise who conducts his automobile odysseys around the country in a perpetual flight from society and self. And by focusing on his status as "small, private businessman," Watts detracts from the epic-heroic stature of Kesey's Hank Stamper in *Sometimes a Great Notion*.

One's final impression is that Watts is out of tune with her subject. The businessman in this study is utilized to show how philistine he is, or to furnish proof for the thesis that he is depicted as indigenously corrupt. Held captive by this thesis, Watts gives no due to the significant body of probusiness or procapitalist literature produced since the Civil War that offers an altogether different image. The figure of the businessman has been employed by American writers for both ends, to support as well as condemn the capitalistic system. Nor is any due paid to the fact that many American writers have had a double-edged view of the businessman, mixing sneering parody with deep fascination or grudging admiration. The book's chapters, which average about nine pages in length, speak of an economy of research and a penury of scholarship. Favorite words such as "unbelievable," "incredible," and "striking" suggest the gush, as do "most," "many," and "some" the imprecision, expected from an undergraduate English essay. In sum, Watts's work conveys the effect of a topic uninvestigated and the idea of an opportunity wasted.

Notes

1. Walter Fuller Taylor, *The Economic Novel in America* (Chapel Hill: Univ. of North Carolina Press, 1942); Michael Millgate, *American Social Fiction: James to Cozzens* (1964; rpt. New York: Barnes & Noble, 1967).

2. *American Social Fiction: James to Cozzens*, p. ix.

3. Sacvan Bercovitch, *The Puritan Origins of the American Self* (New Haven: Yale Univ. Press, 1975). Actually, it was post-Weberian scholars, not Weber himself, who promulgated the notion that Puritanism spawned capitalism. Weber is not so wrong-headed as Watts alleges since he repeatedly stresses in *The Protestant Ethic and the Spirit of Capitalism* that it was the capitalistic ethos (not capitalism or American capitalism per se) that was a by-product of religious influences and that capitalism actually took root as early as Babylonian, Roman, and Indian times. Watts pounces on Weber's only direct reference to America at the very conclusion of his book and upon that builds her case against the validity of his theory.

4. Leon Edel, *Henry James, The Conquest of London: 1870-1881* (New York and Philadelphia: J. B. Lippincott Company, 1962), p. 253.

Two Stylebooks: An Editor's View; or, The Outlook from the Trenches

Gerald Trett

Joseph Gibaldi and Walter S. Achtert. *MLA Handbook for Writers of Research Papers, Theses, and Dissertations.* New York: Modern Language Association, 1977. xii, 163 pp. Student Ed., 1977; Reference Ed., 1979.

The Chicago Manual of Style: For Authors, Editors, and Copywriters. 13th ed., rev. and exp. Chicago: University of Chicago Press, 1982. x, 739 pp.

In a 1979 review of, appropriately, four style manuals intended for scholarly authors and editors, the writer remarked that "on an editor's dark days, it may appear that we are rapidly approaching an age in which it will no longer matter how words are spelled, sentences are constructed, paragraphs are organized, or manuscripts are presented for publication."[1] Five years later this writer wonders whether the reviewer, an able, experienced, and respected editor, might not wish to update her statement by dropping her opening qualifications and beginning simply, "We are rapidly approaching . . ."

In 1984 one could add to "this depressing trend" almost any number of ominous actualities: a printing technology in continuous flux, new and treacherous methods of composition (ranging from word processors to magnetic tapes to floppy disks to OCR-scannable typescripts, to say nothing of laser technology), rising costs (and book prices) at precisely the time university underwriting of publishing evanesces, as faculty salaries attenuate and library funding plummets.[2] All indices agree. In scholarly publishing these are dark, cold days.

Of the many, often conflicting suggestions proposed for meeting these problems (and let us not call these suggestions solutions—there are none), there appears to be emergent agreement in one area: scholarly publishers are going to have to ask more of their authors, especially in manuscript preparation—considered broadly and in all its ramifications.[3] It is in this context that I shall be examining the two stylebooks that are subjects of this review. The point of view is that of a working university press editor. While I shall touch on the manuals under consideration as wholes, my focus is selective: a handful of crucial sections that address problems any university press editor struggles with virtually every working day in almost any manuscript.[4] My organization is parabolic: I begin and end with discussions of both books; the body of the paper treats them more or less separately.

The Background

Despite obvious large differences, these two manuals yield nice comparisons. Both began modestly enough, the *Handbook* in 1951 as a densely packed thirty pages in *PMLA*, the *Chicago Manual* in 1891 as a single sheet of typographic fundamentals for in-house use by copy-readers. Both over the years came to dominate their respective fields of publishing, the first edition of the *Style Sheet* (as the *Handbook* was then named) selling nearly two million copies, the *Chicago Manual*, in its twelve published editions, achieving "the status of a kind of lingua franca among publishers."[5] Both manuals, finally, in their present manifestations, are the result of radical revision, rewriting, and expansion of their immediate predecessors—with the authorities responsible for both responding to outside suggestions for revision (but in different ways and with different results, as we shall see). This revision of the *Manual* was almost entirely the work of Bruce Young and Catharine Seybold.

Both manuals have been reviewed professionally. The magisterial Elsie Myers Stainton uncharacteristically gave the *Handbook* the back of her hand: "The disappearance of the old succinct style sheet is a loss to writers and editors." Naomi B. Pascal's judgment was more balanced. She found the *Handbook* "unnecessarily ugly even for so utilitarian a book. This handy paperback, however, delivers exactly what it promises."[6] In her first judgment I concur: the *Handbook* is not only ugly, it is a singularly (and unnecessarily) bad piece of bookmaking.[7] And while I regret disagreeing with a respected colleague, I am constrained to say that analysis does not support her second judgment. Fulfilling its promises is exactly what it does *not* do. To come straight to the point: this editor sees the *MLA Handbook* as a serious miscalculation that its distinguished editorial committee, sporting such names as Thomas Clayton, John H. Fisher, John C. Gerber, William T. Lenehan, and Harrison T. Meserole, should have strangled in its cradle or, failing that, withdrawn after publication at first opportunity. The thirteenth *Chicago* delivers what it promises: "It reflects the impact of the new technology on the entire editing and publishing practice, and it spells out, in greater detail and with many more examples, the procedures with which it deals" (p. vii). And no matter how carefully and understandably its authors-editors may shy away from the appelation, the thirteenth will remain, at least in most of its editorial recommendations, the bible of scholarly book publishing. As we shall see, in its greater openness and flexibility, the newest *Manual* may well be thought of as the "New Testament," as a fulfillment and correction of the Old twelfth.

MLA

The *Style Sheet*

The evolution of the *MLA Style Sheet* into the *Handbook* is worth a careful look, for two reasons. Most, perhaps nearly all, younger scholars in language and literature have probably not seen, let alone worked with, the MLA version of the "Old Testament." More important, while some of the manifest inadequacies of the *Handbook* are clearly traceable to its authors, other problems may be the outcome of the evolutionary process itself.

As noted earlier, the original *Style Sheet* began in 1951 as thirty-two pages in *PMLA*.[8] It was largely the work of the late William Riley Parker, secretary of the association, 1947-56, and its unprecedented success was surely the result of his brilliantly conceived manner of proceeding. "This is not," Parker insisted, "another scheme to achieve uniformity." Rather, the project was a *"compilation."* Through study of stylistic practices of a number of manuals and scholarly journals, "majority usage" was determined and various draft style sheets sent to the editors of appropriate journals in the fields of languages and literatures. The editors were instructed to note what they found unacceptable so that "all variant practices could be accurately recorded and a 'variorum' style sheet result."9 The published result was an astonishing performance, a model of compression, concision, and logical organization. The scholarly author is systematically taken all the way to publication, from stipulations on proper typing of manuscript to beautifully clear instructions for reading and marking proof, with, of course, interim stops at preparation of text and documentation.

Now, the modest parade of superlatives above omitted the word *clarity*, for a reason: it was the one quality some scholars found the *Style Sheet* deficient in. It seems to me that the complaint is more a function of the user's background, experience, and patience than it is a question of the compiler's presentation. "These directions," he said, "have been compiled [to facilitate] the preparation of *learned* articles and books."10 Parker's writing is always that of a man addressing colleagues, one scholar talking to other scholars. Even when he is obviously speaking more as teacher than as compiler, his tone is such that one is impelled to belief, or at least acquiescence (as in the sentence that ends the footnote on the bloody question of the naturalization of foreign words: "No matter what the audience, the scholarly author does not italicize such words as 'cliché,' 'enjambment,' 'genre,' 'hubris,' 'leitmotif,' and 'mimesis'").11 Parker was one of those teachers who never say anything twice, and say it succinctly the first time. This principle informed not only his instructions in the *Style Sheet* but also the manner of presentation. "It deliberately leaves much unsaid," he warned (and with a vengeance, some have thought).12 Consider this sequence from the documentation section.

From the revised edition:

1 Archer Taylor, *Problems in German Literary History of the Fifteenth and Sixteenth Centuries* (New York, 1939), p. 213.

[The simplest form of reference; the publisher (the MLA) might have been reported also.]

   1 *Problems in German Literary History of the Fifteenth and Sixteenth Centuries* (New York, 1939), p. 213.

[See above; use this form if the author's full name has been given in the text.]

   1 New York, 1939, p. 213.

[See above; use this form if the work's title and the author's full name have been given in the text.]

Or this, a subtler example (from the 2d ed.):

1. An article in a journal with continuous pagination throughout the annual volume—the simplest form of reference.
   45 David E. Bynum, "Themes of the Young Hero in Serbocroation Oral Epic Tradition," *PMLA*, 83 (1968), 1296-1303.
   46 Bynum, p. 1298.

[If there are several short references like this, they may be inserted in the text. A short title may be added if more than one piece by the author is referred to in your study.]

Perfectly clear, but only to the reader who *sees* what Parker is doing here: in each instance teaching by demonstration something unrelated to, and not mentioned in, his bracketed comments, these "somethings" being rules to be observed but deemed unworthy of formulation or separate treatment. To make full use of the *Style Sheet*, the scholar had to make two assumptions: (1) every sample, or model, note was there for a reason, often unspecified or without comment; (2) every note with an explanation taught something in addition to and beyond Parker's explanations or comments.

   Of course, one reason for the *Style Sheet*'s wide acceptance was the nature of Parker's audience (and his canny estimate of its limitations). By today's numbers the world of scholarship in the fifties was relatively small and intimate, the number of publishing scholars and important doctorate-granting institutions few; and despite such ideological divisions as that between "critical" and "scholarly" that agitated members and split departments, Parker could assume a commonalty in cultural and educational background of the scholars he was addressing. But—given that setting—there is more to it than that.

I said earlier that the unprecedented success of Parker's compilation came from his "manner of proceeding, " meaning his drawing a consensus through the polling procedure he employed. But I was also looking ahead to the finished work: the *Style Sheet* is best seen as what Kenneth Burke has called a symbolic action, or better, "the dancing of an attitude." The *Style Sheet* was never just the sort of reference work where you could passively "look something up." Hence the complaints about the difficulty of finding some things in it; hence the experience of all who have used it, of seldom finding a given item quite where we remembered it being situated. Learning to use the *Style Sheet* was—and continued to some extent to be— the active process I have described above, of always looking *at* the item presented and *beyond* the discussion of it. Learning to use the *Style Sheet* was, then, an initiation into the arcana of the world of scholarship, and through gaining mastery over them, into full participation in that world. (That some initiates never fully penetrated *all* the mysteries is revealed by the continual violations in scholarly manuscripts of the unformulated rules generated in my two examples' above.)

The *Handbook*

The 1977 *Handbook*, based on the second edition of the *Style Sheet* (which was the work of a distinguished committee that "completed the revision begun by William R. Parker"), is virtually a new book, almost entirely rewritten, with its contents somewhat reorganized.[13] Nearly three times the length of its predecessor (five times that of the original), the *Handbook* attempts to "amplify and illustrate matters only touched upon in the earlier work." "Every effort," we are told, "has been made to clarify the ambiguities of the revised *Style Sheet*"—this because many instructors, "not surprisingly . . . have complained about its inadequacies as a classroom text or as a supplementary reference guide." Hence the new, changed function of the *Handbook*: it aims to "incorporate the recommendations of . . . the *Style Sheet*," for publishing scholars, and to "serve as a supplementary text in a writing course or as a reference book for undergraduate or graduate students to use independently." A *writing course?* Surely a slip of the pen. Not so, unfortunately, for we are told in the next paragraph that "the instructor who wishes to use the [book] as a text will find sections on selecting a topic, using the library . . . and so on" (Preface "For the Instructor . . ."). Such a statement is, on its face, a prescription for disaster. How, conceivably, can one contrive a work that will at one time meet the needs of the college freshman faced with his first "research" paper and the scholar preparing a learned paper for publication? How—but to raise further questions is to belabor the obvious. Let us see, first, how the *Handbook* approaches the freshman and his task.

The first nine sections of the *Handbook* treat the whole research process, from defining the "research paper," as it is improperly called, it seems to me, to "writing drafts" and concluding with "guides to writing." These nine sections consume precisely eight pages. Here is section 1, "The Research Paper," in its entirety:

Like other forms of writing, the research paper should be characterized by lucid, coherent exposition. No set of conventions for preparing a manuscript can replace lively and intelligent writing. Unlike some other forms of writing, however, the research paper requires writers to seek out and investigate sources of information other than their own personal knowledge and experience. Research into a topic will yield new information, sharpen perception of a problem, and lend authority to some hypotheses. The research paper, the final product of research, is not a collection of other persons' opinions but a carefully constructed presentation of an idea—or series of ideas—that relies on other sources for clarification and verification. Learned facts and borrowed opinions must be fully documented in the research paper, usually through endnotes or footnotes, but always in such a manner that they support rather than overshadow the paper itself.

It would be difficult to fault any one of the ideas set forth here— the definitional sentence, for instance ("The research paper . . . is . . . a carefully constructed presentation of an idea") is admirable. That surely is one way of saying what every instructor wants. But it would be difficult to conceive of the student who could understand, let alone learn from, this presentation. The crucial relationship between the process of research and the resultant paper is not addressed, here or in subsequent sections; what seems to emerge is the notion—and it is faulty for this assignment—that research is the verification of a preconceived idea through documentation.

Consider for a moment a different, more patient, introduction to the process of research. Here are the opening words of the first section ("Purposes of a Reference Paper") of the classic treatment by the late Porter G. Perrin:

A reference paper is a record of study in some special field, scientific, social, historical, literary. Genuine or "original" research is the discovery and discussion of material that has not been generally known; undergraduate research is usually based on published information that has been gathered by someone else. Most undergraduate papers are primarily a record of intelligent reading in several sources on a particular subject.

Since a good deal of college work consists of acquiring and discussing the information and ideas of others, a standard method of discovering material, making notes of it, and presenting it has been developed. Preparing a reference paper gives practice in using this method. The paper in composition courses often emphasizes method and form and so prepares a student for later papers in other courses. Advanced work in literature, history, and the social sciences especially depends on this sort of study, and in sciences a laboratory experiment is often supplemented by research in what has been previously done. The same methods, more elaborately developed, are the basis of graduate work in the various professional schools, the means by which theses and dissertations and monographs are manufactured. . . . A freshman "reference paper" is a start on the road of scholarship that extends through the advanced courses in college to the work of professional people who are steadily adding to the knowledge and understanding of the past and the present.[14]

To employ a useful old cliché: this is writing with a purpose. Unlike the *Handbook*'s presentation, which in its high-level generalities reads like an outline or, at best, an introduction to a presentation, never completed, Perrin's astutely paced opening places the reference paper in a context of research, both academic and professional, and honestly distinguishes it from the real thing by calling it what it is, a practice, a dry-run emphasizing "method and form." *Then* he eases the student into the paper and the process by showing "how large a part the individual [writer] really plays [in producing such a paper]" (I cite in part the conclusion of this section):

Furthermore, a reference paper is not necessarily a series of facts alone. Facts must be *interpreted*, for only the most common knowledge can stand without some comment on its meaning. Questions of causes, of results, of importance are not settled by recording information; a mind must work on the data to find the proper relationship between them and to see their meaning in perspective. No one can gather and present intelligently research materials without leaving his mark on them.

The main purpose of a research paper, from the point of view of a composition course at least, is to give training in college writing, in gathering, reflecting on, organizing, and putting in readable form material gained from study.[15]

Only those who as beginning instructors have struggled with "teaching" the reference paper to unhappy and mostly uncomprehending freshmen can appreciate the quiet brilliance of Perrin's way of introduction, the almost uncanny skill with which he quiets the fractious donkey, awakens the drowsy sloth, soothes the sulky wahoo, and sends them to their task. By beginning with the pupose of the paper, Perrin succeeds as well as one can in removing the hex from a mandated exercise that, artificial as it is, must still be done.

A harmful brevity informs too many of these sections.[16] That on using the library, for instance (sect. 3), gives a total of only nineteen reference works. Perrin provides a list of twenty magazine indexes alone. Conversely (and curiously), section 9 (guides to writing) lists thirty-one composition handbooks and usage guides, most of them standard freshman texts and references. Surely the instructor has already chosen one. For whom is the list intended?

But language is the major problem in these sections. Over-generality vitiates whatever useful information is given (the discussion of plagiarism, sect. 6, excepted). Two examples suffice. On writing drafts (sect. 8) the *Handbook* blandly advises: "Most [writers] begin with a quickly executed first draft that follows their outline and presents their ideas in rough form. In subsequent drafts, they may add or delete material, improve the wording, make the style consistent, and correct mechanical errors." Of course.

Section 2 (selecting a topic) ends: "Before beginning any writing project, make sure you understand the amount and depth of research required, the degree of subjectivity permitted, and the type of paper expected—a report on the *process* (what

you did) or the *product* (what you discovered) of your research."
The last phrase is probably meant to be a tip of the hat to
William Riley Parker since it is a rephrasing of part of his advice
on the question of audience to graduate students preparing
theses and dissertations.[17] One wonders what it means to *this*
audience, especially since, as we have seen, the *Handbook* has
earlier defined the reference paper as *product*. As for an
instrument that would measure "the degree of subjectivity
permitted"—ah, cousins, could I but be instructed in what that
instrument is—could I be told where to look for it—I know not
the fathom line that ever touched a descent so deep as I would be
willing to bury more wealth in than Croesus had, or the great
Jew R _____ is supposed to have, to purchase it.

The *Handbook* concludes with an appendix of four and a half
pages on the specific requirements of the preparation of theses
and dissertations. Unlike the sections on the reference paper, the
appendix is not new but is rather an expanded rewriting of a
supplement of less than two pages that Parker added to the first
revision of the *Style Sheet*. Here, perhaps, the greater length is
justified. The sections on the physical layout of the dissertation
(divisions of text, pagination, etc.) and the discussion of
permissions are useful because they are specific and normative.[18]
Section E, however, on special requirements for theses and
dissertations, expands Parker's twelve lines on the typing and
spacing of footnotes and quotations into nearly a page by
mentioning other matters that every graduate school in the
country mandates differently. And in the section on selection of
a thesis topic gratuitous expansion becomes gaseous bloating.
The graduate student is told, in part: "Representing a new
departure in either subject or method, the thesis or dissertation
ought to make a substantial contribution to your field.
Preliminary discussions with instructors, especially the thesis
adviser, are invaluable in selecting a topic" (p. 135). This is
mindless noodling (propriety forbids the proper application of
the previous figure). Was there ever a graduate student anywhere
who needed such advice? So much, then, for the new expanded
treatment of research for both freshmen and graduate students.
One would have expected better from the *Handbook*'s authors,

who are assistant director and director of Research Programs, Modern Language Association.

In addition to the section on plagiarism, mentioned above, there are other welcome additions. The presentation on tables (sect. 23) is short and simple. This is all to the good because the construction of good tables, especially statistical ones, is more a knack than it is the result of intellectual effort (as all editors know). A full explanation of the mechanics of constructing statistical tables is best left to comprehensive treatments, like the one in the *Manual* (especially pars. 12.3-11), which starts almost literally from scratch. (The new treatment accorded tables in the 13th ed. of the *Manual* is a welcome addition there; the chapter on tables in the 12th ed. was one of its weakest.) The illustrations in the *Handbook* of the proper format of a reference paper, the spacing and indention of notes and bibliography (pp. 161-63), and the like (e.g., sects. 24 and 30) are clear, economically handled, and well worth the space. (But why the needless refinement of typing superscript numbers in *endnotes* when the numbers are clearer typed on the line, with periods?) Better worth the space given to symbols and abbreviations used in proofreading (sect. 50) would be a slightly updated reprinting of that section in the second edition of the *Style Sheet*, one of William Riley Parker's happiest contrivances. I can pull from my bookshelf at least twenty different sets of instructions on marking proof, all beautifully and expansively laid out and professionally written, and not one comes close to the terse clarity of Parker's one-paragraph explanation-demonstration. In fact, I cheerfully confesss to having lifted copies, by Xerography, for use by authors anxious about marking their proofs (or for authors about whom *I* was anxious because they weren't—all this before the new copyright law took effect in 1978, of course). Parker's demonstration was for me, and remains, directions-of-choice. The decision to supplant it with a listing of symbols available in any desk dictionary can be accounted for only as revision for its own sake.

The index is new, and new, alas, in ways beyond those required by the expanding of older material. The indexes of the various editions of the *Style Sheet,* which form the core of the new index, reflected an American consensus encoded in the *Manual* treatment and such handbooks on indexing as Sina Spiker's in all but capitalization of the first word of the entry. That aberration, though stubbornly maintained for nearly three decades, was a mere irritant that in no way affected the usability of the material. The indexers of the *Handbook* seem to have been hell-bent on innovation for its own sake, for they have not only retained the lower-casing of the *Style Sheet* indexes but have jettisoned the comma separating the title of the entry from its folios. The result is entries like this: "© 48"—and no reader should be forced to decipher this: "z.B. 48 *under* e.g." This last would read, in the *Style Sheet,* "z.B., 48 s.v. 'e.g.'" To be sure, the latter requires two more characters, but if the purpose was to save space, why does the index employ indented form? The general absence of punctuation (commas are employed for inverted phrases) leads to the desperate strait of perverting any known use of capitalization in cross-references: "laws *See* legal references." Or to easy misreading: a subentry of *dissertations* reads, "abstract of App. E." Or to outright confusion because commas *do* separate folios, as in another subentry of *dissertations*: "footnotes of 30, App. E" (*two* references: sec. 30 and an unspecified section of the appendix, this latter the result of assigning the topics of the appendix their own letters in place of numbers—a mistake Parker was too clever to fall into). Only this time the master sorcerer was not here to rescue his apprentices and we have another episode of *Fantasia.* The sad thing about this index is that hidden in the mass of ineptitudes and eccentricities is a scrupulous accuracy. Spot-checking turned up not one faulty reference.

There remains for consideration only the core of the old *Style Sheet*: documentation (sample notes) and various instructions. A selection of the latter will be discussed in the next section as editorial problems, promised earlier. Here we shall be concerned with the sample, or model, notes and the accompanying commentary. The "MLA forms," as they are popularly referred to, have proved durable over three decades and do not require much analysis. Since the *Handbook* introduces some modifications, a few comments are in order.[19]

The sample notes. The 30 models of the original *Style Sheet* grew to 88 in the second edition to over 125 (with separate matching bibliographical forms) in the *Handbook*. The 125 notes break into forms for published books, periodicals, and other sources, such as manuscripts and lectures (sects. 32, 34, and 35, with 66, 18, and 43 notes, respectively). Most of the 88 samples of the last *Style Sheet* are retained in its successor, with some updating (and correction) and the addition of a number of new models.

The majority of the new notes for books provide models for citing public (government) documents and legal works. Although one might wonder whether the literary scholar needs these forms, the "content" of several notes (e.g., n. 53, the congressional investigation of the Dec. 7 attack on Pearl Harbor) goes some way to meeting the objection, and these forms are welcome and probably useful. Yet one wants and needs more. There is a curious avoidance, in all sections on documentation, of the difficult and irregular. Surely there was room for at least one example of the proper handling of one of those thirty-five-word Renaissance or seventeenth-century titles (with instructions on capitalization and punctuation). Chicago has several (see par. 16.37). And why, if only as a tocsin sounded for the overzealous graduate student, is there no example of the proper handling of a title from one of the great Victorian compilations, which may go so far as to have volumes within parts within series, such as the following:

¹"Hakon Saga," Hakonar Saga, *and a Fragment of* Magnus Saga, *with Appendices,* ed. Gudbrand Vigfusson, Vol. II of *Icelandic Sagas and Other Historical Documents Relating to the Settlements of the Northmen on the British Isles,* Rerum Britannicarum Medii Aevi Scriptores, or Chronicles and Memorials of Great Britain and Ireland during the Middle Ages (Rolls Series), Vol. LXXXVIII (London: H.M.S.O., 1887; Kraus rpt., 1964), p. 32.

This perhaps gives a bit more than is required! Yet absent a cross-reference to "Rolls Series" in some large card catalogs and the fact of the listing of the above under "Orkneyinga" in the Library of Congress system, the anxieties reflected in that near parody of documentation are understandable. Examples from literature before 1700 are far too rare in the *Handbook*.

Moreover, a few notes recognizing the irregularities and just plain quirkiness (let us politely call them errors) in the layout of several standard large editions would go a long way toward assuaging authorial uncertainty (and editorial crankiness). Two examples that are invariably troublesome: (1) the economical but clear citing of Pope's *Essay on Criticism* in the *Pastorals* volume of the Twickenham Edition (placement of title of edition? typeface? cite all three editors?; (2) consistent handling of volume and page numbers in the Yale Edition of Johnson (where the two Shakespeare volumes, 7 and 8, are paginated continuously, whereas the *Rambler*, vols. 3-5, unaccountably receives separate pagination). Small matters, but the recurrence of problems with such bread-and-butter items suggests that there are areas the major stylebook in literature and language should be handling and is not.

Section 34, periodicals, is essentially a reprinting of materials from the last *Style Sheet*. Here especially the absence of any real expansion is to be regretted. The preface promises "information that ranges from the elementary to the esoteric," and one may ask, particularly of this section, Where is the esoteric? The American scholar's fascination, in the last twenty years, with Continental critical activity was readily apparent in 1977, yet the scholar is given little assistance with the sometimes very odd organizational systems of many European periodicals. For instance, knowing that *heft* numbers of the German periodical *Text und Kritik* have no discernible relation to dates of publication would forestall some editorial queries and authorial head scratching. The bizarre system of numbering, whereby Heft 2-3 (1970) precedes Heft 1-1a (1971) or Heft 46 (June 1980) follows Heft 64 (October 1980) and is followed by Heft 67 (July 1980), can only raise the hackles—and anxieties— of the American-trained scholar. On this severely Germanic logic, Mark Twain's favorite pronouncement is appropriate: "It's French." Or, turning to the Mysterious East, one would like to know whether the *Tamking Review* really utilizes volume, issue, and part numbers. And it would be a real courtesy to have a sample note or two illustrating typeface, placement, and capitalization of the English translation of a title citing a Polish, Russian, or Czech journal (Chicago provides several; see pars. 16.122-23).

Section 35, the last on documentation, treats "other sources." The first of these, manuscripts and typescripts, is so skimpily handled—only four sample notes—that only the initiated will know what is missing. No form of documentation is more demanding, especially on the question of what information to repeat in subsequent references, on which the *Handbook* has not a syllable. The interested scholar should consult the superb material on manuscripts in the *Style Sheet for Authors,* rev. ed. (Williamsburg, Va.: Institute of Early American History and Culture, 1973), pp. 26-28.

Another group of miscellaneous sources consists of the usual—lectures, letters, films, musical compositions, and works of art—and is unexceptionable. A third group, however, all new to the *Handbook,* is eyebrow-raising: we are given model notes for theatrical performances, radio and television programs, recordings (including jacket notes, librettos, and other material), and personal and telephone interviews.[20] For whom can these notes be intended? Surely not the serious student of language and literature! I fear I detect the dead hand of American Studies plying its trade in pop culture. Yet even for the freshman, for whom the opening research sections of the *Handbook* are intended, the provision of these models is questionable. Record jackets? The great Haydn scholar H. C. Robbins Landon has indeed provided copy for occasional record jackets, as has Ralph Kirkpatrick for his Bach recordings. To allow the young student to stop there when both authorities have also produced scholarly monographs on their subjects is to miss the opportunity to teach a first lesson in research: evaluate your sources. "The point," Perrin said, "is to find the best books." [21] This enshrinement of the ephemeral in model notes is another example of what Richard D. Altick called, five years ago in the pages of this journal, "the fun-and-games approach to learning" "of the juvenile *Zeitgeist* of the present moment." However unwittingly the authors of the *Handbook* have contributed to the idea that "Research Can Be Fun," the damage is accomplished.[22] The very presence of such models in an official MLA publication sanctifies and invites the use of the kinds of materials they codify.

Commentary on the samples. What I am calling the "commentary" on the sample notes (for lack of a better collective term) was, in the *Style Sheet*, the brief, pithy editorial asides, comments, or outright dicta pronounced on individual notes, always enclosed in brackets and printed below the sample. In the *Handbook* these have become the text of the documentation sections; in addition to retaining much of Parker's commentary, the new text is considerably expanded, in keeping with the expressed objectives of the *Handbook*. Much of the new material is just what it should be, clear and helpful, spelling out much that, as we have seen, was assumed by the *Style Sheet*. For instance, the careful discussion of the intricacies of citing a book with no publication data and no pagination (sect. 32t) is first-rate. And the warning that pieces in collections of essays and articles often change or drop their titles (sect. 32h) is a neat touch, an indirect warning to be alert to bibliographical detail where it *is* important. Especially welcome are the various reminders sprinkled throughout that "p." must be used in citing many periodicals and with some book titles, even when "vol." is given. The expanded information on citing reference works (sect. 32i) is valuable—even with the loss of *s.v.*

Finally, one important change in instructions deserves separate comment: citing titles of periodicals. On this MLA has over the years done an almost complete about-face (and one wishes that more senior scholars were aware of this). Whereas the first *Style Sheet* recommended (with carefully drawn qualifications) using the abbreviations utilized in the MLA "Annual Bibliography" (rev. ed., sect. 27), the second edition (sect. 29) drew back somewhat ("abbreviate only those titles likely to be familiar"). The *Handbook* changes the emphasis: "Unless your intended audience is familiar with these acronyms [those used in the MLA International Bibliography, and they now number in the hundreds], do not use them. Instead, abbreviate common words in order to save space" (p. 123). This formulation is close to the Chicago presentation, unchanged in the thirteenth edition (pars. 16.101, 16.102), and it is a needed and thoughtful tightening of position.

Yet there are also more puzzling moments than there should be in a work of this kind. The proper placement of the abbreviation "ed." is fuzzed because the question is never addressed directly. Thus the difference in meaning between placing the abbreviation before the name, as opposed to after, is lost and one now encounters, in manuscript, constructions like this—(Title), eds. Bowers and Levenson—because the implicit *by* is neither explained nor exemplified (as it is in the *Manual*, par. 17.36).

The new sections on citing public documents and legal materials have more serious problems: explanation simply fails. The citing of all government documents is jammed into twenty or so lines, without a hint of the one vital piece of information on which these difficult citations depend: the forms follow in sequence the information given on the catalog card (Library of Congress system). The similar attempt to discuss some aspects of legal references in only twenty lines beggars description or explanation. Yet one may need some threads through the legal labyrinth, and the concerned scholar should consult the carefully selective, well-focused section in the *Manual* (par. 17.76).

There is one instance where the sample note contradicts the instructions in the text. The latter specify capitalizing, and abbreviating in documentation, such words as *preface* or *introduction* (p. 67). Note 39 has "Henry Nash Smith, Introd.," but note 40, an alternate form of the preceding, reads, ". . . introd. Henry Nash Smith." The corresponding bibliographic form for note 39 reads, curiously, "Smith, Henry Nash, introd." (sect. 421). Minutiae, to be sure, but the otherwise flawless proofreading makes one wonder whether the *rule* was stated correctly to begin with.[23]

Finally, there are, again, language problems that should not occur, especially in these sections, "commentary" and instructions. Occasionally Parker's clear instructions are muddied by loose and careless phrasing—revision, apparently for the sake of revision. Two instances: The new *Handbook* instructions for citing a book with two or more authors read: "Cite all authors as they appear on the title page—not *necessarily* in alphabetical order" (p. 59; my italics). I challenge anyone to defend the need of the last clause, and to explain the function of the italicized adverb (cf. Parker's phrasing in the *Style Sheet*, 2d ed., sect. 23a). On the other hand, the end of a new and well-considered explanation of the handling of titles within titles (sect.13c) explodes in this piece of razzle-dazzle: "When a normally underlined title appears within another underlined title, the *shorter* title appears neither underlined nor in quotation marks" (my italics), with this example (without quotation marks, for clarity, though I am quoting): *The Art of David Copperfield* (book). This is a piece of Parker-like instruction the *Handbook* was supposed to be correcting. Unless the reader grasps at once the full import of the key preposition *within*, the word *shorter*, especially given the inept example, can only seem wrong, or at best puzzling (cf. Parker's wording of this, ibid., sect. 23c).

At times the authors worry too much about the uninformed sensibilities of their junior readers and fall into wordiness: "Use three such periods (. . .), *leaving a space before and after each period*";"capitalize *the first letter* of the first word" (pp. 24, 29; my italics). Or, on citing titles of works: "Always take the title from the title page, not from the cover or the title printed at the top of each page" (p. 54). That last "title," gentlemen, is called a running head and there is no reason not to use the term; it is self-defining in the context provided. On the other hand, the term *half title* is not self-explaining, yet it arrives and leaves, without warning, on page 55, probably its first instance in the text.[24] The authors' almost grim insistence throughout on the redundant *square brackets* grates. An American editor wonders when, if ever, American bibliographers will feel their debt to the British repaid and eschew those special spellings, word forms, and terms they seem to relish so much.

Finally, the authors of the *Handbook* lack Parker's happy

knack of tucking unobtrusively into their instructions small but important bits of information. For instance they might have dropped into their discussion of publishers' names (sect.31h) the fact that the proper shortening of "Charles Scribner's Sons" is "Scribners," since they are aware of it and do so in their booklist in section 9. Parker's clear notice (*Style Sheet*, rev. ed. sect. 27) that *PMLA* and *ELH* are titles, not abbreviations, has been so fuzzed with a wordy rephrasing in the *Handbook* (sec. 46) that only the keenest-eyed will know the information has been imparted.

Some Procedures

I turn now to a consideration of those procedures, promised earlier, that editors see as problems, and are problems, because the implied questions the procedures attempt to answer admit of a variety of solutions. The focus is on the instructions provided in both stylebooks, and my choice is highly selective.

Names of authors. Names of persons are, and obviously will remain, problematic because many considerations are involved. Still, we should all of us, authors and editors, be handling them better than we are. The *Handbook* presentation (sect. 31a) is simply a rewriting of the old *Style Sheet* and shows its age. Too much is left open to be of much help: "Common sense will have to guide the author . . . ; 'Thomas Stearns Eliot' . . . instead of . . . 'T. S. Eliot' . . . might confuse the reader." Nowadays it won't, but its pedantry certainly may offend, as the use of brackets *does* offend when names are supplied, as in C[live] S[taples] Lewis. Parker's (unfortunately qualified) recommendation to give names in their "most usual form" is pretty much what Chicago's careful treatment boils down to and seems eminently sensible and clear.[25] Could we but follow that rule of thumb we might in future never again encounter in the same set of notes "W. J. Bate," "W. Jackson Bate," and "Walter Jackson Bate"—only the last, even though Bate as coeditor of *The Rambler* in the Yale Johnson is listed as "W. J. Bate." *Webster's Biographical Dictionary* is the standard American authority, and it should have been listed in the *Handbook*.

Titles of works. The *Handbook* instructions on citing titles of books are, again, a slightly enlarged and better exemplified version of those in the *Style Sheet.* These instructions were never adequate (Parker assumed an audience well versed in the arts of bookmaking) because they failed to mention the governing rationale: titles must be punctuated. The Chicago presentation shows just how much is involved:

Punctuation. Add punctuation if necessary. (Title pages are usually designed to require a minimum of puncutation; elements of a title may be set on separate lines or in different type sizes. When such titles are cited and run in one line, they must be punctuated for clarity.) Insert a colon (not a semicolon or a dash) between the main title and the subtitle (be sure it *is* a subtitle and not a part of the main title requiring only a comma before it). If there is a dash in the original title, retain it. Add commas in series, including one before the *and* preceding the final word in a series. Set off, with commas, dates not grammatically related to the rest of the title. [par. 7:126]

Identifying subtitles can be difficult; and, given the MLA rule on citing full titles only in bibliography, important. The stylebooks under review here are cases in point (see the opening listing). The titles are remarkably similar in grammatical structure and typography (two typefaces each), yet the *Handbook* is cited without a subtitle (perhaps erroneously). In the absence of clarifying punctuation (and citing of the whole title in the *Handbook*'s acknowledgments)—in short, lacking any real evidence, I made the conservative choice.

I have a modest proposal that may help others to resolve this dilemma. The Library of Congress Cataloging in Publication Data (now included in virtually all scholarly books—it was not available in 1977) lists, by convention, only the main title of a work (in the CIP data, usually printed on the copyright page), never the subtitle. Thus, when in doubt one can at least test one's hypotheses by comparing them with the title listing in the CIP data. (*Verification* is not possible, because occasional errors do slip through.) That is what I did with the Chicago title. The CIP data give only "The Chicago Manual of Style"; hence the different way of listing the *Manual* at the beginning of this review.

The CIP data are useful in another way, not having to do with title, that may well be mentioned here. In 1980 the University

Press of Virginia decided to produce an unedited reprint of Poe's complete *Marginalia*. The late John Carl Miller was commissioned to write an introduction. He did, and that was his only connection with the project. He was duly credited on the title page of the finished book and in its acknowledgments. To no avail: reviewers have unanimously listed the book, and discussed it, as *edited* by Professor Miller—with one exception, a much-published Poe scholar who knows how to read frontmatter. Had these otherwise competent and well-meaning scholars simply examined the CIP data in *Marginalia*, they could not have gone wrong. For while names of editors expressed on title pages are picked up in the CIP, writers of forewords, consultants, and other assistants are not. As it is, a myth has been created that may not easily be dispelled. Perhaps the malevolent spirit of Griswold yet lingers. Whatever, I am duty-bound to report that my proposals have met with less than universal acclaim from fellow editors.

The MLA rule on typeface for citing, in documentation, italicized titles within italicized titles needs a reconsideration it did not get in the *Handbook*. Where the inner title comes in the middle of (*Thomson's* The Seasons *and the Language of Criticism*), or closes, the outer title (*The Unfolding of* The Seasons), there is little chance of confusion. But where the opening of inner and outer titles coincides or where the inner title dominates the outer, the absence of expected italics may confuse—it certainly puzzles momentarily with *this* title: the title page reads: "Beowulf │ *and* │ The Fight at Finnsburh │ *A Bibliography*". The rule produces this odd-looking (shortened) note: [1] Fry, Beowulf *and* The Fight at Finnsburh, p. 3.

The *Manual* now recognizes this MLA procedure as an acceptable alternate to its preferred method (quotation marks for all inner titles) but goes on to warn that "some titles within titles are clear enough without being set off" (par. 16.35). Fry's bibliography is one of these titles, and there are more of them than one would expect. The *Handbook* should have considered these anomalies and perhaps modified the rule, as Chicago does. Yet another case of tilting toward the undergraduate, going for the simple, regular, and uncomplicated.

Quotations. No stylebook I know of has equaled or surpassed in clarity and fullness of presentation that of the *Manual* on the handling of quotations (12th ed., revised and slightly expanded in the 13th). Conversely, nobody has assumed greater sophistication, and said less, on a difficult topic than William Riley Parker in the various editions of the *Style Sheet.* The new presentation in the *Handbook* goes a long way (though not all the way) toward remedying what was lacking (sect. 14, pp. 20-29). The differences between quoting prose and poetry are carefully explained; spacing and paragraphing of extracts are exemplified, discussed, and well illustrated, as are inter-polations, and placement of end punctuation is specified. The handling of ellipsis receives unusually careful attention, with six different examples provided.

Along with many other editors, I had hoped that the new presentation of quotations in the *Handbook* would include a rethinking of the MLA rules on ellipsis and a dropping of the use of four periods to *close* a quotation. That has not occurred. In holding to the rule, the *Handbook* now leaves MLA as the only major scholarly body I know of still adhering to a procedure that has proved needless. Even the legal profession, the prissiest of the prim on quotations, has dropped final ellipsis.[26] The *Manual* states the majority position well: "After all, unless it is the opening or closing sentence in a work that is being quoted, something precedes and follows the passage, and it is not necessary to emphasize the fact" (p. 295).

Almost as an afterthought the *Handbook* concludes its discussion of ellipsis with the remark that "some scholars prefer to indicate whether what is omitted is the last part of one sentence or the first part of the next sentence by [spacing all four periods] if the last word of the first sentence is not quoted" (p. 26). I have not the slightest doubt that I speak for all editors, everywhere, when I say that the answer to those scholars is NO! IN THUNDER! This is an un-thought-out adaptation of legal style lacking, as presented, either a rationale for the procedure or a full explanation of it. This sort of typographical suicide may begin as a dalliance with eagles, but it often ends as a feasting with panthers—great big ones in the forms of cost overruns and authors' alteration clauses enforced by courts of law.

Lacking in both stylebooks is any suggestion of how to handle one particularly sticky problem with ellipsis. Consider these two sentences as text to be quoted: Jones distinguishes the "conventional" from the "real," and denies any connection. But that is a distinction without a difference. If in quoting one wanted to shorten the two sentences at *real*, how is ellipsis to be handled? (1) "Jones distinguishes the 'conventional' from the 'real.' . . . that is a distinction" etc. Or is it (2) ". . . 'real'. . . . "? An authoritative statement would prevent many angry words and overingenious arguments.

To close this section, I return to the caveat planted earlier. Improved as the new *Handbook* presentation on quotations is, without a full discussion of related problems in capitalizing the quoted material, the presentation remains a torso with arms and legs but no hands or feet: the reader gets neither a rationale to stand on nor rules and examples to grasp with.[27] The Chicago presentation (pars. 10.12-18 and 10.49) is exemplary and should be consulted.

The Manual

The 739 pages of the thirteenth edition of the *Chicago Manual* (up nearly 200 pages from the 12th ed.) dictate a different look at its recommendations.[28] I suspect that most authors are a bit daunted by the book, not just by its length, but by the comprehensiveness of the presentation, specifically, the amount and kinds of materials having little or nothing to do with the scholarly author's concerns. My focus, accordingly, will be on those parts of the *Manual* that are (or, with some nudging, should be) of interest to scholars in the "humanities"—readers of this journal.

Three sections, all expanded and updated, commend themselves to all scholars, however well published. Earlier I recommended William Achtert's piece in *PMLA* on the new uniform copyright law. Here I qualify that by suggesting that it is best considered a starting point for grasping the essentials, to be followed up by the more comprehensive treatment of permissions in the *Manual* (chap. 4), especially for the writer whose work utilizes an unusually wide range of sources or is faced with the dull duty of editor, whether of journal, anthology, symposium, or festschrift. In addition to such things as duration of copyright and the problems with, and opportunities of, the doctrine of fair use, well covered by Achtert, there are useful paragraphs, mostly warnings, on the complications of ownership in manuscripts and personal letters, and the *real* complications involved in reproducing photographs and works of art. With the recent discovery by archivists and heirs that there is gold back there in the stacks, one would welcome a more detailed discussion of these matters, along with the traps to be avoided in dealing with European picture sources. The sample letter for requesting permission to quote or reprint is a model of its kind, easily adapted to any circumstance.

The sections on physical preparation of manuscript (pars. 2.1-50) have been slightly rewritten and expanded to reflect authors' increased responsibilities vis-à-vis current technology, such as tape or floppy disk or typescript to be scanned by an optical character recognition scanner (OCR). These materials are wisely restricted to discussion of the "manuscript" requirements involved; technicalities of the process are mostly avoided. An instructive question arises about this chapter: Is it bad luck or just an irony of the times that in the months, or perhaps years, required to go from manuscript to finished books, OCR scanning was found to be too inaccurate to be used for books? The remainder of this material on manuscript preparation is a reprinting of the presentation in the previous edition, often a bit condensed but still one of the best statements ever written. The list of procedural violations that render a manuscript unusable by editor or compositor (par. 2.36) is impressively thorough, yet it has grown by one item since the twelfth edition and will grow more for a future fourteenth edition, such is the nature of American ingenuity. Still, an editor can only wonder why some manuscripts are submitted with even some single spacing. Perhaps the cause is dissertation hangover, never recovered from. Whatever the reason, I have another modest proposal, this one a long-range one.

In graduate school a friend happened to take a course in

Shakespeare from the great G. B. Harrison, a visiting professor in summer school. Harrison began every class, my friend insisted—that is, every *class period*—with an invariant ritual. "Class," Harrison would intone, "what three things do we need to read Shakespeare?" To this the class would respond in hushed reverence, "The text. The text. The *text.*" Maybe Harrison had something. What wonders could we not achieve if we adopted his ritual for use by every English and foreign language department the country over in, specifically, the course called variously Introduction to Graduate Study, Bibliography, or Research Methods. The catechizer's introit would be: "Class, what three things must we do to get our scholarship published?" The catechumens would respond, "Double-space text and quotations. Double-space notes and bibliography. Double-space *everything!*" I dream, but given the failure of sweet reason and patient explanation, ritualizing the message is all that is left.

The third section of the *Manual* that will interest authors is Chapter 3, "Proofs." While following the organization of this chapter in the twelfth edition, the editor responsible has rewritten the standard material with an experienced and very shrewd eye on the problems resulting from computerized typesetting. Early on, for instance (par. 3.16), the would-be proofreader is warned that "where many errors occur in a line or two, it is best to cross out the whole passage containing the errors and write it all correctly in the margin because the typesetter will need less time to read the rewritten passage than to figure out where each of many small corrections should be made"—something no careful scholar who did his proofreading apprenticeship on linotype-produced material would think of doing. This kind of alert, clear instruction, with attention at every step in the process to changes required by the new printing technology, informs all aspects of the chapter. Superb as the presentation is, I wish that a theme that is implicit throughout had been stated explicitly, or at least received greater emphasis. The author who approaches contemporary typesetting with the notion—perhaps only suppressed or held as an unconscious assumption—that "the manuscript is good enough—I'll catch remaining errors in proof"—is likely to be the baffled and infuriated author whose finished book contains new errors, even bits of garbage (in the technical sense). Every time the computer runs to correct an error, lines, paragraphs, chapters, even the whole text, may be reset, with new decisions on line breaks and hyphenation. Even when a publisher's production manager instructs his or her printer's representative to make only line corrections at a late stage of proof, there is no way to guarantee that that is what will happen. "Theoretically impossible" things happen, and no one can be blamed. It is the nature of the technology. The remedy is a forearmed author: like a chain-smoking, alcoholic pregnant woman who gives up nicotine and alcohol for the duration, the prudent author puts away any idea of catching errors in proof and grimly concentrates on producing an error-free manuscript and then spotting all errors in first proof, as if the production of an unblemished "baby" depended on it, as indeed it does. It is in the context of the forearmed author that I suggest every publishing scholar read Chapter 20 of the *Manual*. "It is intended only to supply a reader who knows little or nothing about the technology of bookmaking with enough information to picture what goes on, and to avoid making the worst mistakes" (pp. 586-87).

A few words, finally, on the new treatment of documentation in the *Manual*. The aim, the editor responsible has told us, is a "unified exposition of all the possible ways to document one's material," along with hosts of examples.[29] The result is Chapters 15-17, "Documentation," "Bibliographic Forms," and "Note Forms," respectively, with the *new arrangement* more nearly matching the order in which the tasks are performed and the added *model forms* providing the "wealth of examples" (pref., p. vii). Of the latter there is no need to comment except to say that they are as promised. The expanded treatment of public documents (pars. 16.141-75) would be enough to justify the claim. The new arrangement was probably unnecessary, but it will trouble only those utterly addicted to the layout of the old twelfth.

For what really unifies the presentation is new Chapter 15, "Documentation." It pulls together, and arranges in a coherent sequence, much information *about* documentation that was somewhat scattered in previous editions (such as endnotes versus footnotes, relation of both to bibliography, etc.). What is noteworthy and important about the new presentation is a new open, or even permissive, attitude not found in earlier editions. This new attitude has been commented on by all reviewers. Here I wish to reflect on some of the implications of this relaxation that are not dealt with in the text itself, specifically, in an otherwise brilliantly clear and open-handed presentation of alternative methods of documentation.

Briefly, the important alternatives boil down to two: (A) notes keyed in text with reference numbers and printed either as footnotes or endnotes, with or without a supporting bibliography; and (B) an author-date system utilizing in-text references keyed to a reference list printed at the back of the book. The *A* forms are of course those long used by the humanities, the *B* forms those used in the natural (and, to a lesser degree, social) sciences. The discussion of these methods carefully lays out the trade-offs involved, and the presentation of the recommended forms of citation in the succeeding chapters scrupulously allots equal time and space to *A* and *B* forms of the same material. But, while carefully granting the need to match method of documentation to manuscript, the text makes clear the direction of the prevailing winds. The *B* forms are generally to be preferred because they are "most economical in space, in time . . . and in cost" (p. 400). "The footnote method of documentation must be considered a difficult luxury" (p. 410). "Authors in other fields [than the natural sciences] who are willing to adjust their documentation to this system are encouraged to do so" (p. 401).

In absolute terms this argument cannot be faulted. There can be no doubt that the author-date system, with its typically shortened bibliographic forms and in-text coding of references, saves space and costs (I am not convinced it saves editorial time). If we then throw into the mix such typical space-savers as endnotes (optional but probably needed in a "humanities" text), which will allow going straight to page proof, the omission of "p." and "pp." in citations where possible (par. 17.18), and the use of modular design (not discussed in the *Manual* but much used by Chicago; think of it as being like the design of a prefabricated house), then there are considerable savings in relative terms.

Even so, there are reasons to question the use of an author-date system in "humanities" publications or the almost automatic stipulation of any of the other time-saving recommendations. Several years ago the annual meeting of the AAUP (i.e., University Presses) featured a number of sessions devoted to cutting costs in publishing. Over cocktails I asked a press director known for getting everything possible from every dollar spent what he thought of such proposals as those mentioned above. "Not much," was his wry answer. "Every speaker we heard today forgot why we exist. The way to save money is to produce fewer and better books and do them right."

Choosing a system of documentation involves more than finding the economically cheapest presentation of research. Suppose, for instance, to choose an easy example, that in the noted neo-Marxist scholar Robert Weimann, Akademie der Wissenschaften der DDR, Berlin, an American publisher found an author "willing to adjust" to the author-date style. To the complexities of a difficult, almost baroque style in text would be the added complication of encountering mostly unfamiliar names in documentation, with titles of works in four languages other than that of the text buried in a reference list, and, at the same time, reference numbers to *end*notes that further support the text, or qualify and carry on the argument, all with further quotations and documentation. Such a travesty of procedure nearly guarantees a baffled and infuriated reader, wearied by the necessity of pagethumbing and placeholding. Historians insist on having full bibliographies in their works because such listings reveal at one time what is of first importance to them: the depth and range of research. Literary scholars often prefer bibliographic footnotes because their first concern is not scope but adequacy and relevance, and these need to be graspable almost immediately. For the natural scientist timeliness is all. Important publication takes place in journals, not books (as a rule), and there is no hierarchy of prestige among scientific journals, as there is in the humanities. Anything more than name and date, such as full publication data, would merely impede.

My point is simply that the choice of a system of documentation is less a matter of habit and tradition than the *Manual* suggests, and more a reflection of how the scholars of various disciplines approach and use the written record. To confuse these distinctions when they are important is to forget what we are about. That, I gather, is what the press director meant. To the scholarly publisher and his staff the finished book is an end in itself; to the constituency he serves, the product is never an end, only a means. I would not willingly confuse the two, even in these worst of times.[30]

As codetta, I invoke the reviewer's right to hang out a modest wish list—a few things I would like to see in future editions of the *Handbook* and the *Manual*. My wishes are modest, all having to do with the minutiae of documentation. As scholars range farther and farther afield in their research, cross disciplinary lines, and work their ways deeper and deeper into archives, documentation grows ever richer and more complex— and confused and confusing. The machinery itself is starting to break down as parts are mistakenly put to uses they were not intended for. The word *see*, for instance, is now virtually meaningless because it is used to mean almost anything. The stylebooks should explain and restrict it to a proper use, as the *Manual* has so successfully done with its stipulative definition of *idem*. More important, the *ordering* of items in a complex note needs a thorough airing. We would have better-looking text pages (and more economical footnoting), for instance, if what I like to call the "omnibus" note (consolidation of references) were better understood. I suspect that many authors shy away from them because they worry, properly, about going wrong and grudge the time they can take to construct. Both *Handbook* and *Manual* have models (sect. 36 and pars. 15.62-63, respectively), but they are too simple to be of real help. A related but slightly different question is the hierarchy, or rank-order, to be accorded the various *kinds* of data that may legitimately demand expression. When, as happens, a single note must give the sources of several quotations in text, several references documenting a single fact or assertion in text, and in addition corroborating secondary sources (with further attention to contrary views), with these requiring further discussion and argument with further quotation and the documentation of *those* quotations, then we *all* need something to lean on. The *Manual* touches on these (pars. 15.48-52), but all too easily. And I didn't even mention the exquisite pains of trying to produce a readable extract in a note set in 7- or 8-point type.

But I would not have the *Manual* grow much more than it has. Unless Chicago is willing to produce an oversize book in a fourteenth edition, I fear that any further tightening of lines and reduction of type size will only enrich the country's ophthalmologists as its editors line up for trifocals.[31]

In Sum

The thirteenth Chicago serves its constituencies well. This is so because, in part, at least, the Press for the first time asked for, and got, evaluation of the twelfth edition and suggestions for change from colleagues at other presses. More important, the editors responsible for revision proved themselves both willing to listen and capable of working critically with the data they received.[32] The well-thought-out organization of new material (along with reorganization of old), the crisply clear instructions, the overall clarity of presentation—these result from and are a tribute to the professionalism of the entire Chicago staff. There are a few more inconsistencies and typos than one wants to see, even in a first printing, but these are trifles, mere flyspecks that in no way obstruct the view.[33] The new *Manual* sets a new flexible American standard for scholarly publishing.

The practically errorless *MLA Handbook* cannot be so commended. Though I have spoken warmly of its predecessor, there is no denying that *its* constituencies need something different. The *Handbook* is not it. In attempting to provide something for everybody, in neglecting "the fact that each of [its] audiences . . . has its own particular requirements" (as Altick said of another bad reference book),[34] the *Handbook* simply falls to pieces as a result of the linguistic and conceptual centrifugal forces at work in it. The audiences involved are not just different but, I think, irreconcilable. Hence the language problems exhibited throughout the book: here overgeneralization, there the overspecific; the easy term defined, the unfamiliar skipped over—all the inevitable (and understandable) result of the authors' anxieties in trying to find *an* audience.

The undergraduate needs the regular, the normal, the simply clear, so that the design of the system emerges and is grasped fully; the scholar requires the complex, the "esoteric," as the *Handbook* has it. Whether the answer is two different books is another question altogether, one I cannot answer, though I am troubled by the ethics of one of the great American scholarly organizations setting itself up in the college textbook market. One thing is clear, however: the scholarly author is not well served by the *Handbook* in its present form, even granting the materials salvaged from the *Style Sheet*. He or she needs a "reference edition" that is truly that, fully reflecting the rich complexity of the best of today's best scholarship.

It would be churlish to hold the authors entirely responsible for this misfiring. Their mistake was to accept an impossible assignment. The editorial committee who, presumably, made the crucial initial decisions share much of the blame, for not thinking through the implications of their decisions. There was no William Riley Parker to pick up the pieces for them, as indeed there could not be. Nevertheless, it was the authors who put their names on the title page *as* authors, and on them must fall most of the responsibility. As Dr. Johnson might have expressed it, What was said of Rome, adorned by Augustus, and of English poetry, embellished by Dryden,may be applied by an easy inversion to the *MLA Style Sheet*, amplified by Gibaldi and Achtert, "marmoream invenerunt, lateritiam reliquerunt." They found it marble, and they left it brick—piles of them.

Elsie Myers Stainton has the penultimate word (and here I quote her fully): "Maybe the wordy new book will sell more copies, but the disappearance of the old succinct style sheet is a loss to writers and editors." That it is, and in a dimension untouched-on but relevant. In the thirty-three years since the first *Style Sheet* was issued, the price of it, as represented in its successor, has risen precisely 9,500 percent. I would guess that older "writers and editors" are holding on *dearly* to their style sheets. I know I am.

Notes

I need to thank Francis P. Glosser and Nicholas C. Edsall, friends and colleagues at the University of Virginia. However inadvertent their assistance, it was of value in the preparation of this article. Dr. Glosser, a member of the staff of the university library, pointed me toward the European periodical, discussed herein, whose singularly apt handling of publication data clarified and materially shortened my presentation. Professor Edsall's reflections on the rationale of historical documentation forced me to reopen and rethink the whole question of scholarly documentation. The result, however oversimple the paradigm I ended with, is a more thoughtful consideration of the books reviewed.

1. Naomi B. Pascal, "Four More Enchirada," *Scholarly Publishing*, 10, No. 4 (1979), 351.

2. Ibid., p. 352.

3. Symposium, "Strengthening the Shrinking Dollar," *Scholarly Publishing*, 14, No. 1 (1982), 29-32. The whole piece (pp. 29-48) is worth reading as a useful crystallization of numerous similar proposals.

4. It should be obvious, but, for the record: the judgments expressed here are mine. Not even by inference can they be attributed to the staff, Director, or Board of the University Press of Virginia.

5. Pascal, "Chicago's Thirteenth," *Scholarly Publishing*, 14, No. 1 (1982), 87.

6. Stainton, "Some Pointers on Style," *Scholarly Publishing*, 12, No. 1 (1980), 86; Pascal, "Four Enchirada," p. 355.

7. Facing pages sometimes do not align or are of noticeably different lengths. As a result the drop folios float freely and unintentionally (see, e.g., pp. 72-73, 74-75, 76-77). Page 97 witlessly carries over from the *Style Sheet* one of its few layout blunders, the placing of a reference number with a subheading. Another carry-over, the use of section numbers (not pages) as the main finding device, both in the index and in text (where they align with the running heads), does not work well in the longer *Handbook*. Section 32, e.g., now spans sixteen pages and finding, say, section 32i requires some page-flipping that could have been avoided if the subsection letters appeared with the section numbers on each page. A further irritant in this respect is the misuse of the "dictionary" method in establishing the running section numbers. The correct number for page 2, e.g., is *3* not 2. Finally, the 5-color accent stripe running across the cover seems inappropriate. "Research is fun!" it suggests. It's not. More on that topos later.

8. "The MLA Style Sheet," William Riley Parker, comp., *PMLA*, 66 (April 1951), 1-32.

9. The information in this paragraph comes from Parker's own account of the style sheet's origin and preparation, p. vi of the *PMLA* printing. At a time when the preparation of a festschrift can take ten years, one can only marvel that, from initial study and first draft through consultation with nearly 120 editors to publication, the process required only two years—and Parker apologized for his tardiness.

10. *MLA Style Sheet*, rev. ed. (1951?; June 1963 printing), p. 3; my italics. I guess at the date (and apologize for the pedantry of the citation) because the detailed printing history of the *Style Sheet*, here printed on the verso of the title page, fails to distinguish this, the revised first edition, by date or anything else.

11. Ibid., 2d ed. (1970), p. 12n.

12. Ibid., rev. ed., 1963 prt., p. 3.

13. Ibid., 2d ed., p. 2. The *Handbook* has become a bibliographical tangle. The front matter of the first printing, a 1977 paperback, contains three discursive sections: a signed Acknowledgements and two prefaces, the first "for the instructor and thesis adviser," the other "for the student." The third printing, designated "reference edition" (1979), drops the first preface and retains the second *as* preface, without further title and with two word changes: in the last paragraph "undergraduate" of the first printing becomes "inexperienced" in the reference edition; "graduate student" becomes "experienced." Except for these changes, and the substitution of a laminated case for paper covers and a price increase of nearly three dollars, the contents of the reference edition appear to be the same as the two previous printings. Subsequent paperback printings revert to the format of the first printing but are now designated "student edition." Technically and legally, of course, these are all reprintings of the first edition, properly labeled that on the copyright page. Unless noted, all quotations from and references to the *Handbook* are from the reference edition.

14. Perrin, *Writer's Guide and Index to English*, rev. ed. (Chicago: Scott Foresman, 1950), pp. 365-66.

15. Ibid., p. 367.

16. Note that Perrin's presentation requires thirty-eight pages, six on notes and bibliography.

17. See *MLA Style Sheet*, rev. ed., sect. 40, or 2d ed., sect. 46.

18. The authors cannot be faulted for the problems of the section on permissions. It was probably written in 1976, when many details of the copyright act were unknown or unclear. Achtert's later account, "The New Copyright Law," *PMLA*, 93, No. 4 (1978), 572-77, is first-rate. In future printings of the *Handbook* it should replace the present material, which is seriously, even dangerously, over-generalized.

19. Here it is interesting to note what has *not* been retained in documentation. The abbreviation "s.v.," illustrated in old notes 69 and 75 (*Style Sheet*, 2d. ed.), has met the same fate that awaited "op. cit" and "loc. cit." in the first *Style Sheet*: retirement to a decent desuetude. That the decision on "s.v." was hasty and ill-considered, as Parker's was not, is disclosed by the writers of the *Handbook* itself. As Kenneth Burke might observe, having thrown the abbreviation out the front door, they then find it irreplaceable and have to sneak it in the back door (into the index) disguised as "under" — and, of necessity, in italics no less! On the other hand, the *Handbook* pointlessly retains (notes 41 and 47) special citation forms for published dissertations. If the dissertation is *published*, it becomes nothing more than a book with a single title and should be so cited, if only because publishers nowadays do anything short of outright falsification to disguise the origins of the few dissertations that are published.

The most notable change in documentation is the treatment of the abbreviation "ibid." On page 91 it is proscribed: "do not use." Yet on pages 125-26 (in the list of abbreviations) the (good) full treatment of the *Style Sheet* is retained, with the additional phrase "avoid using." Second thoughts? There should have been some. "Ibid." can be a real mischiefmaker, but that is merely a sign of its lively versatility. The authors are apparently unaware of the use of the abbreviation *within* a note, where it is not merely useful, but irreplaceable. The *Manual* has an example of this use (par. 17.14), though it can be faulted for failing to illustrate the range of uses.

20. The *Manual* too considers sound recordings (par. 16.177-78), but the examples given there justify the listing, as those in the *Handbook* do not. And why are there no samples for handling microfilm and microform?

21. Perrin, *Writer's Guide*, p. 283.

22. Altick, "This Will Never Do," *Review*, 1 (1979), 59.

23. There may be another divergence on page 29. Is STC's most famous poem now considered long enough to require italics in citing the title?

24. For this kind of slip one can only commiserate with the authors. It is difficult to avoid when new material must be integrated with old, as here. Their board and their readers have the responsibility of acting as editors, and they have let their clients down. *Everyone* must have been nodding when they let through this sentence with its two freshman English errors: "Every field has its preferred format or "style" (p. 95). You bet. That's why we have "hand" books.

25. *MLA Style Sheet*, 2d ed., sect. 23a.

26. *A Uniform System of Citation*, 13th ed. (Cambridge: Harvard Law Review, 1981), sect. 5.3(iv.)

27. In fairness I note that the sort of linguistic rot exemplified here set in in the second edition of the *Style Sheet*. The first edition had at least a brief statement on the principal problem: capitalization of quoted material varies with syntactic function. See the footnote (No. 6) to sect. 13a.

28. For an informative, behind-the-scenes account of the *Manual's* whole development, see Catherine Seybold, "A Brief History of *The Chicago Manual*," *Scholarly Publishing*, 14, No. 2 (1983), 163-77.

29. Ibid., p. 176.

30. I would not be willfully misunderstood. The *Manual* is, after all, Chicago's and is planned for the use of its staff. I cannot imagine Chicago producing anything like the nightmare volume I sketched above. The problem with Holy Writ, however, is that True Believers like it simple, straight, and uncomplicated—no complications or subtle theological distinctions. And no leap of the imagination is required to see some Born Again publisher or author come swinging down the sawdust trail shouting "Eureka! Salvation! Free of footnotes! Henceforth let all books be author-date books!" I only wish that the *Manual* had recommended such a system a little less *enthusiastically*.

31. There has been so much talk, here and elsewhere, about the changes in the *Manual* that, for balance, I mention a few instances where it does *not* relax its old procedures. On inclusive numbers: The Chicago system "is unnecessarily complicated, say some. In reply Press editors would point out that the system is only complicated enough to produce graphic displays that are consistently easy to grasp at a glance. . . . So until someone invents a simpler system offering the same advantages . . . we expect to stick with it" (par. 8.70). So do we. On forming the possessive of polysyllabic names ending in *s* or *z*: The "Press prefers its own rule" and wickedly points out some of the absurdities of the rule espoused by "a highly respected learned association," as in Thomas' poetry (pars. 6.23, 6.21-22). And as an editor I appreciate the playful pedantry of this model note: *A Manual of Style*, 13th ed. (Chicago: University of Chicago Press, forthcoming) (par. 16.96).

32. In preparation for revision, Chicago sent out 75 questionnaires to editors and got back 129 (Seybold, "Brief History," p. 174). Similarly, proposed revisions of the first edition of the *Style Sheet* "were sent to every journal editor, university press director, and department chairman" (2d ed., p. 3). This time, however, MLA seems to have avoided consultation on the proposed *Handbook* and relied on "the thinking and . . . suggestions of teachers, scholars, and students throughout the United States and Canada" (Acknowledgments). Whatever the reality, that phrasing suggests to me a mere counting of noses outside any intellectual framework. Hence the ad hoc character of many of the changes, such as dropping "ibid." and relaxing the rule requiring the serial comma before *and* (sect. 10d), this last an invitation to inevitable confusion. Any editor would have vetoed that change, had the chance been offered.

33. The William Strong of page ix is surely the William S. Strong of page 692. The cross-reference on page 448 (par. 16.36) should read 7.145, not 7.144. The word *not*, in the second *B* style note (par. 16.114) is still an adverb (traditionally at least) and should be capitalized. The reference numbers in the running heads on pages 228 and 229 are wrong. And there are a few typos.

34. Altick, "This Will Never Do," p. 48.

Contemporary Images of Richardson: The Poststructuralist-Marxist-Feminist in the Closet

Lennard J. Davis

Terry Castle. *Clarissa's Ciphers: Meaning and Disruption in Richardson's* Clarissa. Ithaca: Cornell University Press, 1982. 201 pp.

Terry Eagleton. *The Rape of Clarissa: Writing, Sexuality and Class Struggle in Samuel Richardson*. Minneapolis: University of Minnesota Press, 1982. ix, 109 pp.

It is not unusual that a literary work of the past that is considered dead and buried will be resurrected with a kind of renewed vigor as a "find" of a particular time and a particular ascending discourse. Observe, for example, T. S. Eliot's discovery of the Metaphysical poets or Pound's misprision of Chinese poetry. Samuel Richardson's *Clarissa* has recently become such a work. To be sure, Richardson has been studied and written about in academic circles over the years. But it was hard to imagine that a book like *Clarissa* would be the terrain over which heated debates about the nature of literature and the nature of reality might be fought. (Of course, we except here the initial debates over Richardson's work in the eighteenth century.) *Clarissa* has rarely been thought of as a favorite read, and, to steal Johnson's remark about *Paradise Lost*, none ever wished it longer. Nevertheless, in the post-structuralist era the work has become a sort of intense battleground for conflicting literary and political discourses from deconstructionist to feminist to marxist. The actual marginality of the work has made the debate even more ferocious. I say marginality because,

despite its most ardent defenders, few outside the university
would ever claim that *Clarissa* is one of the central works of our
culture. It is as if in the marginality of criticism, competing
groups out of power will seize not on the central works—few
battles of this type will ever be fought over Shakespeare—but on
the unclaimed territory of the obscure. Two recent books are
cases in point. Terry Castle's *Clarissa's Ciphers: Meaning and
Disruption in Richardson's* Clarissa and Terry Eagleton's *The
Rape of Clarissa* are both attempts to claim Richardson to their
particular discourse. Why Terry Castle should have claimed
Richardson for the deconstructionist camp is perhaps more
obvious than why Terry Eagleton should have claimed for
Richardson a quasi-revolutionary role. The epistolary form of
Richardson's work tends to thrust language into the foreground,
and in an age of linguistics and semiology, Richardson might
seem like a natural focal point for language studies. Of course, it
might well be said that *any* epistolary novel would manifest
many if not all of the proto-semiological traits one might find in
Richardson.

Castle's point in *Clarissa's Ciphers*, however, is that
Richardson's novel is uniquely obsessed with language, that
most of what happens in the book occurs because of
misperceptions, competing theories, and textual strategies
having to do with reading. The epistolary form of the work
more or less focuses our attention on language and on reading
since it is so dependent on the mechanics of letter-writing and
reading, so reliant on the artifice of the text. After all, a novel
made of letters is actually a collection of texts, and in this light
Castle reads with a deconstructive eye, saying, "In a sense,
everyone in *Clarissa* is an exegete; everyone is caught up in a
world of 'cyphers'" (p. 19).

In order to appreciate Castle's reading, one has to accept a
basic set of premises that might be called "pop deconstructionism." First, all texts are multivalent, polysemous—that
is to say the reader really creates the text, and each reader creates
his or her own text. As Castle writes, "It follows that there are,
finally, as many versions of this text as there are individual
readers and readings" (p. 53). This truism we own to Roland

Barthes, particularly in his tour de force S/Z. And this insight leads us to the second premise that all literary works are more properly texts than works. A text exists without an author, it simply is a set of signs. We are not interested in trying to intuit what the author means in trying to deduce the theme of a story; we simply set about interpreting the signs of the text. Obviously we become the authors of the text in the act of reading, which is really the act of interpretation. But the third premise of pop-deconstructionism is that writing is essentially a futile endeavor—writing is the sign of loss of meaning; it is a substitute, a trace, a grapheme without meaning. Once articulated, meaning is lost. We thank Jacques Derrida for this last belief. So, if there are many readings to a text, and the intention of the text is relatively unimportant, then the meaning of the text is in some sense less important than what the text can tell us about the process of signification or, as Castle puts it, the work "invites us to examine the grounds of our own hermeneutic activity" (p. 29). What things signify, however, is less important than the fact that meaning is interrupted, skewed, destroyed, or misperceived in the process of reading. "Clarissa reads naively, deciphering both letter and experience by dint of a compulsive benevolism [while Lovelace] violates her faith in the natural significance of things" (pp. 21, 83).

These premises of pop deconstructionism bear examination. Barthes's notion of the polysemousness of reading, the distinction between what has been translated as "writerly" and "readerly" texts, is here banalized into the sophomoric notion that all readings of a text are valid (as in the oft-heard phrase "Well, that's only *your* opinion"). The emphasis on the isolate nature of the text harks back to "new criticism." And the depiction of Lovelace as the emanuensis of Derrida who teaches the naive Clarissa that experience is not legible sounds too much like an autobiographical allegory about the naive graduate student who used to think that language meant something and then went to the English Department at Yale for a few years only to be deconstructed into better sense.

My real objection to Castle's work is that it rather humorlessly sees Richardson as a writer engaged in a full-fledged deconstructionist project (p. 19). The Harlowes do not simply confine and harass Clarissa, they "inscribe her with a range of oppressive meanings" (p. 24). Or more impressively: "*Clarissa* offers no 'Story' in any conventional sense, but is concerned, on some level, with a problematization of the very notion of 'Story' itself. More than has been previously acknowledged, *Clarissa*, like *Tristram Shandy*, is a fiction that investigates fiction making. It is a narrative concerned with the nature of meaning—how it is produced and how it is frustrated" (p. 40). It is difficult not to laugh at the thought of Richardson, the old hypochondriacal printer, imagining himself writing about the nature of meaning and its production. I do not doubt that it is possible to "read" *Clarissa* as a deconstructionist treatise, but I need to be led to the understanding that the rather sophisticated set of observations that Castle makes would be intelligible even to Richardson. Castle puts this problem another way, "Richardson either could not or would not see the hermeneutic paradox *Clarissa* embodied [and so] . . . a belated, partial recognition of the indeterminacy of fiction came to him only gradually . . ." (p. 172). Stubborn man that one.

What I am saying is that it makes a certain amount of sense if you are, say, a psychoanalytic critic, to claim that certain works may be replete with concealed psychodynamic material that only the critic, like the analyst, may be permitted to find. This material may be said to be put there deftly by the unconscious while the conscious hand manipulated things like plot and character. But the deconstructionist critic who works in the eighteenth century can hardly claim that writers in this period intuitively understood the premises of books like *La dissemination*. This lack of explanatory material places a work like Castle's in serious trouble. What is actually going on is a form of cultural imperialism that launches its own explanations as colonizing forces to take over the historical text.

Since I raise the question of historicity here, let me stop and observe that Castle rarely pauses to investigate whether any readers in the eighteenth century reacted to Richardson's work in the way she does. There could have been a somewhat dubious but interesting analysis about the nature of signification as it was conceived by philosophers and linguists, since there is a good deal of speculation about how language signifies in the work of Locke, Berkeley, Condilliac, and some more obscure grammarians and lexicographers. Some work has been done in this field by scholars like Hans Aarslef. Or there might have been some investigation of how readers in the eighteenth century perceived the linguistic problems presented in *Clarissa*. But the direction here is strictly textual, a ploy which alleviates the necessity of coping with historical reality.

The lack of historicity is actually part of a larger problem that I might call "literary devoteeism" or "graduate-studentitis." This disease or fanaticism fosters the conception that any work worthy of a dissertation being written on it alone must therefore be capable of bearing the weight of any analysis. As in the case of religious devoteeism, the text is seen as sacred and therefore endlessly polysemous—all words, events, and even morphemes are actually significant. The work in this sense is a plenum of meaning, awaiting only the bright intelligence of the clever graduate student to decipher. Castle is without shame in this regard. Any word, phrase, or sentence is seen as directly relevant to the work of Jacques Derrida. It is pretty clear that when Richardson had Arabella say to her sister Clarissa "O, thou art a—And down she flung without saying what," he did not expect that Castle would imply that this breaking off in mid-sentence was part of a general plan among family members to prevent Clarissa from being able to "recuperate the language of the family [so that] they [could] reduce her, in effect to the preverbal condition of the infant . . ." (p. 73). And when Arabella begins to "doodle" on the harpsichord or hum a tune, Castle interprets these actions as "a parody of meaningful speech . . . yet in a deeper sense, they are also a revelation of the nature of discourse in Clarissa's world" (p. 73). The book is slowly built up on an overabundance of such dubious examples. And in an effort to make the text become this plenum of meaning, Castle inflates her text with ennobling adjectives. So Richardson's work is "massive, yet often baffling," "remarkable," with a "unique power," "justly celebrated," a "masterpiece" whose "form . . . simultaneously alludes to hundreds of fictional acts of interpretation," a "great project," "richly perverse," with "archeological dimensions," a "problematic text," but a "fallen text," or more "a paradigmatic text," but ultimately "a text [that] itself is always fragmentary."

Aside from the linguistic and epistemological issues already mentioned, Castle introduces what in her mind is a political note, saying that Clarissa's language is devalued not only because she believes that language can express meaning but because she is a woman. Lovelace, like Derrida, understands on the other hand that language is merely a deconstruction of meaning, a tactic, a ploy. Lovelace performs the act of deconstruction not only with Clarissa's language but also with her gender—culminating in the ultimate "reading" of her through rape. In this sense, Clarissa is seen as a victim of a male-centered power and language system. Her readings are incorrect because she is a woman, and her value to the reader comes largely because her fate points out the problem of helplessness and victimization.[1]

The anti-feminist side of this debate picks up with William Beatty Warner's *Reading* Clarissa: *The Struggles of Interpretation* (New Haven: Yale University Press, 1979). Warner's reading is a deconstructive one too. But Warner combines his deconstructive textual reading with a fiercely male-centered, quiddical reading of the work that has Lovelace come out as the hero of hermeneutical analysis—his rape of Clarissa being in effect his logical attempt to deconstruct her. Castle's difference with Warner centers on her feeling that Richardson is in essence condemning the deconstruction as a way of talking about the way power is inherently part of any social use of language. Warner merely approves of Lovelace cum Derrida doing the old naughty act of analysis wherever he will. Castle's disagreement actually comes as a kind of addendum because she seems to have read Warner's book only at the last moment. We must take seriously Castle's points about women and their lack of access to language; indeed, as Castle says, "Clarissa's rape is a primal act of silencing" (p. 115). But one is frustrated in reading *Clarissa's Ciphers* by its rather limited understanding of the political. Castle seems to feel that she can intuit what is political by simply referring to the linguistic level. But the oppression of women in the eighteenth century has some very real consequences besides their silence in language. (And why is there no mention of the contradictory relationship between the profusion of women novelists and their powerlessness in the late seventeenth and early eighteenth centuries? The index of Castle's book is more likely to list Emile Benveniste or Roland Barthes than Aphra Behn, Eliza Haywood, Mary Davies, Mrs. Manley or any other female writer.) Furthermore, the omission of Michael Foucault's work in this context is surprising. One would assume that any discussion of language and power would include works like *The Order of Things, Discipline and Punish*, or Foucault's essays on knowledge and power. The absence of this interesting and central body of work is puzzling.[2]

The more seriously political issue is taken up by Terry Eagleton in *The Rape of Clarissa: Writing, Sexuality and Class Struggle in Samuel Richardson*. Eagleton's analysis is overtly marxist, and, unlike Castle, he sees Clarissa not as a victim of language and power but as a strong opponent of that political and cultural rule. She, and Richardson by default, are seen as revolutionaries foisting a new enlightened bourgeois view of patriarchy and language. Eagleton does not like Warner much and seems not to have had time to read Castle before going into print. Eagleton too hits all the structuralist—if not poststructuralist—points about textuality and reading, but adds to this an interest in how Richardson, by being so textually centered, was in fact embodying bourgeois ideology.

Citing Antonio Gramsci, Eagleton's point is that "any revolutionary class, in addition to seizing political power, must secure *cultural* hegemony over its opponents . . . in the realms of religion, philosophy, art, morality, language and manners" (pp. 1-2). Eagleton then discerns that Samuel Richardson was one of the "organic" intellectuals of the English bourgeoisie—a point that takes a bit of proving since it takes a particular act of will to see Richardson as an intellectual at all. Richardson *must* be an intellectual for this argument to work. The problem with Eagleton's reading of *Clarissa*, like Castle's, is that he tends to see his own image in the rediscovered text. If textuality and language are central, then Richardson must be a kind of Eagleton or Derrida—not simply an unconscious and perhaps unwilling obsessive who focused on the epistolary for complex personal and cultural reasons—or even merely by chance.

Eagleton's way out of this search for a hero is to say that there is a contradiction between the "discursive formation" called "'Samuel Richardson' [who] denotes a powerhouse of vital ideological interests [and] enmeshes English society, connects with the power structures and spreads to catch the sensibility of Europe in its sway" and the man "shadowlily inaccessible, a self-effacing entrepreneur in some ways more akin to the periwig-makers of his precinct than to the mighty whom his fictions enthralled" (p. 9). The reason for this contradiction lies in the very nature of printing, which was on the one hand an artisanal craft and on the other the discourse of public statement and ideology. A book launched by a few workers can have "unfathomable effects." This is a clever and significant way out of the problem that Castle merely avoided, but it still seems more of an excuse for having to pin on Richardson the weight of bourgeois revolution.

Of course, what is said of Richardson's novels might be argued persuasively for any of the thousands of middle-class novels that make up the canon of English literature. Eagleton tries to say that Richardson's devotion to writing, his correspondences, his circle of literary devotees, created a "partially collective mode of literary production" that turns his texts into "pretexts—into occasions for sharply nuanced debate, forums for continuous mutual education, media for social rituals and relations." Therefore, Richardson "produced, not simply a set of novels, but a whole society in minature . . . he converted the process to his art into an act of ideological solidarity "(p. 12). This argument is persuasive, although somewhat overstated. Richardson was probably the first novelist to generate a huge audience and use that audience in turn to recreate his own works. Dickens might be considered the next major author who fed back on his audience's response, as he did, for example, when he sent Martin Chuzzlewit off to America in an attempt to boost flagging serial sales. In this sense,

Richardson's footnotes, insertions, prefatory material, inserted letters, and so on are a testimony to a wider participation in his works.

We are asked to see Richardson's novels not simply as entertaining stories—or even hermeneutic revelations—but as "themselves a material part of those struggles, pitched standards around which battle is joined, instruments which help to constitute social interests rather than lenses which reflect them. These novels are an agent, rather than mere account, of the English bourgeoisie's attempt to wrest a degree of ideological hegemony from the artistocracy" (p. 4). To the extent that Richardson's works became public events, this statement is undoubtedly true. And with Laurence Stone's assertion that novels were important in creating the revolution in affective behavior he documents in *The Family, Sex and Marriage*, one certainly has the right to say that novels were not simply reflections of society. But it seems equally unsettling to say that Richardson was consolidating the power of the bourgeoisie as it was to say that he was deconstructing language and meaning.

Ideology is a central concept to Eagleton, and by it he means not only the belief system of one class but the very way that a given society signifies meanings to itself. In this sense, ideology is a mass signifying system. But Eagleton, like many contemporary marxist literary critics, fails to locate the particular ways that ideology works. Instead, ideology is just seen as a kind of big, scary bogey whose motives can be assigned freely as Eagleton does in the following discussion of the bourgeoisie: "Emboldened by its political and economic advances, it is now emerging from the privacy of business and bedroom to impress its ideology on society as a whole" (p. 6). Nevertheless, some readers will appreciate Eagleton's theoretical formulations on the workings of ideology in the introduction to this book, although the practical historical research is frustratingly absent.

Surely, even Eagleton appreciates the act of cultural imperialism he is performing when he notes the paradox that Richardson, "more akin to the periwig-makers of his precinct than to the mighty whom his fictions enthralled" (p. 9), should have such a powerful role to play in the making of ideology. But we are constantly fed lines that test our credibility in which Richardson is made to seem a revolutionary intellectual in the ranks of Bertolt Brecht—converting "art into an act of ideological solidarity" (p. 12). Eagleton's strange kind of ahistorical marxism is weakened by excessive attention to ideology as a history of ideas rather than as a kind of political and material practice. This means that often for Eagleton ideas beget ideas alone, and that history really does not need to come into play as long as we can impose on the past our own image of it. For example, he writes: "Protestant individualism and Protestant ideology entail a new 'turn to the subject,' inseparable from the 'nuclear' reorganizing of the family. In bourgeois philosophy, a militant empiricism discredits the coldly rational and embraces the raw stuff of subjective sensation. Post-Lockeian political theory, distressed by the sectarianism of civil war, espouses a 'moderation' more traditionally associated with mildness of women than with the aggression of men" (p. 15). This kind of language, one might note in passing, is all the more troublesome because it is so general. Where is the listing of the elements of protestant ideology that are presumed to be self-evident? Where are the historical proofs or even references with which the reasonable reader might seek to find alternate interpretations? Post-Lockeian political theory is stressed here, and what is absent is the people who thought about that body of ideas, the conditions that helped bring those ideas into use and power.

I am not interested in devaluing Eagleton's analysis, which in some very important ways is fascinating, but in pointing out that his reading of *Clarissa* is itself part of a larger current than his own blend of marxist criticism. Eagleton's avowed purpose in this book is to combine textuality, sexuality, and class struggle. That is to say, he would join semiotic, feminist, freudian, and marxist criticism. In so doing, he must make Richardson a kind of combination of Derrida, Elaine Showalter, Lacan, and Marx. And, in this sense, Eagleton must combine some disparate but not mutually exclusive traditions. The claim in all these analyses is that the object of criticism—poor bewigged and beleaguered Samuel Richardson—is in the camp of the modern reader and that these more or less powerful discourses are in the camp of the current user of the critical apparatus. By having Richardson display this particular combination of discourse badges, we are supposed to feel more comfortable about these ways of describing the world. But this very synthesis provides its own undoing by diluting marxism, say, with deconstructionism—or vice versa.

There are too many correspondences, despite all the marxist terminology, between Eagleton's and Castle's reading of the text. Eagleton too sees Lovelace as a "post-structuralist precursor" (p. 46) and for him too the letter is "the site of a constant power struggle . . . the function of an ineluctable power system" (p. 49-50), or, more psychoanalytically, he refers to "female sexuality itself, that folded, secret place which is always open to violent intrusion" (p. 54). This combination of the psychoanalytic and the marxist becomes a kind of parody of inclusiveness. One might want to speculate why this group of academics likes to see rape as a linguistic act, or put more properly, why do people who spend a lot of time reading and writing like to imagine language as the site of sexuality? Deconstructing a text or opening a letter is, after all, not remotely like rape any more than opening a dictionary is like performing a triple by-pass. To find sexual adventure behind every act of textuality is possible, but finally a little overwhelming. Eagleton believes that "the sex/text metaphor in Richardson is so insistent that it is difficult to believe it unconscious"(p. 54). Freud would have said that this was all the more reason for it to be unconscious. But can we seriously imagine Richardson openly postulating this post-freudian insight?

Eagleton really loses some credit in the freudian section of this work which culminates in such insights as the one where Clarissa is equated paradoxically with a penis: "Daunted by her 'phallic' wholeness, shaken by this nameless threat to his own gender, Lovelace must possess Clarissa so that he may reunite himself with the lost phallus, and unmask her as reassuringly 'castrated' . . . . Yet the whole enterprise is ironically self-defeating, since by destroying Clarissa Lovelace risks destroying the phallus too. It is no wonder that he defers the rape unconsciously, dreading the loss of the very idea he desires" (p. 59). This novel interpretation remains totally unconvincing, not least of all because it is arrived at without any reference to the text. It is unclear whether Richardson is supposed to have written this allegory from a conscious or unconscious perspective, but that does not much trouble Eagleton. The fact that Lovelace *has* an unconscious at all does not seem to be a problem either.

Eagleton's strength is also his undoing as he moves deftly from the psychological to the linguistic to the political. These leaping theoretical pirouettes are his forte. For example, the rape is seen as a "purely impersonal act of violence which refuses entry into discourse and brusquely unveils language for what it is: a ceaselessly digressive supplement which . . . will never succeed in nailing down the real" (p. 61). Clarissa's death achieves for her "that pure transparency of signifier to signified which she seeks in the integrity of her script" (p. 75), but it is also "a political gesture, a shocking, surreal act of resignation from a society . . . an absolute refusal of political society: sexual oppression, bourgeois patriarchy and libertine aristocracy together" (pp. 75-76). That is to say, "Richardson's importance lies also in his bold experiments with form: the shift from 'language' to 'discourse' belongs with the transition from masculine to feminine and aristocracy to bourgeoisie" (p. 101). The experience of reading a book like *The Rape of Clarissa* is one of constantly switching hobby horses mid-stream as Eagleton leaps from French critical theory to feminism to marxist analysis. Of course, there is no reason why one should adhere strictly to one point of view, and it is refreshing that a freudian-marxist-feminist-structuralist analysis can be made at all. But the effect finally is debilitating—not only to reading but to the credibility of each system. Compared with Castle's rather more limited use of Derrida's work, one can admire Eagleton's willingness to bring competing theories together. But his lack of fidelity to any one system will disappoint even the eclectics among his serious readers.

Notes

1. Castle's interpretation here comes in a line of feminist and antifeminist readings of the work. Some significant works in this regard are Katherine M. Rogers, "Sensitive Feminism vs. Conventional Sympathy: Richardson and Fielding on Women," *Novel*, 9 (1975), 256-70; Judith Wilt, "He Could Go No Farther: A Modest Proposal about Lovelace and Clarissa," *PMLA*, 92 (1977), 19-32; and Jean Hagstrum, *Sex and Sensibility: Ideal and Erotic Love from Milton to Mozart* (Chicago: Univ. of Chicago Press, 1980).

2. Derrida himself never mentions Foucault in his work. Apparently a gulf of sorts separates these two and their followers as well.

The Case of the Two Hammetts

W. L. Godshalk

Richard Layman. *Shadow Man: The Life of Dashiell Hammett.* New York: Harcourt Brace Jovanovich, 1981. xviii, 285 pp.

William F. Nolan. *Hammett: A Life at the Edge.* New York: Congdon and Weed, Inc., 1983. xiv, 276 pp.

In the twenty-some years following Hammett's death in 1961, an increasing number of literary detectives have been searching out the details of his life and works. Bill Ruehlmann, the author of *Saint with a Gun*, first put me on the trail, and I soon met, either personally or by telephone and letter, Joe Gores and David Fechheimer (both real-life detectives and men of letters), as well as Richard Layman and William Nolan (the authors of the books under discussion). These were heady times, filled with shared information and ideas, telephone calls to fellow Hammett researchers to tell them you had just recovered another detail of his life, quarrels over minor issues, consensus in our frustration that Lillian Hellman had refused to help us, and finally drinks and food at John's Grill where Sam Spade had once had lunch and where, we were sure, Hammett himself had also eaten and drunk. It is in this atmosphere of mutual respect and friendly rivalry that my following remarks must be read. Like Hammett, I will not pull my punches.

Comparing Layman's *Shadow Man* with Nolan's *Hammett* is, in essence, comparing two different kinds of biography. Cautious and skeptical, Layman carefully presents the known facts of Hammett's life and work. Although there are implied evaluations and judgments throughout his study, Layman generally eschews praise or condemnation. His work is filled with information. Lacking Layman's caution and skepticism,

Nolan's biography may be read as an imaginative and ebullient defense of the heroic image of Hammett that is brought into question by Layman's revelations. For Layman, Hammett is a mixed bag—a good detective who was even a better liar, a man with a profound social conscience who found it easy to neglect his struggling family. For Nolan, these tensions are virtually non-existent. For him, Hammett's life has a purity of line, and even his failures are given the aura of a hard-boiled triumph.

Nolan's vision of Hammett is neatly summed up in the following passage:

> The punishing years as a Pinkerton field operative permanently affected Dashiell Hammett. He had witnessed political corruption at all levels, had dealt with most forms of crime, from random street fighting to murder, had been punched, knifed, clubbed, and shot at; he'd dealt with the rich, the middle class, and the poverty-ridden, with stool pigeons, thugs, racketeers, dangerous psychopaths, and elegant blackmailers. He had moved warily through a world of lies, cross-treacheries, and dark, mindless violence, where his only stability was the job itself. To survive, he had learned to curb excessive emotional response, to become hard-shelled and outwardly impassive, to trust no one, to see the world through a cynic's eye. [p. 45]

Even with his emphasis on the "dark, mindless violence" of the detective's world, Nolan's is an imaginative, romanticized view of Hammett and his career, and that romantic vision colors the way Nolan reads Hammett's prose: Hammett "brought the argot of the streets into print, portraying the people of his world with total authenticity, allowing them to talk and behave on paper as they had talked and behaved in his Pinkerton years" (p. 46). To my ear, this sounds rather extreme. Surely we must make allowances for the mediation of art.

Layman is much more cautious in approaching Hammett's life as a detective. "Hammett could not have worked as a San Francisco detective for longer than eight months—half that length of time is more likely," Layman comments, and yet "much more is known about that portion of his career as a detective than about his active days in Baltimore" (pp. 22-23). Why? Because, Layman believes, "Hammett himself is the primary source of most of the stories about his San Francisco detective adventures. The anecdotes about his experiences that he told his friends and his reading audience became grander, more exciting, less accurately detailed, and less plausible as time passed" (p. 23). Noting several real occurrences (e.g., acting undercover as a prisoner, Hammett was infested by lice), Layman comments that these "lacked glamour and made detectives seem less heroic than Hammett liked. He preferred to talk about cases—particularly the big ones—which carried with them an air of romance, adventure, and importance" (p. 23; see also p. 13).

Layman goes on to analyze Hammett's supposed involvement in four of the more spectacular cases: the Fatty Arbuckle rape, the Nicky Arnstein bond theft, the apprehension of Gloomy Gus Schaefer, and the *Sonoma* gold specie robbery. In each, Layman finds some evidence that Hammett's later accounts were exaggerated. Although Nolan must have been aware of Layman's skepticism, he presents each of these cases without indicating that Hammett's descriptions of his vital roles have been questioned. To question Hammett's excellence and heroism as a detective is not a function of Nolan's book.

For Layman, Hammett's character borders on the unsavory. Hammett's story "Who Killed Bob Teal?" reveals "for the first time in his professional life Hammett's tendency to disregard his readers, to play them for suckers who would accept his worst work as readily as his best" (p. 61). This opportunism, "amplified over the next fifteen years, finally caused Hammett to quit writing altogether" (p. 61). Layman emphasizes this opportunism throughout Hammett's writing career. (See, for example, p. 165.) Nolan finds another reason for Hammett's literary silence, a no less sombre one, but one that reflects much less damagingly on the author: "A direct line can be traced from the reluctantly heroic Continental Op, through the more cynical Sam Spade [in *The Maltese Falcon*], to the final emptiness of Beaumont [in *The Glass Key*] and Nick Charles [in *The Thin Man*]. This line of degeneration reveals why Hammett abandoned the crime novel. There was nowhere for him to go beyond *The Thin Man*. He had written himself into a blind corner" (p. 133). Nolan is defending Hammett against Layman's charge of opportunism. Hammett's silence is seen as caused by his own growing cynicism.

Nolan does not question Hammett's personal morality or his relationship with his family. Layman, in contrast, rather subtly builds a case against Hammett. Hammett's father had been a flamboyant ladies' man, and Layman has it that Hammett "declared openly and often that he would never treat a woman the way his father treated his mother" (p. 8). Later in the biography, Layman returns to this early promise. "Jose Dolan was five months pregnant and [Hammett] wanted to marry her. He had a promise to uphold—that he would never treat a woman the way his father had treated his mother" (p. 21). How Layman became aware of this promise he does not tell us, but he certainly shows Hammett breaking that promise over and over again, using and deserting a series of women, including Jose Dolan. Layman's implication is that Hammett, in this respect, becomes almost exactly like his rejected father.

As we might expect, the two biographers do not always use the same details from Hammett's life. Nolan is much more likely to stress the he-man aspects. Thus he notes the "many weekends" that Hammett hunted in Bucks County with Faulkner, Robert Coates, and Nathanael West, pointing out the excellent markmanship of Hammett and Faulkner (p. 135). Layman neglects these Pennsylvania hunting trips, but he does give an account of Hammett's drinking that is far from adulatory: "As Hammett got drunker, he became louder, ruder, and more talkative. Finally, at nearly five in the morning, his date had had enough, and she asked him to call her a cab . . . . When he refused, she hailed a cab herself. As she was entering the car, Hammett begged her: 'Please don't leave me alone'" (p. 204). Although this account was available to Nolan, he does not mention it, I imagine, because it does not put Hammett in a very good light. Apparently the writer could not always hold his liquor.

Of course, the biographies are not always so divergent, but it is even instructive to compare them when they are telling the same story—again about Hammett's drinking—with approximately the same tone. Layman's account of Hammett's buying an Alaskan bar during the Second World War runs like this: "He enjoyed the bars, even with the outrageously expensive liquor, and he took a special liking to a saloon called the Carolina Moon, which he bought. When the war was over and he had no further interest in owning an Anchorage nightspot, Hammett gave the Carolina Moon to the black lady who ran it for him" (p. 194). Nolan sees it like this: "Having been ejected from several bars, and 'fat with cash,' Hammett decided to purchase a drinking establishment in Anchorage. He proceeded to buy out the owners of the Carolina Moon, hiring a black woman to manage it for him. Another friend recalled: 'After the war, Dash just up and signed the bar over to her, as a gift, for running it'" (p. 191). It is interesting to notice that Layman has Hammett buying the bar because he liked it; Nolan has him buy it because he had been thrown out of several other bars and he needed a place to drink. Nolan further spices up his account with a quotation from an unnamed source. The "friend" may be Luther Norris, but Nolan's notes are vague, and it is difficult to tell. The quotation may, indeed, be one of Nolan's imaginative reconstructions.

Take, for example, the following passage, which is purportedly quoted from Hammett's series of vignettes called "From the Memoirs of a Private Detective":

"This business of a detective poring endlessly over clues to solve a crime is overdone," declared Hammett. "The [chief] difference between the [exceptionally] knotty problem confronting the detective of fiction and that facing the real detective is that in the former there is usually a paucity of clues [,] and in the latter altogether too many." [p. 46]

(The bracketed words and punctuation are corrections of misquotations.) If one turns to *The Smart Set Anthology* from which this passage is supposedly quoted, one finds that the first sentence that Nolan quotes is not there.[1] Now Hammett may actually have "declared" what Nolan says he "declared," but he certainly did not declare it *where* Nolan says he did. And so there is, reasonably, some question about the authenticity of this passage.

In another place, Nolan openly bowdlerizes and changes a supposedly quoted passage without alerting his reader. Here is the passage from Nolan:

"In those days," he [i.e., Hammett] wrote, "if you ran a joint in Chinatown you had a bodyguard whether you needed one or not, just to rate. There was this roly-poly Chinese muscleboy offered to me by a friend who owned a dive down there, to use if I had anybody I wanted pushed around—a leg broken or something—but I was not to spoil him by giving him money for this service. 'Five or ten bucks is okay for a tip,' I was told, 'but no more.' I didn't take advantage of the offer—but I *did* write the Chinese into a picture much later in Hollywood." [p. 60]

Here is the passage as it appears in Hammett's final story, "Tulip":

"That was back in the days when if you ran a joint you had a bodyguard whether you needed one or not, just to rate. Bill had a roly-poly middle-aged Chinese pansy whom he offered to lend me if I had anybody I wanted pushed around—like a leg broken or something—but told me not to spoil him by giving him any money. 'Five or ten dollars is all right as a tip,' he said, 'but don't spoil him by giving him any money.' I wrote the Chinese into a picture in the '30s in Hollywood, but we had a he-man director who wouldn't shoot fags, so we had to change him around."[2]

A brief comparison of the two passages should convince anyone of Nolan's extremely cavalier attitude toward quoting verbatim. Hammett's "middle-aged Chinese pansy" becomes Nolan's "Chinese muscleboy," and the whole passage is trimmed of any allusion to homosexuality. There are other changes, too, but one can only wonder for what reasons they were made. I could list a series of other quoted passages silently altered by Nolan, but I will assume that my point has been adequately made.[3] As far as quoted material is concerned, Nolan cannot be trusted.

Layman's biography is also not error-free. Discussing *The Thin Man*, he tells us that Maurice Duke is the author of *Celebrated Criminal Cases of America* (San Francisco: James H. Barry, 1910), obviously thinking of the eminent bibliographer and critic. However, the author is actually Thomas S. Duke, who in 1910 was Captain of Police in San Francisco. At one time Joe Gores and I were attempting to find out if Hammett may have known Duke—a definite possibility—but we reached no conclusion. Layman goes on to say that Nick Charles reads from Duke's book "the entire story" of Alfred Packer "aloud" to Gilbert Wynant (p. 145). Hammett, however, has Nick give Gilbert the book, and while he is silently reading, Nick gets himself a drink.[4] I would not like to generalize from these slips, but it does seem that Layman's work itself must be read with a bit of skepticism.

In discussing Hammett's manuscript fragment "The Secret Emperor," Layman dates Hammett's work on this unfinished piece in 1925 and claims that Hammett "abandoned the novel . . . at the time of Jose Hammett's second pregnancy" (p. 81). Layman does not explain either in the main text or the footnotes how he arrives at these dates. What is interesting about "The Secret Emperor" is that it shows us Hammett at work developing his story from notes, outlines, drafts—a complex procedure. One thing Hammett did was to use scrap paper in writing drafts, and so one page is written on the back of a letter to Phil Cody, editor of *Black Mask*, other pages on the back of a cancelled manuscript of Hammett's story "The Creeping Siamese." These pieces of scrap paper help us to establish an approximate terminal date, but they aren't extremely helpful. First, "The Creeping Siamese" was published in 1926, but Layman suggests that it was "written earlier in his career" (p. 69). Second, Hammett could use scrap paper at almost any date after he considered it scrap paper. He could use it the next day, or two years from that date. I am puzzled by Layman's confidence in dating this seminal piece of work, and I wish he had explained his method.

The literary criticism contained in both biographies is, of course, secondary to the story of Hammett's life, but much of value may be found in both studies. Layman concentrates on close, careful description that contains interpretive implications or comments; in contrast, Nolan concentrates on general interpretation with descriptive details added. As examples, let me quote two passages—one by Layman, the other by Nolan—on Hammett's *Red Harvest*, his first published novel. Layman is particular: "When the op leaves Personville, he leaves his job uncompleted. The gangsters are dead and their mobs are wiped out, but the source of corruption in Personville, weak and greedy Elihu Willsson, remains. Willsson goes unpunished, yet he still has the power of his money, and he still lacks the character required to use his power responsibly" (p. 94). Nolan, commenting on the same aspect of the novel, is much more general, and he tends to see the author mirrored in his creation:

> With a Hammett detective, it was always the job that mattered, the job assigned, the job that had to be done against lawbreakers—the small, near-futile, but necessary acts that shored up the crumbling banks of society against the tides of corruption. Hammett and his Op were fatalistic—they felt that things wouldn't really change (" . . . you'll have your city back, all nice and clean and ready to go to the dogs again")—but someone had to do something, and that was the Op's job. [p. 77]

I think the different qualities of the two critics may be clearly seen in these two brief passages. Layman is much more likely to stick to the facts as he sees them; Nolan has a penchant for taking the broader view.

In discussing *Red Harvest*, Nolan comments that the Op, though "he drinks with the town's brassy playgirl, Dinah Brand," does "not make love to her" (p. 76). On the surface this does seem to be the case, but a close and imaginative reading of one passage in the novel seems to indicate that Nolan is wrong. The Op and Dinah are in the woods, hiding from pursuers, lying under a blanket. Dinah says, "There's a mouse or something crawling under the blanket." The Op replies, "Probably only a snake." The moderately sensual reader, I believe, will find phallic implications in the Op's snake, and if the Op and Dinah are preparing to make love, Dinah's next question, which otherwise is a non sequitur, makes sense. "Are you married?"[5] Since Hammett had to be careful about including sexual encounters in his early novels, I think this exchange was as close as he could get to implying what the couple is doing out in the woods under a banket. And this passage, if I read it correctly, surely calls into question Layman's very large and uncharacteristic generalization: "Healthy sexuality is absent from Hammett's work until *The Thin Man* . . . and then it is presented flippantly. More often, sexuality in Hammett's work is distorted or perverted and represents the extent to which a character has departed from a romantic ideal of man's capacity for uncorrupted love" (pp. 86-87). Hammett's suggestion that the Op tumbles Dinah in the woods may be flippant, but it's surely healthy enough, and I for one can find no moral implications in the passage. In fact, Dinah, with all her faults, is presented quite sympathetically.

Layman's worst piece of criticism, however, is of *The Thin Man*. He cannot understand why Hammett includes the story of Packer—the "Maneater"—from Duke's *Celebrated Criminal Cases*. (We earlier looked at Layman's factual slips in this passage.) Moreover, he agrees with Hellman that this story of Packer's cannibalism was inserted in the novel as filler (p. 145). Layman fails to recognize that this story is a metaphor for the social cannibalism—both financial and emotional—that permeates the novel. The characters feed on each other in various metaphoric ways. Nick has married Nora for her money; Nora has married Nick for the vicarious thrill she gets from being married to an ex-detective. The novel centers on the missing Wynant, the man who is so thoroughly devoured that he disappears. Wynant has been almost everyone's bank-roll, and, in the novel, Macaulay consumes him entirely, assuming his identity and taking custody of his wealth. Wynant has effectively been cannibalized. It is strange that Layman misses this aspect of the novel, for he goes on to quote one of the more blatant examples. Alice Quinn bitterly confesses to Nick that she stays with her openly lecherous husband "for his money."[6]

Layman's failure to see the significance of the Packer story, however, serves only to highlight a larger failure, a failure shared by both biographers. They miss the fact that each of Hammett's novels contains passages similar to the Packer story. Steven Marcus noted this fact prominently in 1974. Discussing the Flitcraft parable from *The Maltese Falcon*, he observed that "comparable passages occur in all of Hammett's best work."[7] One is reminded of C. S. Lewis's discovery that each book of Spenser's *Faerie Queene* has an "allegorical core." Hammett's novels have similar core stories that point to leading motifs and ideas. Layman describes in detail the two dreams that make up this core in *Red Harvest* (p. 95), but he fails to interpret them, or to see their larger significance. For *The Maltese Falcon* (p. 112) and *The Glass Key* (pp. 120-21), we must give him high marks for identifying and carefully explaining the core stories. Nolan's interpretation of the Flitcraft story, for example, is weak beside

Layman's. For Layman, the parable is about human flexibility
and adjustment, and is a clue to Spade's character. Nolan sees it
as a simple warning: "Spade is telling Brigid . . . that life is a
series of falling beams . . . . He is telling her, in effect, not to
be surprised when one hits her—as it finally does" (p. 92).
Unfortunately, neither biographer notes that these parables are
an important and recurring element in Hammett's novels.

Another fault I find with the critical commentary of both
biographers is that they underestimate the romantic element in
Hammett's work. They are both very close to understanding and
explaining that this is an abiding part of his vision, but they are
both so preoccupied with demonstrating that Hammett is the
first great hard-boiled writer that they miss the parts of his work
which are sentimentally romantic.[8] This sentimental
romanticism is especially evident in the earlier work; the ending
of "The Girl with the Silver Eyes"—an early novella from
1924—provides a good example of the quality I am referring to.
The Continental Op has just captured the very dangerous
Jeanne Delano, and she is trying to seduce him in order to
escape:

> Her lids had come down half over the silver-gray eyes, her head had tilted
> back so far that a little pulse showed throbbing in her white throat; her lips
> were motionless over slightly parted teeth, as the last word left them. My
> fingers went deep into the soft white flesh of her shoulders. Her head went
> further back, her eyes closed, one hand came up to my shoulder.
>
> "You're beautiful as all hell!" I shouted crazily into her face, and flung her
> against the door.

The Op then thinks of Porky Grout, who had been killed trying
to keep Jeanne from being captured: "Porky Grout, whose
yellowness was notorious from Seattle to San Diego, standing
rigidly in the path of a charging metal monster, with an
inadequate pistol in each hand. She had done that to Porky
Grout—this woman beside me! . . . and he hadn't even been
human! A slimy reptile whose highest thought had been a
skinful of dope had gone grimly to death that she might get
away—she—this woman whose shoulders I had gripped, whose
mouth had been close under mine!"[9] Wow! Certainly not even
Nolan would argue that these passages were written in the

"argot of the streets." Hammett's "metal monster" is, of course, an automobile. Although we may catch glimpses of the hard-boiled here, the excessiveness veers toward sentimentality, and what Hammett writes is really hard-boiled romance. Throughout his writing career, realism and romance were always in tension. By the end of his career as novelist, he had these aspects of his work under control, and in *The Thin Man* he carefully balances the realistic Nick with the romantic Nora. In my judgment, that balance is nearly perfect.

Perhaps one penultimate, minor point will be allowed. Neither author remarks that the novel *The Grand Manner*, mentioned twice in *The Thin Man*, was written by Louis Kronenberger—a friend of Hammett's.[10] The reference may seem gratuitous, and some years ago I asked Kronenberger why Hammett had included it. Kronenberger confessed that he didn't know, but he thought, possibly, that Hammett was merely tipping his hat to a friend. I think, however, there's a more interesting possibility. A reader who had carefully read both novels would see a similarity: *The Grand Manner* is an objective vision of human selfishness; *The Thin Man*, a subjective vision of the same phenomenon. Hammett read everything. At his best, he expected the same high standard from his reader. I imagine that he wished us to understand the connection between his own novel and Kronenberger's.

I greatly enjoyed both biographies. Reading Nolan's book, I became thoroughly engrossed in his vision of Hammett's hard-boiled heroism. I was convinced. Turning to Layman, I was just as convinced that Hammett had greatly exaggerated his adventures as the Pinkerton Op, that it was high time for the revisionist scholar to set the record straight, to present a more accurate and balanced vision of Hammett and his works. Now that I have had time to reflect, I realize that both books are flawed, but that my present view of Hammett owes something to each. The reader who wishes to know as much as he can about Dashiell Hammett will neglect neither.

Notes

1. *The Smart Set Anthology*, ed. Burton Rascoe and Groff Conklin (New York: Reynal and Hitchcock, 1934), p. 89. Nolan (p. 243) gives the wrong page number.

2. *The Big Knockover: Selected Stories and Short Novels of Dashiell Hammett* (New York: Random House, [1966]), p. 252. The title page claims that the volume was edited by Hellman. She did contribute a brief introduction.

3. The curious reader may wish to compare the passages supposedly quoted from Frank Gruber in Nolan (p. 44) with the passages in Gruber's *The Pulp Jungle* (Los Angeles: Sherbourne Press, 1967), pp. 110 and 141. Caution: your mind may boggle.

4. Dashiell Hammett, *The Thin Man* (New York: Vintage, 1972), p. 67: "While Gilbert was reading this, I got myself a drink."

5. Dashiell Hammett, *Red Harvest* (New York: Vintage, 1972), p. 130.

6. Robert I. Edenbaum, "The Poetics of the Private-Eye: The Novels of Dashiell Hammett," *Tough Guy Writers of the Thirties*, ed. David Madden (Carbondale and Edwardsville: Southern Illinois Univ. Press, 1968), p. 102, succinctly makes the point about cannibalism in the novel.

7. Steven Marcus, ed., *The Continental Op* (New York: Random House, 1974), p. xviii.

8. See, e.g., Layman, p. 45, Nolan, p. 39. Both discuss Hammett's "hard realism" (the term is Layman's) in contrast to the work of Carroll John Daly.

9. Marcus, ed., *The Continental Op*, p. 158.

10. *The Thin Man*, pp. 155, 158.

Which Life of Robert Graves?

James McKinley

Martin Seymour-Smith. *Robert Graves: His Life and Work.* New York: Holt, Rinehart and Winston, 1983. xvi, 609 pp.

The major problem facing a biographer, assuming his subject has had a tolerably interesting passage, is deciding *which* life to write, what emphasis to place where. If the subject is someone like Robert Graves, who has lived a long life, gone through sea changes of geography and psychology, and in mid-life added to his personal complexity an equally complex fiction-for-living-and-making-fiction, then that decision is past crucial and hurtling toward destinal.

Unfortunately Martin Seymour-Smith, in his pioneer biography of Graves, seems not to have decided firmly enough which life of Robert Graves was the dominant, or what made that life the one that, when understood, best explained Graves and his work. Too, Seymour-Smith's choice of narrative mode and structure—he describes and summarizes more than analyzes, and he arranges facts peculiarly—adds to a sense of diffusion that mars this otherwise worthy biography.

Let me address these points in reverse order (actually in arbitrary order since what is conveyed is part of how it's conveyed). Take the narrative device called structure. This book is inevitably arranged in chronological order, yet often the chronology is disrupted by *topics*. A minor but illustrative example can be found in the thirteen pages of Chapter 26, Part II, when the reader is carried chronologically through Graves's work-in-hand and from Galmpton, England (where Graves was waiting out World War II), to Deya, Mallorca (Graves's pre-war home when he was living with the American poet Laura Riding; in 1946 he is living with Beryl Pritchard, the former wife of his friend, Alan Hodge). But the reader is also ferried from 1947 to 1948 to 1950 to 1971 by topics ranging from Graves's "intensely romantic and idealistic desire-nature" (I confess I don't know what that means) to the contributions of Graves's secretary over "eighteen years" (more of that later). Here and elsewhere a reader can lose his way and turn to muttering, "What is important now, the time or the state of the man's mind or domestic arrangements?" This organization, used throughout by Seymour-Smith, is a little like ordering a platoon to line up in order of birth by height. You get confusion, and in literary terms, patches of obfuscation.

Another more seriously disconcerting narrative tic is exemplified by this paragraph from page 530, near the end of the book:

> But his [Graves's] main work became, at last, what he always wished it to be: poetry. In 1965 he published his penultimate *Collected Poems*; between that and the final *Collected Poems* (published in America in 1977 with a surprisingly inappropriate introduction by a nonentity) he put out no fewer than ten collections of new poems (not including two more books of children's poems, and a large, useful anthology culled from his own work called *Poems About Love*, 1969). He was more (and too) prolific in the ten years separating his last two collections than he had ever been before. The poetry of these years was—with occasional exceptions—markedly inferior to what he wrote in the years 1929-1950.

What is wrong here? Well, the first sentence flatly disagrees with much of the preceding book, and with what Graves, in fact, always—from age 14, at least—believed and acted on, that his main work was poetry. What Seymour-Smith means is that "at last" enough money was coming in so that Graves didn't have to write pot-boiling prose anymore. Look next at the dissonance created by the summary nature of the first two sentences and the two concluding sentences where we are told that Graves wrote too much of his "main work" in the last fifteen years of his creative life, and that it wasn't as good as the poetry of 1929-1950. Clearly Graves wrote considerable quantities of his main work during these years. Clearly Seymour-Smith doesn't like it. Less clearly, we do not learn here or in the remaining thirty-eight pages of the book *why* Seymour-Smith dislikes these poems (only two are quoted), or what happened to Graves that he should begin to write inferior poetry (a judgment many critics dispute). This tendency to summarize damages the biography, since it slights important works. Seymour-Smith gives two paragraphs to *A Survey of Modernist Poetry*, a seminal study of textual criticism written in 1927 by Graves and Laura Riding. Graves's massive and psychologically revealing masterwork, *The White Goddess*, gets five analytical pages. "The Shout," an extremely important early short story, receives four descriptive paragraphs, even though several Graves scholars think it contains the essence of his mature aesthetic. And the novel *Watch the North Wind Rise* (titled *Seven Days in New Crete* in England), which I regard as revealing key elements of his aesthetic and psychological system, is ignored.

Similarly, Seymour-Smith's inclination to be snide (I am the nonentity who wrote the surprisingly inappropriate introduction to Graves's *Collected Poems*) sometimes injures the sense of this book. In places the penchant for dismissing or denigrating certain people in Graves's story actually warps the account, rendering some surprisingly inappropriate judgements. One important example lies in the appraisal of Graves's first wife, Nancy Nicholson, whom he calls, variously, "uninteresting," "shallow," "obstinate," "difficult," and "a termagant." Seymour-Smith castigates Nancy, who died in 1977, partly it seems to support his notion that the young Graves was dominated by his mother and Nancy to the point where he wrote poetry to relieve a neurotic association of sex and death (i.e., to alleviate the commonplace recognition that sex with a woman, resulting in procreation, was guilty because the new life was born to die), and also to establish Graves as miserable early, thus explaining his vulnerability to Laura Riding when she showed up in England in 1926 and his readiness in 1939 to fall "for the first time" in love with the present Mrs. Graves, Beryl Pritchard Hodge Graves. This is personality in the service of biographical theory, and certainly that is acceptable even if one might argue that Graves's misery was less severe than Seymour-Smith would have it, and that any red-blooded man, miserable or not, would have been vulnerable to the vampirish Laura Riding in 1926. More to the point, these assessments of Nancy are at odds with what many of her letters disclose, and with what Graves, his children by Nancy, her family, and numerous mutual friends testify.

Nor is Nancy the only important person whose character and contributions to Graves's life have been somewhat twisted. Karl Goldschmidt, the German-born secretary to Riding and Graves, then just to Graves (he took the name Karl Gay during World War II when he served with the British forces) gets two paragraphs of compliments for his twenty-four odd years of faithful work. But Seymour-Smith glosses over Goldschmidt's substantial editorial contributions to Graves's *ouevre,* managing to make it sound as though Karl was on the fringe of Graves's life, typing away somewhere. In fact, Karl was professionally and personally a member of the family until Graves, partly inspired by one of his less-admirable incarnate Goddesses of the 1960's, sacked him.

Others who suffer Seymour-Smith's disdain are: Alastair Reid, the poet and essayist who destroyed a deep friendship with Graves by running off briefly with another of Graves's incarnate Goddesses; T. S. ("Tom") Matthews, an intimate of the Graves-Riding circle, and later a frequent visitor to Graves, whose account of his impressions of Graves and Riding is dismissed by Seymour-Smith as falsehood (not least because Seymour-Smith alleges that it inaccurately portrayed him);[1] Ruthven Todd, the poet and novelist who was a sometime confidant of Graves on Mallorca and who is not mentioned in this book; Isla Cameron, an actress and folksinger who is alluded to once but never identified as a onetime *intime* of Graves, one who was nearly dubbed a Goddess and who was critical of Graves's behavior toward his wife in the Goddess-plagued 1960's; and Schuyler Jackson, who won Laura Riding in 1939, and is contrary to what others say described here as of "minuscule" intelligence, questionable talent, and dubious honesty. Several others— eccentric and normal, dervish-like and distinguished—have been omitted or distorted, so that part of the texture of Graves's variegated life has been excised. Even the editor and writer Alan Hodge, while getting warm praise as a close friend of Seymour-Smith's and as Graves's able collaborator and steady friend, is wrongly depicted as not much minding that his wife Beryl went off with Graves in 1939.

Granted, no biographer can or should mention every person with whom his subject has contact (and it's sure that many sources about Graves requested anonymity). Yet I find it interesting that Seymour-Smith's roster of undesirables conforms closely to Beryl Graves's. I base that judgement on my many conversations with Mrs. Graves (incidentally, some concerned Martin Seymour-Smith's tenure as tutor to two of Robert and Beryl's children in the early 1950's; he left on shaky terms with Graves, a fact discreetly elided from the book). This raises the question of Beryl Graves's influence upon this biography.

In his introduction Seymour-Smith first thanks Robert Graves for all his help during the biography's writing, meaning about the last six years. To my certain knowledge, and despite the fiction advanced by Seymour-Smith, Graves has been unable to help with any kind of writing for almost all of that time. We can therefore presume that most of the help came from Beryl. Indeed, Seymour-Smith next writes: "I am equally grateful to Beryl Graves for her cooperation in all the foregoing; and for her unfailing hospitality while I was working at Deya; for her kindness and patience and sense of humour. She went over every word of the final draft of this book with me, and over the proofs, and made many invaluable suggestions—but resolutely refused to try to influence me in any of my interpretations. She only corrected errors of fact." I too can and sincerely do affirm Mrs. Graves's intelligence, kindness, generosity and sense of humor, and I attest to her willingness to aid acceptable students of Graves's work. But I must also say that her love for Robert Graves understandably colors her interpretation of his life and work in the sense of emphasizing her share of that life and work. Some of that attitude, it seems to me, has seeped into Seymour-Smith as "influence," despite his manly attempts to resist it.

This attitude is, I believe, most noticeable in one of the book's fundamental structures (here we move from questions of narrative mode to those of emphasis, of which Robert Graves we are given and in what measures). Put in the baldest terms, this book divides in two. Part I might be called Robert Graves's Trial Through a Miserable Youth, "Ill-Considered" Marriage, and

Masochistic Affair with Laura Riding. This goes from Robert's birth in 1895 to 1939, and comprises about sixty percent of this biography. Part II, the remaining forty percent, might be called Robert Graves's Resuscitation Through Beryl and His Greatest Happiness and Achievement. This period extends from 1939 until 1975, when Graves stopped writing. Seymour-Smith is at pains to introduce the Beryl Period with a flourish. He writes near its beginning that the then Beryl Hodge "had as strong and unusual a character as any of the members of the party" (i.e. of Graves, Riding, Alan Hodge, and Beryl who were moving in 1939 from England to Brittany). He lauds her, oddly, as "too naturally humane to attach herself to any specific doctrine" (meaning, one supposes, that she was not idea-ridden like the rest of them) and as one "as remarkable—though in no way as spectacular" as Laura Riding. He also writes (in what to me is an astonishing assertion about a time when Graves was still in emotional bondage to Laura), "For he dared not acknowledge to himself that he had fallen in love, for the first (and only) time in his life with a person [Beryl]—rather than with someone who represented something needed, such as a wife, or a Muse." We can ignore the dues-paying character of the first assertions to marvel at the cleverness of this last one. It of course assumes that someone—Seymour-Smith or perhaps Beryl—knew what acknowledging Graves was doing even if he didn't. It also obliquely disposes of Nancy as just a wife (shrewish at that) and of Laura (the idea-bound Muse), at the same time finessing the question of just what this new loved person would be if not a wife or Muse.

In fact Beryl has been both, as Seymour-Smith later is glad to point out, except when he is stating—against much observation and textual evidence—that Beryl is not the familiar Gravesian "Vesta" figure, that aspect of woman "good as bread" who stands in solid, domestic opposition to the cruel, capricious Laura-like Goddess. Altogether, then, I think the Beryl Period is marked by Seymour-Smith's too frequent bowing to her exemplary character and by overstatements of her profound effect upon Graves. (She, it's said, made him a more careful prose writer—a function, as I noted before, that certainly was often filled by Karl Goldschmidt at those times when as practiced a prose stylist as Graves, who wrote *Goodbye to All That* in 1929, needed help.)

Nevertheless, Seymour-Smith is right that Graves's post-Laura life was happier and remarkably productive. And that Beryl unquestionably helped make it so, even though I believe it was Graves's unflagging drive to work and work well that was the main engine of the time. That, and the whole synthetic understanding of the poet's task in the world that came with *The White Goddess*. Seymour-Smith gives his customary good glosses of several notable novels of this time (*Wife to Mr. Milton, The Golden Fleece, King Jesus*) and of the poetry which he admires (except, as we're seen, of the last years of Graves's writing career). He is particularly good on the mythological works like *The Greek Myths* and *The Nazarene Gospel Restored*, and in charting Graves's obsession in the 1950's and 1960's with movie and stage successes. For me, this whole period is better handled than the first part of the life, perhaps because Seymour-Smith was himself part of it. For this period, as for the entire book, he also had excellent research sources. The files in Graves's Deya home, Canellun, were open to him as were Graves's diaries, correspondence, and notes. Seymour-Smith also conducted numerous valuable interviews with people he had known with and through Graves over the nearly forty years since Seymour-Smith sent schoolboy verse to Graves for criticism. And he has conscientiously read Graves. Thus, even if his Beryl Period emphasis is arguable—several Graves scholars, including me, would hold that Graves's pre-1939 work is his most important, while simultaneously arguing that the love poetry of his last years is powerful—it is true that Seymour-Smith forthrightly, skillfully, and confidently advances his beliefs.

Yet, that said, I must again say that these beliefs do not in my view constitute a completely satisfactory system for understanding Graves's life and work. For that reason this substantial and often incisive biography falls somewhat short of effectively picturing who and what Graves has been. Some of Seymour-Smith's descriptions through biography-time will, I hope, make this point.

Early in the book Graves is described as having tremendous "emotional pressure" on him, brought on by the probity of his German mother, Amalia von Ranke Graves. This pressure, in tension with his Irish sense of "beauty" (from his father, Alfred Perceval Graves) and "purity" created a "terror" that destined him to be a poet. How? Well, in his seeking to reconcile a desire to be pure and beautiful, like a poem, with his normal human sexuality made guilty by his mother's preachments on religion and morality. This neat duality is not the last.

Next comes the thesis, reprised in the Beryl Period, that Graves abnormally feared a latent homosexuality and to combat it (he had experienced a "chaste" love at Charterhouse, his preparatory school) married the nagging feminist Nancy Nicholson. (But later it's said that the "aggressive" heterosexuality of *The White Goddess* is a related reaction against the buried homosexual desire.) The overt reason, when Graves is twenty-one, is that "he did not know the difference between lust and love or between friendship and love." Remember, this is Graves after four years of The Great War, and at least some second-hand experience of the difference. Still, Seymour-Smith's analysis can be defended—and is at least partly systematic, in that throughout Seymour-Smith has Graves either not knowing what his motives are or innocently watching while some submerged neurosis surfaces. We recall Robert not quite knowing he loved Beryl, and, as the book has it, being more worried in those crucial days of 1939 about Beryl's two pet cats than about the impending end of his time with Laura Riding.

A prime example of the "unknown motive thesis" comes in an account of the early life, when Seymour-Smith contends that Graves's well-known and severe post-war neurasthenia was not caused by the war. Rather, Graves's deep pathology was "relentlessly" uncovered by the war, in turn causing the poems of the 1920's. I respectfully disagree—the war certainly caused Graves's nightmares and fears, and many of Graves's poems of the time came out of those fears. Even accepting Seymour-Smith's premise the careful reader is bound to ask: what, precisely, was this nearly innate pathology, and why isn't it

operative later in Graves's life? When we get to a later Graves, of
the Riding-ridden 1930's, we are given another explanation for
Robert's creating—namely, his resentment of Laura Riding's
bad treatment of him and her sexual withdrawal from him.
(Again I must differ, for it seems clear that it was his worship of
Riding as muse, mentor and lover that produced central poems
like "On Portents.") Then when it is time in the mid-1940's for
The White Goddess—after Laura has deserted him for the
American (a term of opprobrium for Seymour-Smith) Schuyler
Jackson and he has discovered his overwhelming heterosexual
love for Beryl—we are told that his mind flashes back to his
chaste but abhorrent schoolboy love, resulting in the vow
"Always women in the future no matter what."

This conveniently explains away Graves's coming
sexagenarian infatuations with young "Goddess" women while
allowing Seymour-Smith to postulate a psychological,
mythological, poetic difference in Graves's affections between
"the one true love" Beryl and the other women whom he has
publicly and privately said he loved. We may ask, in fact,
whether Robert Graves at the time of *The White Goddess*—age
fifty, thrice married-in-fact, the father of seven, a war-veteran
and author of over fifty books—really was still haunted by a
Charterhouse love-that-was-not. Or whether, as I believe, he
became intellectually and emotionally obsessed with
transcultural associations (see *King Jesus, The Golden Fleece,*
etc.) that culminated in the great synthetic fiction-for-
fictionmaking that is *The White Goddess*. We may even
speculate that Seymour-Smith is, in another premise, to the side
of accuracy when he asserts—putting aside The Great War
(1914-1918), Nancy Nicholson (1918-1929), Laura Riding (1926-
1939), *The White Goddess* (adumbrated as early as 1936), the
incarnate Goddesses (scattered infrequently through 1950-1969),
and "The Black Goddess" (1965)—that "Graves's love poems to
Beryl are his most powerful."

Still, it is here that Seymour-Smith comes close to resolving
Graves. He posits a Graves whose true work comes from an
attachment to the concrete, whether Beryl or a historical-mythic
problem, and what could be called an anti-Graves whose less-

true work comes from obeisance to abstract qualities, like Laura Riding's dicta about poetry and history, or the "Goddesses," whom Seymour-Smith says represent ideas, not emotions or desires or mythology-come-alive. This is fair enough, and adequately documented, but in my opinion falls short of a comprehensive view of Graves—meaning, again, that *life* of Graves which best explains him.

What is that life? It manifests itself, as Seymour-Smith often suggests, in duality. This biography has Graves at many odds, like "generous" and "petty," "ever-fearful" and "courageous," "necessarily dramatic," and "refused to display his real feelings," etc. But it lies more, I think, in a genuine personality division than in opposing aspects of the same personality (see Graves's musings on this problem in *The Meaning of Dreams* [1924] and *Poetic Unreason and Other Studies* [1925]). Graves is to me a man who could and did operate on two entirely different levels—like artistic, intellectual, emotional—and maintain total separation between them, as if living with two different sets of neurons. The lines were down, the connections severed between one Graves and the other, between Romantic and Rationalist, between Muse-blasted mystic and ambitious author, between a man outside of Time, in poetry's trance-like Eternal Now, and a man caught in the web of personal and planetary history. Certainly, as Seymour-Smith acknowledges, the two warred. Certainly the poetry on the one side and the prose on the other are like the remains on the battlefield.

But equally certainly one side had to win. The victor was the mystical, I think, the out-of-time. Its slow, gradual victory is the life of Robert Graves. Its arc in his arc, moving through cycles of death and rebirth, from his grievous wounding in World War I through myriad affairs of art and several of the heart to a final rest in the certainty of his aesthetic construct, that Idea he called the White Goddess. If this war, this arc, produced pettinesses, vast generosities, callous acts, loves with and without reason and season, all the contradictions of Robert Graves's life, then all too obviously it is the measure of the man. Seymour-Smith's assessment is then not wrong; its emphasis is merely misplaced, the balance-beam askew.

For all that, Seymour-Smith's book is a mighty stride toward understanding Graves. The writing is lively and literate, the interpretations mostly defensible, the documentation as solid as any research can make it. I have quibbled with several major points and could go on to do so with several minor ones, as when Seymour-Smith slights poems like "To Juan at the Winter Solstice" and several good poems of the 1960's, or when he states that only Beryl received the loving transmission of "telepathic communication" (I'll bet Laura Riding did, too). But on the whole I earnestly thank Seymour-Smith for this book, and for his devotion to a man we agree is the best love poet of our century. We are fortunate that in 1943 the young Seymour-Smith wrote to the accomplished poet, and that Graves graciously responded. The favor is repaid.

Note

1. *Jacks or Better* (New York: Harper and Row, 1977). Seymour-Smith dismisses Matthews for inaccuracy, yet *Robert Graves: His Life and Work* also contains several howlers, as when Seymour-Smith writes, "Like every poet in the romantic tradition Graves felt guilty because he wrote poetry" (p. 114).

The Poet as Fascist: Pound's Politics and His Critics

Robert Casillo

Massimo Bacigalupo. *The Formed Trace: The Later Poetry of Ezra Pound.* New York: Columbia University Press, 1980. xviii, 512 pp.

Alan Durant. *Ezra Pound, Identity in Crisis: A Fundamental Reassessment of the Poet and His Work.* Brighton: Harvester Press, 1981. x, 206 pp.

Wendy Flory. *Ezra Pound and The Cantos: A Record of Struggle.* New Haven: Yale University Press, 1980. xv, 321 pp.

Forrest Read. *'76: One World and The Cantos of Ezra Pound.* Chapel Hill: University of North Carolina Press, 1981. xii, 476 pp.

In the late 1940s Ezra Pound's reputation suffered considerable damage as a result of his Fascism and anti-Semitism. It reached its nadir after he was charged with treason in 1945 and escaped trial only through his confinement for insanity. Nonetheless, in 1949 Pound received the Bollingen Poetry Award for the Pisan *Cantos*. Although many liberal critics had argued that Pound's poem was vitiated or compromised by its inhumane attitudes, the event marked the beginning of Pound's rehabilitation. Pound's apologists followed New Critical assumptions: political opinions are irrelevant to a poem, while a poem's ideas lose their noxious character once transformed by sensibility within the autonomous context of a work of art. Poetry and politics thus remain separate.[1] Over succeeding decades, however, it became evident that neither Pound nor *The Cantos* could be understood fully through exclusively New Critical

methods. Critics and scholars now treat *The Cantos* as a
personal document and a didactic exploration of numerous
extrapoetic contexts: history, economics, culture, society,
religion. For many critics Pound has proven himself a
transhistorical prophet, an apostle of permanent values
necessary to the survival of modern society. No Fascist and anti-
Semite, he is the enemy of the "capitalist-imperialist state."[2]

Even those critics who acknowledge Pound's Fascism and
anti-Semitism generally consider them incidental rather than
central to the main operations of his language. They figure as
mere "error[s]," "embarrassments," and "aberrations" of
Pound's writing and career.[3] But given the fact that Pound is
best known to the public as a Fascist sympathizer and that he is
also the most notorious of modern literary anti-Semites, one
would at least expect scholarship and criticism to have seriously
addressed these issues in an attempt to set the record straight.
The opposite has happened. We have no full-scale study of
Pound's Fascism or of the relation of anti-Semitism to his poetry
and psychology.[4]

The four books examined here devote considerable attention
to Pound's politics and may therefore serve to measure
contemporary understanding of the subject. In *Ezra Pound and
The Cantos: A Record of Struggle*, Wendy Flory offers a new
version of an old argument. In 1949 some critics dissociated
Pound's poetry from his ideas to insulate his language from
crudely discursive "contaminations." By contrast, Flory has no
difficulty in discussing most of Pound's ideas. However,
Pound's Fascism, anti-Semitism, and totalitarianism are special
cases, requiring the erection of artificial barriers around his
poetry and the poet himself. Flory sees two Pounds. One is the
good, Taoist, and "essential" (p. 78) Pound, who is emotional
and intuitional, and who instinctively inclines towards
"humanitarianism" (p. 5) if he keeps in touch with his "true"
(p. 4) feelings. When Pound writes great poetry, he expresses his
deepest, truest emotions. The other is the inessential or bad
Pound, who, impatient and fearful of introspection, and thus
"losing touch" with his "emotions" (p. 5), gets lost in theory
and propaganda, opinions, abstract formulas, and dogmas, and

"make[s] choices on a theoretical rather than on an emotional basis" (p. 56). Nor is Flory disturbed that Pound's radio broadcasts, presumably a flagrant example of his theoretical abstraction, compel his "anger," "hatred" (p. 5), and outrage. Having it both ways, Flory says that Pound either lost control of his emotions or else misplaced his benevolent ones. Thus separating Pound's "poetic self" and his "propagandizing self" (p. 5), Flory can dismiss as insincere his intolerance, Fascist authoritarianism, or anti-Semitism.

Flory's distinctions are vague, arbitrary, and psychologically dubious. *The Cantos*, besides being lyrical and thus emotional, are didactic, and Pound's didactic purpose informs many important lyrical passages. Meantime, even Flory recognizes that the broadcasts contain emotional content. The ideology of the broadcasts, a demotic version of *The Cantos*, intersects with and illuminates the poem's themes. Again, instead of being purely theoretical, the broadcasts are perhaps the most psychologically revealing of Pound's works, a "repellent analytical session," as Massimo Bacigalupo calls them (p. 102). Although Flory traces Pound's errors to lack of introspection, she curiously believes that his verse, with its voices, masks, and imagistic surfaces, manifests emotional truth. If anything, the broadcasts contain self-revelations which Pound rarely permits to enter the guarded terrain of *The Cantos*.

Flory further believes that Pound's worst excesses result from his prolonged yet "unconvincing" (p. 32) imitation of Wyndham Lewis. Thanks to Lewis, Pound acquires the dangerous "habits" of indulging in "invective" and "overstatement," of suppressing emotion, and of affecting a callous "pose" (pp. 86, 82, 69). The reprehensible Mr. Lewis encourages Pound's dislike of introspection, thus diverting Pound from his true self; fills Pound with loathing of the masses, whom he really adores; and inspires Pound's "pose" of anti-feminism (pp. 68-75, 83). This is a preposterous attempt to make Lewis into a scrapegoat for Pound, and Pound into Lewis's zombie. Pound's distaste for introspection precedes their acquaintance and persists after they part. One finds it in Pound's fascination with masks and imagistic objectivity, arrived at independently of Lewis,[5] as in his later attacks on psychoanalysis and introspective Taoists. There is no evidence in these instances that Pound is following a mentor, but even had he done so, would this not have shown an affinity? Pound's contempt for the mob appears as early as *Patria Mia*, and it is one source of common attraction among Pound, Lewis, Eliot, and Hulme.[6] If anything this contempt intensifies over Pound's career: Pound "sincerely" believed that the "goyim are cattle" (Canto 74, 439).[7] As for Pound's attitudes towards women, Flory acknowledges the anti-feminist passage in which Pound refers to woman as "A chaos, / An octopus / A biological process" (Canto 29, 144). But for Flory this reflects only the borrowed "rhetoric" of Lewis, who believed that women were "lower forms of life," a "jellyish diffuseness" that "spreads itself . . . [over] everything." By contrast, Pound sanctifies women and celebrates ritualized sexuality ("inluminatio coitu") in Cantos 39 and 47 (pp. 139, 72).

Flory ignores Pound's phallocentric and patriarchal mythology. For Pound the sun is phallic, a divine symbol of masculine authority and origination, fecundating, shaping, marking, and differentiating feminine Nature. Likewise the ideal artist must imitate the sun and "charge" and shape the "passive . . . female chaos" (PD, 204) of mere matter (the Hyle of Canto 30), while in ritual woman has the inferior "role that holy nature had given her" (SP, 55).[8] The profoundest horror of the Hell *Cantos* is not usury per se but the fact that Hell is a swamp or "bog" (Canto 14, 63), a place of parthenogenetic (feminine) and hence undifferentiated generation ("scission"), like usury; repeatedly Pound invokes the phallus of order against all forms of swamplike confusion. As for Pound's ritualistic celebration of feminine sexuality, this in no way negates his view of the feminine as adventitious, inferior, secondary. Pound "worships" the feminine only when, as in Canto 39, the feminine swamp is brought under an agrarian, patriarchal, and hence masculine order. Odysseus' mythical encounter with Circe in Cantos 39 and 47 parallels the more historically truthful Canto 41, in which Mussolini (the "bullock") drains swamps near Circeo for agriculture, and

Canto 40, in which Hanno conquers the African "bayou" and kills and flays three native women. In spite of their overlay of myth, which contrary to Flory is far more "evasive" than "exploratory" (p. 14), Pound's attitudes towards sexuality resemble those of the most honest Lewis. They also resemble those of Fascism, which ridicules the pliable and "feminine" masses.[9]

According to Flory, Pound's emotional "stability" kept him from "the excesses which . . . invalidate much" (p. 78) of the later Lewis. Actually, Pound was just as "abrasive" (p. 59) as Lewis during the *Blast* period, and Lewis sometimes thought that Pound had gone too far.[10] Pound also admitted his attraction to "violence" (L, 182-83).[11] Nor does Flory mention that the later and "extreme" (p. 32) Lewis, whom she blames for Pound's Fascism, became somewhat disenchanted with Hitler in the late thirties. Pound made his broadcasts in the forties, broadcasts whose violence surpasses anything in Lewis. If Pound was so completely bound to his model, one wonders whom he was imitating in the radio broadcasts.

With these dubious assumptions, Flory can easily disentangle Pound from Fascism. His Fascism exists in a realm of circumstance, delusion, or "evasion" (p. 180). Not only are Pound's excesses attributable to the "events of his time" (p. 5) (rather than to just Lewis), but Pound misunderstands Mussolini's and Hitler's aims and convinces himself that they are mainly "monetary reformers" (p. 180), usury-slayers. In truth, Pound understands the broad scope of Fascist values and celebrates them in the broadcasts and *The Cantos*: authoritarian hierarchy and "functional" corporatism, ritualistic mobilization of the masses, subordination of the feminine to the masculine, contempt for the "feminine" herd, solar worship and pagan Christianity, antimonotheism, and a hatred of transcendental modes of thought. One should add biological racism and eugenics, two major examples of that naturalism which Pound shares with Fascism.[12] As for Pound's Confucianism, although Flory repeats the myth that *L'Asse che non Vacilla* (Pound's translation of Confucius' *Unwobbling Pivot*) was confiscated because of the "suspicious" (p. 25) but innocent "axis" of the title, Pound often identifies Fascistic and Confucian order, and the play on the Rome-Berlin Axis is no doubt intentional. Like Fascism, the Confucian China of Pound's *Cantos* is a "corporate," "functional," ritualistic, and hierarchical society in which women are subordinate to men and men are, like the fasces, "rods in a bundle."[13]

Pound's anti-Semitism similarly dwindles into an embarrassing aberration, without connection to Pound's thought or psychology. At worst Pound is only an economic anti-Semite: his "extension of his criticism from Jewish bankers to the whole race [as in Canto 52] was, in large part, an act of bravado" (p. 181). Yet it was not an act of bravado (or ignorance of Hitler) that led Pound to say that "the Nazis wiped out bad manners in Germany" (RB, 32), or to support Nazi eugenics (RB, 140), or to denounce the Jewish "poison" (SP, 320) in Europe. The term "poison" includes not just Jewish bankers but "Jewry" (RB, 310) in all its manifestations, economic, cultural, and biological. Pound's anti-Semitism is a massive ideology with deep-laid foundations in paganism, the Middle Ages, the Enlightenment, Romanticism, and modern biological racism and naturalism. Nor is its presence adventitious or parasitic to Pound's text. Whether of Jews or Buddhists and Taoists, outgroup scapegoating is indispensable to Pound's effort of social and cultural differentiation, his attempt to establish a ritualistic, sacrificial, and corporate order.[14]

Another work which fails to do justice to Pound's politics is Forrest Read's *'76: One World and The Cantos of Ezra Pound*, which unearths a long-hidden key to *The Cantos*. According to Read, *The Cantos'* argument derives from the American Constitution, the Declaration of Independence, and the Bill of Rights. Its symbology derives from the Great Seal of the Constitution of the United States, and a pagan calendar which Pound published in 1922 in *The Dial*, in which he announced the "End" of the "Christian era" (pp. 10-51). These last devices define an heraldic, symbological, and geometrical schema which Pound encodes everywhere in *The Cantos* and which governs its language at all levels. Its message, meanwhile, is "'76," world history as a continuing movement towards unification and justice. This movement, argues Read, follows ideal political principles which the Founding Fathers recognized in 1776 and which Pound renews in his idea of "continuing revolution" (p. 111)—a phrase of Mussolini's.[15]

Read's ideas would seem merely whimsical were they not argued so obsessively and arbitrarily. Pound nowhere states that he had adopted this master plan, and there would have been no reason for keeping it secret. Read also ignores Pound's distrust of too "exact" allegory and even of symbolism and metaphor, not to mention his statement that he lacked a Dantescan "Aquinas map."[16] Nor is it likely that Pound would have adopted Read's rigid scheme, since adherence to its details would have posed immense historical and aesthetic difficulties. Critics generally agree that *The Cantos* develop through personal, poetic, and historical accretion around certain themes, leitmotifs, and general axes of composition.

But for Read *The Cantos* are all arcana, "special arcana" (p. 78), a fantastic allegory. When Pound flees Hell in Canto 15 to Pater Helios, he is a "renewed" American "Eagle" (p. 171). Canto 16 "allegorizes" justice and "fair trial," while the heroic imaginative actions of Cantos 17-27 allegorize "the right to bear arms" (pp. 172, 176) in the Bill of Rights. Again, the mythical "Compleynt of Artemis" adumbrates neither Pound's Fascistic naturalism nor his eugenics but tallies with the "natural rights" (p. 194) tradition of the American Revolution. The Circe episode, in which Odysseus literally "dominates" Circe (with his sword), astonishingly signifies not the Fascist domination of the feminine "swamp" but "government by consent" (p. 218).

Even so, Read by no means completely distorts Pound's ideology or his historical views. Pound finds the American spirit of "'76" compatible with Fascism, the reforms of Justinian, Confucian China, the Renaissance, and other important periods. Read is true to the spirit of Pound if not the letter. Thus the most serious weakness of his book lies in his willingness to accept Pound's historical, social, and economic views uncritically.

Read misunderstands Pound's economics. Besides thinking that Pound opposes capitalism, he ignores the historical analogues for Pound's anti-usury. Pound's Hell is "presided over by imperialistic . . . capitalism," which erects "hollow monuments" (pp. 170, 219); while Mussolini "deals summarily with capitalist profiteers" (p. 223) in Canto 41. Actually, Pound never attacks capitalism as a whole, only usury, which threatens the "rights of ownership" (SP, 298). He thus makes a crude, reactionary, and anti-Marxist distinction between "bad" capital, or finance, and honest capital, which encompasses industry and labor. This distinction between usurious "exploitation" and "production" links Pound to European proto-Fascism and Fascism, to Hitler, Gottfried Feder, Drumont, de la Tour du Pin. One cannot expect Read to clarify Pound's Fascism after this error.[17]

Read acknowledges that *The Cantos* celebrate the Axis, and that the radio broadcasts reveal an "incredible misunderstanding of . . . twentieth-century history" (p. 286). Indeed, the broadcasts mainfest "something like madness" (p. 288). Nonetheless, Read denies that the myths, rituals, and ideology of *The Cantos* belong to Fascism's unique historical movement. Insisting that the broadcasts fail to represent Pound's "proper" voice, and that Pound remained an American (and hence presumably not a Fascist), Read dehistoricizes Pound's Fascism. Fascism is the "error" of a poet whose "sympathy for the underdog and . . . revolutionary attitude" transcend the ideologies "of various stripes, liberal, fascist, or Marxist" (p. 435). Read agrees with Pound's statement that he stands above "warring factions" and sees "the boundless dimensions of time" (p. 432).

Fascism thus figures within a great historical process which Pound synchronizes and organizes from the perspective of the Nous, the eternal mind. Having "the eye of Horus" (p. 192), Pound apprehends history not so much chronologically or causally as a series of waves of usury and anti-usury. Thus the twentieth century inherits Renaissance Amor in Fascism's "ongoing . . . revolution" (p. 199), while Social Credit, without any historical affiliation, succeeds the Sienese Monte dei Paschi, which also provides (in Pound's novel interpretation) the "ancestral model" (p. 227) for Fascism.

Likewise the nearly mythical voyage of Hanno "precipitates" '76, and the Leopoldine Reforms in eighteenth-century Tuscany anachronistically combine the best of Renaissance Revolution and the best of Marxism. In spite of seeming differences, these causally dissociated phenomena belong together because each continues the supposedly millenial war on usury. Seen from this synchronic perspective, the historicism of *The Cantos* appears static and ahistorical. History is a spatial panorama of repeating and interchangeable types. It seems like myth.

This would suggest that Pound, for many a radical conservative, cherishes only historical continuities, permanent values. But Read also portrays Pound as the poet of "'76," continuing revolution into a "one world" (p. 6) culture. Pound surveys "different phases of the same revolutionary process occurring (SIMULTANEOUSLY) in different parts of the world at different levels of civilization."[18] These conceptions— historical continuity and revolutionary change—stand in opposition. One implies sameness and evolution, the other abrupt transformation of society. Though Read correctly defines Pound as a revolutionary, he never clarifies what he means by revolution, which is the central concept of his book.

Banally and tautologically Read asserts that true revolution "met emergencies" and "evolved in accordance with conditions of their times and places" (p. 174). Thus Pound rejects the Russian Revolution, which, however extensive its effects, is the masses' accidental and too abrupt rejection of their "cultural heritage" (pp. 174, 233), and which is less revolutionary than the heroic individualism of an obscure and narcissistic Italian despot, who culminates a "millenial European tradition" (p. 174). Meanwhile, the American revolution is a continuation of European Revolution. One wonders why Read even needs the concept of revolution to describe Pound's thought. At once ahistorical and anti-revolutionary, his conception is indistinguishable from the idea of tradition and assimilates to the timeless patterns of myth. Pound favors those governments which grow out of the "millenial traditions or paideumas" (p. 118). One can therefore find a "mythic source" for the "premise of government by consent" in the story of Circe, who consents to "accept male sexual dominance," or a model for heroism (Mussolini) in the story of Hanno, who follows the sun's mythical "periplum" (p. 118, 220). Instead of embodying an escape into the timeless world of Nature, myth, and ritual, the Chinese Book of Rites (*Li Ki*) "provides an ideal revolutionary model for amending dynastic violations" (p. 249). Thus "revolution becomes ritual" (p. 239) and ritual revolution.

Although Read ignores these conceptual difficulties, he inadvertently discloses a major problem in Pound's historical thinking, which hovers between a nostalgia for myth and a desire for revolutionary change. Read's and Pound's uncertainty concerning myth and history affords a good argument that Pound's "super-ideology" is Fascistic. Indeed, equivocation between myth and history pervades Fascism itself. As historians now realize, Fascism was a revolutionary rather than reactionary or conservative movement. But to conceal its abrupt departures from the past, Fascism represented itself in mythical terms as a return to permanent origins (Italy to Rome, Germany to the forest).[19] Likewise in Pound the appeal to myth is a necessary strategy for a self-professed radical conservative who has ceased to be one. Only by subsuming Fascism under transhistorical myths can Pound dilute its revolutionary implications and aims. Thus Odysseus' domination of Circe reflects not Fascist anti-feminism but mythically validates government by consent.[20] Thus the rituals of the *Li Ki*, rather than reflecting Fascism's fascination with sacrifice, inseparable from anti-Semitism, or its regressive nostalgia for pre-historical oneness with Nature, embodies nothing more specific than an organic and timeless order attainable even by technologically advanced societies. Thus Hanno's voyage, rather than figuring as a "prophetic" image of Mussolini's conquest of Ethiopia, absorbs Il Duce within the repeatable patterns of solar mythology.[21] Thus Fascism, far from being a unique response to unique historical events (the rise of Marxism, the crisis of capitalism), culminates a corporate tradition of intelligence which, though its material and causal affiliations are most tenuous, extends from Byzantium to the Monte dei Paschi to the Piazza Venezia.

Pound believes that Fascist corporatism assimilates to

American values in the spirit of "continuing revolution." Not only had Mussolini "rewritten the Declaration of Independence" (p. 225), but Pound also believed that the Constitution must be kept "modern" by conforming to corporate practice. It is easy to see the resemblance between Pound, who wants to institute social changes by means of "the machinery provided in the Constitution" (p. 295), and the supposedly conservative right-winger, who wants to "tinker" with the Constitution for radical ends.[22] Pound's reforms would actually entail the end of the essential liberalism of American politics. When Pound blithely proposes to reestablish voting rights on the basis of vocational corporations rather than geographical and individual representation, he would eliminate the concept of the citizenry, which derives from the French and American Revolutions.[23] Similarly, when Pound denounces the liberal "Rights of Man" in favor of the functional, corporate, and "statal" (SP, 296) doctrine that liberty is a "duty not a right," he rejects not just liberal tolerance but the French Revolution, which Fascism sought to nullify.[24] One cannot take seriously Read's argument that Pound reveres the Bill of Rights. As everyone knows, the First Amendment guarantees free speech. Convinced by the late twenties that usury had corrupted parliamentary debate and journalistic opinion, Pound answers liberal corruption by endorsing Mussolini's suppression of all but state-controlled opinion.[25] So much for this Italian "emender" of the Constitution. As for Pound's appeals to free speech during and after his trial, these are self-serving in defense of his broadcasts, which assert that freedom of speech belongs only to the qualified. Pound's main interest is not political liberty but the constitutional right of Congress and the people to nullify debts and to control the money supply, which Pound considers the true freedom. But Pound's interest in "economic democracy" (SP, 210) should not blind us to his relative indifference to democracy's other forms.

One also wants to know what led Read and Pound to connect Oriental despotism with the Bill of Rights and the Western traditions of democracy and tolerance. Perceiving the "pivot" or "axis" (which no doubt imports Fascism), Y Yin utters the "Bill of Rights" (p. 361) of the Chinese tribal clans. The Chinese Emperor makes sure that each man and woman is free to work for the "common good"—a banal injunction to impose a rigid corporate hierarchy rather than democratic or vocational freedom. Comparable absurdities emerge in *Rock Drill*, in which the *Sacred Edict of K'ang Hsi* figures as an "urbane Bill of Rights" (p. 392), and in which Pound (self-servingly) denounces "cruel punishments" (p. 385). Such denunciations are ironic given that the *Sacred Edict* is an authoritarian, persecutory, and ethnocentric text, recommending cruel punishments (which Pound repeats) against Buddhists and Taoists, the "Jews" of Confucian society. The expulsion of these religious enemies, remarks Read unblinkingly, aims at "social and political unanimity" (p. 395)—but at what cost? For all the talk of "Broderode" (John Adams's "brotherhood") and Apollonius of Tyana's Amor in the later *Cantos*, these claims are not credible in view of Pound's incorporation of a theme of Aryan and anti-Semitic imperial tradition extending from Sargon's Sumeria to Hitler's Germany.[26] For Read, who ignores Canto 91, where American universities are a "kikery" (Canto 91, 614), there is nothing sinister in the fact that "a Sumerian [and hence Aryan] seal visibly suggests the American" (p. 349).

Read recognizes that Pound demanded "to be judged intellectually, ethically, morally, and legally as well as aesthetically" (p. 431). Any scheme of poetic history incapable of clearly discriminating between parliamentary freedom under the Constitution and the ritualistic mass mobilizations of Nazi and Oriental depotism, or between "We the people of the United States" and the "folk" of China or of Central and Southern Europe, is not so much dangerous as silly. Although Read considers *The Cantos* a source of permanent values, Pound weaves together phases of history only as they suit his tastes and interests. Apart from certain lyric sections, which will live as anthology pieces, much of *The Cantos* belongs on the rubbish heap of Fascist metahistorical crankery, along with such monstrosities as Chamberlain's *Foundations of the Nineteenth Century* and Rosenberg's *Mythos of the Twentieth Century*, which they resemble.

In one sense Read's study resembles Massimo Bacigalupo's *The Formed Trace: The Later Poetry of Ezra Pound.* Bacigalupo believes that *The Cantos* are "on the whole" (p. 46) allegorical. Their allegory, however, is neither rigid nor "exact." Nor does Bacigalupo project *The Cantos* onto a mythical plane. Rather, "In many ways *The Cantos* . . . are, among other things, the sacred poem of the Nazi-Fascist millenium . . ." (p. x). *The Cantos* thus have a "definitive" historical ideology, one whose "progress" may be "traced" over the poem. Disturbed by his findings, Bacigalupo views Pound as a part-time peddler of "hatred in the thoroughfares," and *The Cantos* as his "tragedy" (pp. 52-53).

This book contains some old and new evidence showing that the poem encrypts Fascist or proto-Fascist content. In Canto 3 Pound's youthful economic and "erotic deprivation" leads to fantasies of the victimization of Jewish pawnbrokers by El Cid, a prototype of such "factive" (GK, 194) personalities as Malatesta and Mussolini. In Canto 51, a most important "turn" within the work, Hitler attacks usury and harmonizes the German and Italian folk ("volkern") (pp. 63-64). Meantime, in Canto 48 Pound allegorizes insect predation: "three ants have killed a great worm" (Canto 48, 243). Bacigalupo reads this as an allegory of Germany, Italy, and Japan rising by intelligent "instinct" or "genius" (J/M, 18, 19; read Hitler and Mussolini) to destroy Usury (pp. 91-92). Thus is the axe of Fascism concealed within the structure of *The Cantos.* Later, after the fall of Fascism, Pound appears obliquely as a Fascist "martyr," while Hitler is a Sibyl and Eva Braun his Castalian Muse (pp. 268, 297). Bacigalupo also notes that Pound equates the Fascist axe with the Confucian *hsin* and uses Fascist phrases in translating Confucian texts and Chinese histories. He therefore asserts rightly that *L'Asse che non Vacilla* links Confucius' "pivot" ("asse") and the Hitler-Mussolini "axis" (pp. 184-85).

Pound's poetry further conforms to Fascist assumptions even where its content seems "non-ideological." In their implicit denunciation of modern contraception, abortion, and non-eugenic marriage, Pound's invectives against Usury in Cantos 45 and 51 "accord" with Nazi demographic policies, racial theories, and eugenics. Bacigalupo's assertions gain support from the radio broadcasts, where Pound advocates eugenics and racism to protect nature from Jewish usury. So too, Pound's idealization of agrarian society, coition, and procreation consort with Mussolini's agricultural and demographic policies (p. 71). Bacigalupo also seems aware that the obsession with "Jewish" loan capital enables Pound and other Fascists to attack "capitalism" without demanding any major change in production or class structure.

In the end, though, Bacigalupo fails to show that *The Cantos* are the "sacred poem" of Fascism. This failure traces to his undernourished conception of Fascist ideology; to a limited interest in historical values and research; to a neglect of Pound's broadcasts as merely pathological; and to his own contradictory assumptions about the place of ideology in his poem. Bacigalupo treats Fascism at a level of abstract generality: Pound wanted "order" and an "absolute" (p. 80). Thus Bacigalupo ignores many features of Pound's thought which fall within Fascist typology. Like many critics, he reads Artemis' "Compleynt against Pity" allegorically and innocently; far from being murderous against the weak and malformed, Artemis eliminates "all in the past" that is "dead" (pp. 19-20). Actually, not only is such deprecation of pity reminiscent of Nietzsche's and Hitler's naturalism, but it anticipates the broadcasts, where Pound would "prune" or "purge" (RB, 74) human "rubbish."[27] Bacigalupo fails to note that Hanno's voyage in Canto 40 mythifies Mussolini's invasion of Ethiopia, while Canto 48, where three ants kill a "great worm," evokes Fascism's fascination with the instincts.[28] However, the fascination is combined with fear of the instincts and the unconscious: Bacigalupo never explores the Fascistic implications of Pound's attacks on Jewish "Mitteleuropa" (Canto 35, 172) or "Freud-land." Nor does he follow up his own suggestion that Pound's interest in the Byzantine *Book of the Prefect* derives from Fascist corporatism; seeking a Fascist "tradition," Italian Fascists were drawn to the state capitalism or socialism of the late Roman period, whence Pound's Byzantium derives.[29] And, while Pound's fascination with "concrete" definition seems a given to his temperament, these values consort with Fascism's insistence on categorical signification, its hatred of abstraction, its desire to install man within the natural "manifold," and its fear of transcendence of the natural and local.[30]

Although Bacigalupo mentions "the irrational and mystical feeling which is the constant facade of Fascism" (p. 46), this statement remains an historical cliche. Like other critics, he ignores the resemblance between Pound's paganistic desire to replace (Jewish) monotheism and the anti-monotheism of such Fascists as Maurras and Rosenberg.[31] Nor does Bacigalupo see Pound's affinity with Nazi "positive" Christianity. Like the Nazis, Pound in Canto 83 distinguishes the "good" Christ, as the vital, rising, and solar god of pagan religion, from the "bad" Christ, a sadistic figure of Pauline sacrifice and intolerance whom Pound (like the Nazis) traces to the Hebrew religion.[32] Moreover, though Bacigalupo notes Pound's obsession with light and flame, and with the sun as the unmixed center of the cosmos, he fails to connect Pound's solar religion and Fascist solar mysticism.[33] So again, Bacigalupo removes the Monte dei Paschi *Cantos* from their true historical context. Undoubtedly these *Cantos* reflect Pound's admiration for Fascism: the continuous mass celebrations in honor of Ferdinand III in Canto 44 resemble Mussolini's hysterical mimetic rituals in the Piazza Venezia.[34] Finally, Bacigalupo never explores Pound's fascination with ritual and blood sacrifice. Many students of Fascism recognize it as a sacrificial religion, and relate such sacrificial impulses to anti-Semitism.[35] Pound's quest for a timeless and ritualistic society masks and depends on sacrificial victimage, whether of Jews, Buddhists, or Taoists.

Ironically, Bacigalupo finally dehistoricizes *The Cantos* and undercuts his claim that they are the sacred poem of Fascism. Convinced that Pound's narrative time coincides with historical time mainly in the Pisan *Cantos*, he says that *The Cantos* "make contact" with historical time "only in the middle section" (p. 2). This excessively formalistic requirement is belied by the above examples, in which Pound touches modern history even when not writing "to the moment." Bacigalupo also views Hanno's voyage as a trip to the "Nous" rather than a doubling of

Mussolini's Ethiopian invasion; he thus seems to accept the poem's claim to transhistorical values. As for Pound's borrowings from L. A. Waddell, Bacigalupo connects this anti-Semitic writer only with Pound's more innocuous themes of cultural transmission. In truth, Waddell enables Pound to introduce within *The Cantos* a tradition of Aryan kingship, agrarianism, and solar religion, along with a myth (dear to the Nazis) of Aryan migration.

Bacigalupo equivocates over the place of history in *The Cantos* and retreats to the false distinction between poetry and ideology, sensibility and "opinion," the true and insincere Pound. Pound's Fascism is an "infatuation" and "aberration" (pp. 347, x): "The only connection I can see between Pound's stature as a poet and his political aberrations is precisely the abnormality of both" (p. x). Meanwhile, Bacigalupo's historical interest hardly consorts with his critical assumptions, which derive from Derridian deconstruction, and which lead him to consider *The Cantos* as a purely linguistic artifact. His main subject is Pound's interest in "the (previously) written" and with the endless and "irregular" play of linguistic differences. So *The Cantos* become all text and fashionably lose all definable content. Pound's words "attach themselves to memory in the manner of musical phrases" (p. 182). Obviously, Bacigalupo wants it both ways. *The Cantos* have political significance and yet are only "a reverie of signs" without historical meaning (p. 303). Nor do Pound's linguistic assumptions and practices have political implications.

Bacigalupo's study raises the question whether *The Cantos* carry a Fascist import at the linguistic level. The first work to consider that question is Alan Durant's admirable *Ezra Pound, Identity in Crisis: A Fundamental Reassessment of the Poet and His Work*. This study generally ignores the content of Pound's political ideology and its historical contexts. Durant's major assumption is that Pound's modes of writing "bespeak a particular conception of language" which "*necessarily* spills over" into his politics (p. 5). Pound's view of language, argues Durant, follows his belief in a real and objective world "preceding linguistic formulation" (p. 22) and subjective interpretation. Rather than producing meaning, language transmits "preexistent truth" (p. 23). The relation of signifier to signified is one of verifiable "correspondence" or similarity rather than one of difference and absence. Through "correct denominations" (GK, 16; Cheng Ming) man creates an organic, hierarchical, and discursive structure or "pattern" mimetic of Nature's "preordained" hierarchy. Pound thus envisions a language of "original" presence, of total objectivity and "efficiency," in which words deliver univocal meanings and all false or uncontrolled linguistic productions are eliminated. However, this empiricist epistemology depends on a questionable view of the subject. Pound's self implies neither a subjective and hence ambiguous relationship to external reality nor an entity in continuous formation through the processes of its own and others' language. His ideal self is a "neutral" and "static" observer, an "homogeneous," unified, and continuous consciousness which attains self-presence and "self-possession" in correctly naming itself and the external world (pp. 22, 85, 23, 59). The self masters reality through words as the eye, in looking, masters the visual field. Language is the transparent vehicle of its intended meanings. Durant further notes that critics have shown an "unacknowledged complicity" (p. 2) with Pound's assumption that language transmits "facts," references, sources, self-evident truths. No less disturbing is the tendency of Pound critics to think of politics and poetry as "distinct" realms of discourse, so that politics become a mere "content" and "irksome parenthesis" rather than an immanent function of the text.

Durant follows the psycholinguistic theories of the French psychoanalyst Jacques Lacan. In Lacan the structure of language prevents closure between signifier and signified, meaning and intention. Language is not a system of "correspondences" (p. 76) between words and things but a symbolic structure of differences among the signifiers which compose it. In order for the subject to speak, he must select certain signifiers and exclude others, which continue to exist in the unconscious. Thus both the unconscious and repression are "necessary constituent[s] of the possibility of signification";

linguistic differences have to be repressed "in order that we may speak at all" (p. 76). Meantime, the subject is constituted as a difference within the space "cut out" (p. 84) by the choice of certain signifiers rather than others. This means that the self, which emerges through repression, is never self-sufficient. The unconscious always exists as "another scene" (p. 7) of repressed signification and desire, a lack or difference within the self. Nor can the self's utterances fulfill its intentions. Not only is language an endless "chain" of signifiers, but the unconscious constantly invades discourse through the uncontrollable operations of metonymy and metaphor, whose "displacements" onto continuous members of the chain disrupt the possibility of a "denotative" language. By creating a "surplus" in the signifier, these tropes reveal the emergence of difference, insufficiency, and hence desire within the subject. Always there is "one signifier more, the condition of metonymy and desire" (p. 90). The self arises out of its own mobile and unstoppable linguistic production.

In Lacan language and identity emerge with the subject's discovery of genital variation. At first the child identifies with the all-powerful phallus in an attempt to become the object of the mother's desire and thus to "complete" the castrated mother. Since this stage is marked by the child's narcissistic refusal to differentiate itself from the phallus and the mother, Lacan refers to it as the Imaginary. But with the paternal interdict on incest and the castration threat which it implies, the child renounces its desire to be the phallus and hence the object of its mother's desire. More than a symbolic castration, this moment marks the child's emergence as a separate identity within the symbolic order. In acceding to the Name of the Father, the child defines a space for itself within the system of differences which is language.[36]

With the ascent to the symbolic the phallus signifies difference. Submitting to the father, the possessor of the phallus, the child recognizes the phallus not as an object to *be* but as an object to *have*. The desire to be like the father replaces the desire for the mother and identification with the phallus. Lucan emphasizes, however, that the child's desire to have the phallus originates from its perception that it has been symbolically castrated. Lacan also emphasizes that the phallus or Phallus is an abstract signifier beyond any object which might represent it. It is a symbol or idea, implying presence and self-possession, the filling of space, power, language, and the paternal, as opposed to "feminine" absence, emptiness, lack, and difference. And so the subject's desire for the phallus that excludes lack is a mythical quest, for no full presence exists. The phallus can be known only through marks and traces, through real and imaginary substitute objects, none of which can overcome the sense of lack and desire.[37]

Durant applies Lacan to Pound's much-neglected postscript to Gourmont's *Natural Philosophy of Love*. Speculating on the relation between the human brain and the male genital fluid, sexuality and creative intelligence, Pound posits the interchangeability of sperm, language, and light. He also refers to the "integration of the male in the male organ" (PD, 204)—an image of total self-possession. Just as the spermatazoa organizes the "ovule" (PD, 202), so the male mind "charges" the "female chaos" (PD, 204) and moulds it to its will. These speculations imply a natural hierarchy in which the phallus is a unified and controlling center, and in which the feminine signifies lack and hence desire: absence of order and telos, need of the organizing phallus (pp. 104-105).

Lacan also helps to explain the relation between Pound's phallocentrism and his ideas of conscious language, paternal origination, and hierarchical differentiation. In Pound man's control over language reflects the differentiating powers inhering in a unified, phallic, and paternal origin. Pound speaks of "Pater Helios" (Canto 113, 95) and refers to the sun as a source of intelligence and language: "god's mouth" (Canto 77, 466). Interchangeably with logos, thought, and seed, Pound's sun surveys, fecundates, and differentiates reality. Again, Pound thinks of man's essence as light or sperm and thus imitative of the creative, paternal phallus or the ordered plenitude of the "Nous"; "Man's phallic heart is from heaven / a clear spring of rightness" (Canto 97, 697). Where "the phallus perceive(s) its aim" (Canto 99, 702) and men observe "correct denominations," they attain the static perspective of the Nous (Canto 40, 201), from which all unregulated linguistic production is banished, and where there is no lack, difference, or desire (p. 49).

Durant's main thesis is even bolder. Pound cannot accept himself as a subjectivity formed through difference and driven by unconscious desire (pp. 130-31). He therefore seeks to deny the castration complex and to maintain the "narcissistic consistency" (p. 81) and the "original" self-presence of his world. Indeed, "only a successful resistance to castration might preserve" Pound's "domination over sight, language, and cultural order . . ." (p. 91). In its extreme form this project entails a return to the Imaginary, the narcissistic and presymbolic state of undifferentiation which precedes the castration complex, and in which the subject identifies completely with the phallus. This withdrawal from verbal differences is Lacan's "foreclusion" (p. 13). But Pound never chooses this solution, except perhaps in the last silent years. He compromises with the symbolic order by means of fetishism, which permits the "partial allowance of difference" (pp. 110-11) and the "ubiquitious inscription of the phallus" (p. 91) through word and image in *The Cantos*. Durant shows that Pound values such phallic substitutes as the head, sun, pen, chisel, artifact, monument, each a symbol for that which excludes lack and unconscious desire.[38]

This escape from difference is impossible. Pound's repeated inscription of the phallus in *The Cantos* only confirms difference and lack. Constantly experiencing desire, Pound looks vainly for the phallic fetish that would exclude it. Meantime, these inscriptions function within the metonymic and metaphoric play of language, which "decentralizes" and "multiplies" meanings beyond the control of any speaker or signifier. Language is constantly "invaded with . . . slips and mistakes" (p. 162), gaps and differences in which intention fails and unconscious desire is revealed. In order to fully eliminate difference Pound must regulate signification through the complete but impossible "repression" of metonymy, metaphor, and the unconscious. Or as Pound says in Addendum to Canto 100: "A pity that poets have used symbol and metaphor / and no man learned anything from them / for their speaking in figures."

Durant's insights lead to a rethinking of the formal nature of *The Cantos*. As Durant observes, *The Cantos* are modelled after Odysseus' return to the recoverable presence and rootedness of his earlier self and "origin" (pp. 166-68, 48). Likewise their goal is to attain their logocentric origin, a plenitude of meanings unifying the entire poem: the "great [and phallic] acorn of light," "the great ball of crystal" (Canto 116, 793).[39] But this unifying movement is negated by the poem's metaphorical texture, its "dense counterpoint[ing]" (p. 89), and the multiple senses which words acquire in different contexts and in criss-crossing "patterns of association" (p. 89). Thanks to verbal "repetition" and its "intra-allusive" nature, the poem generates a "surplus in the signifier" (p. 89) and produces unmanageable effects beyond Pound's intention. There is no plenitude of self and meaning, only their dissemination, or "knowledge" adrift in "the sea" of "lack" (p. 167). Even Pound confesses that he had "lost" his "center / fighting the world" (Canto 117 et seq., 802).

Durant traces Pound's inability to conclude *The Cantos* not to historical or biographical causes but to the condition of language as an "endless sentence" (p. 40). Yet Durant's examples of linguistic surplus are relatively unimportant. No severe linguistic breakdown is evident when acorns first signify Circe's hospitality, and then stability and growth. Nor is it very disturbing that in Cantos 2 and 17 grapes evoke natural fecundity, and later Sodom and Gomorrah. Durant should have focussed on instances where a seemingly univocal signifier, such as usury, is rendered indeterminate by the contradictory metaphors which constitute it. As Derrida notes, the concept of usury implies the contradictory presence of growth and depletion, presence and absence, fecundity and sterility. The same confusion repeats itself in Pound's metaphors for usury (the swamp, the desert, wasting disease, luxury, excrescence, etc.), and thus renders one of his poem's essential concepts thoroughly indeterminate and undecideable.[40]

Durant's most important contribution is to relate Pound's phallocentrism and his social, economic, and political values.

Repeatedly Pound valorizes structures in which an originating "node" or "point" becomes the unifying and organizing center of a totalitarian system of hierarchical and converging energies. This description fits the Poundian Vortex, the "Nous," and Pound's idea of the "capital," whether the Mediterranean as the originating source of Western culture, or the seat of a centralized government (pp. 27-31). It also fits Fascism, which Pound advocates by the middle 1930s. According to Pound, Fascism "contemplates" the "undivided light" (SP, 307), the origin. More factually, Fascism is a corporate, hierarchical, and totalitarian order subsuming the whole of society under an "apex" (Canto 88, 581) or "summit" (Canto 88, 580)—the dictator, whose name marks him as transmitter of verbal order. There is, moreover, no modern political system more avowedly phallocentric and patriarchal than Fascism. Just as Fascism conceives of the masses as feminine and "malleable" (L, 181), as "lacking" initiative and force,[41] so the dictator represents the phallus; Mussolini is the "bullock," the "Big Stick" (SP, 261), combining intelligence and sexuality. Where liberalism, socialism, and communism tolerate atomistic fragmentation and difference, Fascism forges social unanimity by supplying the lost phallus of authority, without which is neither unity nor hierarchy (pp. 123-25).

Durant shows that Pound's anti-feminism likewise derives from his anxiety over woman as the sign of difference, phallic lack, and hence dangerous desire; as such, she threatens masculine hierarchy and control and needs to be brought within the regulation of the phallus. One thinks of Circe, Helen of Troy, Salome in "Our Tetrarchal Precieuse," the female in "Ortus," and numerous women in Pound. Pound conceives of the feminine as sacred only insofar as the feminine can be installed within an agrarian and patriarchal order, as in Canto 39. Under such circumstances woman is "a disciple who simply absorbs the creativity which emanates from the male genital" (p. 102), her "deep waters reflecting all fire" (Canto 106, 753).[42]

As for anti-Semitism, Durant traces it rightly though reductively to the castration complex. Durant mentions *Moses and Monotheism*, where Freud connects anti-Semitism with

Jewish circumcision, which awakens in the Gentile the repressed memory of the dreaded castration idea. I have shown elsewhere that Pound identifies the Jews with castration, circumcision, and various forms of genital disease.[43] Durant is mainly concerned, however, with passages in which the Jew less overtly represents phallic absence, deprivation, and lack. In Canto 35 Jewish life is associated with the incompleteness of the "maternal genital" (p. 156) (and thus with "Freudian" incest). Absence is no less implicit in "Jewish" usury, to which Pound attaches metaphors of "syphillis," "erosion," depletion, "gnawing into," "interrupted" and abortive procreation, and paradoxically, unbridled growth (pp. 141, 115, 140, 139, 137). Pound further identifies the Jews with the unregulated production of the anus and the swamp. As Pound observes, the humor of (Jewish) Mitteleuropa runs to the anal "orifice" rather than the phallus, and thus subordinates phallic production to the uncontrolled "discharges" of the bowel. But these accusations are not limited to the Jews. Pound hates meddlesome palace eunuchs, and he also despises buggerers, who deny the normal operations of the phallus (pp. 141-42). Meantime, Buddhists are as bad as Jews in their abstract interest in "an originary absence" and in their passive, non-phallic attitude toward the external world (p. 142).

Durant has sought to define the psychological and linguistic "conditions" necessary for Fascism, its "irreducible element of psychological causation" (p. 5). He confirms what historians and political scientists have found through more conventional methods, that Fascism worships male dominance, abhors the confusion of signs, fears the dissolution of the bourgeois subject, and attacks "difference" or alterity. However, Durant has chosen to ignore politics and history as such and thus offers an admittedly partial view of Pound's Fascism. For all its virtues, his study needs to be integrated with a study of Pound's ideology, its historical antecedents, and the historical, social, and cultural circumstances under which it emerged. Though Pound's political views trace in part to his psychological crises, Pound also embraced Fascism because of major catastrophes of social identity, class, economic welfare, family, poetic ambition, politics. Nor can his anti-Semitism be fully understood only in psychological terms, for it reflects his pagan, medieval, Enlightenment (Voltaire), and naturalistic values. Apart from its economic function, which is to deflect violence away from industrial capitalism, anti-Semitic scapegoating serves Pound indispensably in his effort to establish a corporate, ritualistic, and organic society along medieval lines.

This book contains some minor flaws which may affect proper estimation of its value. The worst is a frequent failure of readability, as in this example: "Pound had earlier in this work reviled the need for food coupled with a separation from that food in the moving animal" (p. 153). So too, instead of translating Lacan's tangled but by no means impenetrable thought into accessible English, Durant has riddled his work with Lacanian jargon. He has thus made it easy for conservative critics to regard his genuine insights as eccentric. These strictures, however, should not detract from the book's fundamental importance. Where other treatments of Pound's politics indulge in evasive apologetics, or consider the subject at the mimetic and empirical level of annotation, anecdote, theme, and context, Durant reopens the question at the primary level of language and the unconscious. Pound's politics cease to be extraneous to his work and become a function of his language and personality. Every serious student of Pound should benefit both from Durant's methods and from his insights.

Notes

1. See the opinions of the participants in the *Partisan Review* Symposium on the Bollingen Award, reprinted in *A Casebook on Ezra Pound*, ed. Edward Stone and William Van O'Connor (New York: Thomas Crowell, 1958), pp. 54-66. Also see Archibald MacLeish's argument in *Poetry and Opinion: The Pisan Cantos of Ezra Pound* (Urbana: Univ. of Illinois Press, 1950), partially reprinted in *A Casebook on Ezra Pound*, pp. 90-91, and well-dissected for its illogicalities by Gerald Graff in *Poetic Statement and Critical Dogma* (Evanston: Northwestern Univ. Press, 1972), pp. 172-78.

2. Jerome Mazzaro, review of three works on Pound, *Criticism*, 24 (1976), 388-91.

3. See G. S. Frazer, "Pound: Masks, Myth, Man," in *Ezra Pound: A Reexamination*, ed. Peter Russel (Norwalk: New Directions, 1950), p. 116; Michael Reck, *Ezra Pound: A Close-up* (New York: McGraw Hill, 1967), p. 116; James Wilhelm, *The Later Cantos of Ezra Pound* (New York: Walker, 1977), pp. xvi, 250; Christine Brooke-Rose, *A ZBC of Ezra Pound* (Berkeley: Univ. of California Press, 1971), p. 250.

4. The best-known studies of Pound's politics, John Harrison's *The Reactionaries* (New York: Schocken, 1967) and William Chace's *The Political Identities of Ezra Pound and T. S. Eliot* (Stanford: Stanford Univ. Press, 1973), are brief, general, moralistic, and inadequate. They pursue their subjects unsystematically and without a clear typology either of Fascism or anti-Semitism. Nor do these studies treat Pound's politics as a function or expression of Pound's language. Largely ignoring the complex of Poundian image, symbol, and metaphor, they confine themselves to theme and content.

5. For Pound's attack on psychoanalysis, see *Jefferson and/or Mussolini* (New York: Boni and Liveright, 1935), pp. 100-101, and "Private Worlds," *New English Weekly*, May 2, 1935, 48-49.

6. Noel Stock points out that Pound and Lewis initially responded to each other with a certain wariness, and that their intellectual alliance began in 1914. *Patria Mia* was written between 1911 and 1913. See Stock, *The Life of Ezra Pound* (New York: Avon, 1970), pp. 135-36, 214.

7. The following is a list of abbreviations of works by Ezra Pound cited parenthetically in the text and in the footnotes: C: *The Cantos*, New York: New Directions, 1972 (References in the text give Canto, followed by number of Canto and page; e.g., Canto 99, 697); GK: *Guide to Kulchur*, New York: New Directions, 1970; J/M: *Jefferson and/or Mussolini*, New York: Liveright, 1935; L: *The Letters of Ezra Pound, 1907-1941*, D. P. Paige, ed., New York: Harcourt, Brace, 1930; LE: *Literary Essays of Ezra Pound*, T. S. Eliot, ed., London: Faber and Faber, 1954; PD: *Pavannes and Divagations*, New York: New Directions, 1958; RB: *"Ezra Pound Speaking": Radio Speeches of World War II*, Leonard W. Doob, ed., Westport, Conn.: Greenwood Press, 1978; SP: *Selected Prose of Ezra Pound: 1909-1965*, William Cookson, ed., New York: New Directions, 1973.

8. For Pound's logocentrism and phallocentrism, see my discussion in "Anti-Semitism, Castration, and Usury in Ezra Pound," *Criticism*, 25 (1983), 239-65.

9. For the Fascist conception of the masses as feminine, see Ernst Nolte, *Three Faces of Fascism*, trans. Leila Vennewitz (New York: New American Library, 1965), pp. 150, 518.

10. See Timothy Materer, *Vortex: Pound, Eliot, Lewis* (Ithaca: Cornell Univ. Press, 1979), p. 22.

11. See also Pound, LE, 391.

12. Pound's Fascist values will emerge over the course of this essay. For Pound's eugenic proposals and his racist cultural theorizing, see RB, 132, 140, 165, 168. For Fascist naturalism, see Nolte, *Three Faces of Fascism*, pp. 58, 182-89, 418-20, 527-34.

13. For "corporate" and "functional" as applied to Fascist society, see Canto 97, 698, 707. These are Fascist political terms. For "rods in a bundle," see Canto 53, 372.

14. Flory claims that Pound in the later *Cantos* eschews the brutal intolerance manifested in *The Sacred Edict of K'ang Hsi* toward Buddhists and Taoists. Actually, this persecutory text consorts with Pound's attitudes toward these "heretical" and "disruptive" sects. Not only does Pound countenance murderous violence against these enemies in the earlier Chinese *Cantos*, but in Canto 99 he freely translates *The Sacred Edict* in these lines: "If you don't swallow their buncombe / you won't have to drive them out" (Canto 99, 688). Pound's source is *The Sacred Edict, with a Translation of the Colloquial Rendering*, ed. F. W. Baller (London and Philadelphia: Religious Tract Society, 1924), pp. 84, 86.

15. See Pound, J/M, 113, and Read, p. 211.

16. For Pound's dislike of symbol and allegory, see LE, 9; see also L, 323, and Addendum to Canto 100, 799.

17. See Hitler, *Mein Kampf*, trans. Ralph Manheim (Boston: Houghton Mifflin, 1971), pp. 209, 24; for Drumont, see Edward Tannenbaum, *The Action Francaise: Die-Hard Reactionaries in Twentieth Century France* (New York: John Wylie, 1961), p. 16. For de la Tour du Pin, see Nolte, *Three Faces of Fascism*, p. 175.

18. Pound, quoted in Read, p. 228.

19. See James Rhodes, *The Hitler Movement* (Stanford: Hoover Institution Press, 1980), p. 219, and George Mosse, *Nazism: A Historical and Comparative Analysis* (New Brunswick, N.J.: Transaction Press, 1978), pp. 118-19. For the privilege accorded the origin, see Mircea Eliade, *Myth and Reality*, trans. Willard R. Trask (New York: Harper and Row, 1963), p. 183. See also Mosse, *Nazism*, pp. 128-29.

20. See Max Horkheimer and Theodor Adorno, "Elements of Anti-Semitism," in *Dialectic of Enlightenment*, trans. John Cumming (New York: Herder and Herder, 1969), pp. 69-75. In their reading of Book 11 of the *Odyssey*, Odysseus' conquest of Circe is an act of patriarchal domination.

21. Hanno's expedition in Canto 40 mythifies the impending Italian Fascist invasion of Ethiopia, which it celebrates in advance, as Daniel Pearlman notes

in *The Barb of Time: On the Unity of Ezra Pound's Cantos* (New York: Oxford Univ. Press, 1969), p. 166.

22. See Richard Hofstadter's "The Pseudo-Conservative Revolt," in *The Radical Right*, ed. Daniel Bell (New York: Doubleday Anchor, 1964), pp. 79, 80.

23. Pound makes this proposal as late as *Impact*, ed. Noel Stock (Chicago: Henry Regnery, 1960), pp. 145-46; see also RB, 324, 134, and J/M, 5.

24. For Pound's rejection of the Rights of Man, see J/M, 143, and GK, 254. For the Fascist rejection of the legacy of the French Revolution, see Nolte, *Three Faces of Fascism*, p. 511; Herman Finer, *Mussolini's Italy* (New York: Grosset and Dunlap, 1965), pp. 172-73, 184, 192. Pound speaks of the French Revolution as a "chaos" brought about by the Jews in RB, 320.

25. See Read, p. 224, and Charles Norman, *The Life of Ezra Pound* (New York: MacMillan, 1960), p. 364.

26. See L. A. Waddell, *Egyptian Civilization: Its Sumerian Origin and the Sumerian Origin of the Egyptian Hieroglyphs* (London: Luzac, 1930), *passim*. Pound borrows from this work in the later *Cantos*.

27. See Friedrich Nietzsche, *The Anti-Christ*, in *The Portable Neitzsche*, ed. Walter Kaufman (New York: Viking, 1967), pp. 570, 583-84, 573; Hitler, *Mein Kampf*, pp. 287, 132, 289, 247, 132.

28. For Fascism's controlled fascination with instincts and the primitive, see George Mosse, *The Crisis of the German Ideology* (New York: Grosset and Dunlap, 1964), p. 316. See also Peter Nathan, *The Psychology of Fascism* (London: Faber and Faber, 1943), p. 83.

29. See Frank W. Walbank, *The Decline of the Roman Empire in the West* (New York: Henry Schumann, 1953), pp. 46-47n.

30. For an equivalent of the Poundian doctrine of calling things by their right names, as well as abhorrence of "blind" abstraction, see Charles Maurras in *Romanticism and Revolution*, partially translated by John Fears in *The French Right: From de Maistre to Maurras*, ed. J. S. McClelland (New York: Harper and Row, 1970), p. 260. For the Fascist opposition to transcendence in its various senses, see Nolte, *Three Faces of Fascism*, pp. 185, 537-43.

31. For the Fascist hatred of monotheism, see Nolte, *Three Faces of Fascism*, pp. 186-87. See also Rosenberg, *Race and Race History and Other Essays*, ed. Robert Pois (New York: Harper and Row, 1971), pp. 108-18, for a celebration of Nordic paganism and a denunciation of Jahweh, the "remote" god to whom one prays in "fear and trembling."

32. Canto 83, 533. See also Canto 74, 443, where Pound speaks of the "cross" which, like the swastika, "turns with the sun." For the Nazi distinction

302   REVIEW

between positive and negative Christianity, see Rosenberg, *Race and Race History and Other Essays of Alfred Rosenberg*, pp. 68, 100, 72, and Peter Viereck, *Metapolitics: The Roots of the Nazi Mind* (New York: Capricorn Books, 1965). For the swastika as solar symbol, see *Race and Race History*, pp. 108-09n.

33. For Nazi sun worship and solar occultism, invariably linked to the same sort of seasonal mythology as appears in Pound, see George Mosse, *The Crisis of the German Ideology*, pp. 71-72, and Norman Cohn, *Warrant for Genocide: The Myth of the Jewish World Conspiracy and the Protocols of the Elders of Zion* (New York: Harper and Row, 1967), pp. 176, 168. See also J. Mehlman, "Blanchot at *Combat*: Of Literature and Terror," *Modern Language Notes*, (1981), 817-21.

34. For Fascist ritual, see Ernst Cassirer, *The Myth of the State* (New Haven: Yale Univ. Press, 1946), pp. 277-96 ("The Technique of Modern Political Myths").

35. For Fascism as a sacrificial religion, see Theodor Adorno, "Anti-Semitism and Fascist Propaganda," in *Anti-Semitism: A Social Disease*, ed. Ernst Simmel (New York: International Universities Press, 1946), p. 136; Horkheimer and Adorno, *Dialectic of Enlightenment*, p. 186.

36. For Lacan on the phallus, see *Ecrits: A Selection*, trans. Alan Sheridan (New York: W. W. Norton, 1977), pp. 5-6, 67-68, 166-67, 175, 189-90, 206-07, 220-21, 236-37, 239, 243-44, 250, 251-52, 258-59, 262-69, 274-75, 281-91, 310-16, 322-24. See especially "The Signification of the Phallus," pp. 281-91. My discussion of Lacan is also indebted to Anika Lemaire's *Jacques Lacan*, trans. David Macey (London: Routledge and Kegan Paul, 1977), pp. xviii-xx, 7, 53, 54, 58-62, 82-89, 95, 164-66. See also Durant, pp. 74, 94n, 1, 130, 13, 111-14, for a discussion of the mirror phase, the Imaginary, and the Name of the Father.

37. This paragraph is indebted to Lacan and Lemaire, cited above. See also Durant, pp. 129-34, 12-13, 161. My discussion necessarily simplifies Lacan's and Durant's thinking.

38. Some of these examples are not Durant's but mine, and are given further discussion in my "Anti-Semitism, Castration, and Usury in Ezra Pound," pp. 241-42, 254-57.

39. See Richard Sieburth's *Instigations: Ezra Pound and Remy de Gourmont* (Cambridge: Harvard Univ. Press, 1978), p. 153. Pound was playing on the Latin *glans* (testicle), which means acorn.

40. For Derrida on Usure, see "White Mythology: Metaphor in the Text of Philosophy," trans. F. C. T. Moore, *New Literary History* 4 (1974), 7, and *passim*.

41. Nolte, *Three Faces of Fascism*, pp. 150, 518.

42. Durant, pp. 102, 147, 151, 158-60.

43. See Casillo, "Anti-Semitism, Castration, and Usury in Ezra Pound," pp. 244-49.

A Contemporary Defense of Poetry

Bruce Bashford

Charles Altieri. *Act & Quality: A Theory of Literary Meaning and Humanistic Understanding*. Amherst: University of Massachusetts Press, 1981. 343 pp.

Sometime in the 1960s, the interest of our profession as a whole in literary theory increased dramatically. In the heyday of the New Criticism the standard formula for a critical essay was to treat any question about a literary work—even one about the work's historical context—as another occasion for a close reading. Today nearly every discussion of a literary work, at least in the prestigious journals, claims to throw some light on a theoretical issue. One has to applaud this shift in interest if only because, in a culture as uncertain about itself as ours, it must be a good thing for our discipline to reflect on what it is and on what it might be. But much of the work aspirng to theory has been mediocre. The reasons for this mediocrity are undoubtedly several; a main one, however, is that the increased interest in literary theory has caused critics to start doing philosophy without dealing in the coin of the realm: argument. And so we have essays and books ostensibly proving momentous things about life and literature, but actually only applying an idea borrowed from elsewhere—applying it, as opposed to making a case for it. Charles Altieri proceeds differently in his *Act & Quality: A Theory of Literary Meaning and Humanistic Understanding*. He has obviously read widely in contemporary philosophy, including Anglo-American or "analytic" philosophy largely ignored by persons in literature departments, and he has patiently sorted out what he does and does not believe. The result is a dense book given over to an unusual degree to sustained argument.

As its title indicates, the book is a defense of a traditional humanistic view of literature and criticism. It is a contemporary installment in a distinguished line of defenses of poetry in English, including those by Sidney, Shelley, and Arnold. The chief stimulus for the defense is Deconstruction's attack on the humanistic position, and the specific version of humanism that Altieri presents is developed by explicitly speaking to this attack.

Deconstruction's main challenge to the humanistic tradition has been to deny the possibility of recovering determinate meanings from texts. A great deal of Altieri's book is concerned with meeting this challenge. Altieri begins by countering Derrida with Wittgenstein. The argument is roughly this: Derrida's arguments for the indeterminacy of language depend on a standard of rigor inappropriate to the subject. The later Wittgenstein warned us not to forget that using language is a form of action. A language is a set of procedures we learn in order to act in concert with each other. Derrida's mistake is to require a tighter bond between sentences and their possible senses or referents than is required for us to accomplish our purposes as language users. Therefore, he has language failing at a test it does not have to meet. (It is worth noting, since my summary might suggest otherwise, that Altieri does not treat Derrida in a dismissive manner. His reconstruction of Derrida's position from various texts implicitly represents it as a serious one. Deconstructionists may—as they so often do—decide that this is not the real Derrida, but they will not find the discussion blindly hostile.)

The next section of the book attempts to locate adequate terms for describing our ability to use language. Some readers may find the close discussions of Anglo-American philosophers like J. L. Austin, Paul Grice, and Donald Davidson heavy going. But the direction and the point of the discussion are not hard to get. Altieri distrusts efforts to describe our competence exhaustively by specifying a set of rules we could consult to determine meaning in particular cases. He casts doubt on even sophisticated versions of this approach by showing that they cannot explain powers of expression and comprehension that we plainly possess. He observes that there are cases in which a speaker's choice of a manner of speaking affects our sense of his meaning and, moreover, in which the speaker can count on and manipulate to expressive effect our attention to his manner. The speaker is *performing* as well as saying. Such cases are too complex to be brought under standing semantic rules and require that we think of our competence in "dramatistic" terms (p. 10). Our competence enables us to place the speaker's performance in the situation at hand so that the performance is intelligible as an attempt to display certain qualities in that situation.

This section ends with a tour-de-force reading of William Carlos Williams's short poem "This is Just to Say." (Readers uncertain about whether the book is for them might well read this chapter first.) It is useful to have this exercise at this point even though Altieri has not yet turned to literary theory proper. For it is in reading literary works that the feature of our linguistic competence that he has been exploring, our ability to attend to saying-as-performing, becomes dominant. In Williams's poem, the speaker explicitly asks to be forgiven for eating the plums that were in the icebox. But for Altieri what is important is the implicit understanding of the nature of forgiveness that the speaker acts out in the note. For example, when the speaker conjectures that his wife was "probably" saving the plums for breakfast, he may momentarily be tempted to evade his guilt by exploiting language's capacity to introduce ambiguity into a description of a state of affairs. But his final explanation of his act, that the plums "were delicious/so sweet/and so cold," reveals both an honest assessment of the sources of his action and the recognition that an appeal for forgiveness is an appeal to the generosity of the other. As Altieri says, "The justness of the speaker's note is its recognition of his weakness and its lovely combination of self-understanding with an implicit faith in the hearer's capacity to grasp and to accept his deed, and, beyond that, to accept his human existence as a balance of weakness, self-knowledge, and concern" (p. 164).

Altieri maintains that as readers we attend not only to the qualities and attitudes displayed by the characters in the work, but also to those displayed by the author who creates and situates those characters. This claim, as unexceptional as it may sound, has significant consequences because Altieri considers what the poet displays as part of the *meaning* of the work. The poet's act has to be assessed in the relevant poetic and intellectual traditions, and that means that shifting our attention to the poet will nearly always considerably enrich the meaning of the poem. To cite just one contention in his complex discussion, Altieri argues that we are to construe the sparseness of Williams's poem as making a negative comment on the highly figurative language of Romantic poetry. That is to say, through his choice of diction Williams is criticizing the Romantics for locating the expressive power of poetry in figurative language rather than in poetry's capacity to represent performances in language.

Altieri begins the latter half of his book by drawing the implications of viewing literary works as performances for a wide range of topics in literary theory. He proceeds by contrasting his position with those of a number of influential figures in the field. And several of these analyses of other critics (for example, the discussion of Ralph Rader) are so penetrating that the book is worth consulting for them alone. One of his main concerns remains the degree of determinacy of meaning exhibited by literary works, and he locates himself between opponents and allies. Against theorists like Paul de Man and Frank Kermode who emphasize indeterminacy, Altieri stresses our ability to adjudicate among claims about the nature of the performance embodied in a work. For him, we have access to literary works in the first place because we have learned the "grammar" of our culture—very roughly, the types of acts, like apologizing, that are intelligible in the culture— and we can test descriptions of a work against this grammatical sense. Considering other figures, like Rader, who argue for determinacy of meaning, he cautions against inadvertently thinning out the work by an overly abstract formulation of the poet's intention. For Altieri, the work's meaning remains tied to the concrete action that displays it; discursive statements can direct our attention to the work in fruitful ways, but they can never lift the meaning off the work.

In the remainder of the book Altieri argues for the value of a literary education. Reading literary works not only draws on our general sense of cultural types, it also sharpens that sense: "The cognitive impact of literature consists largely of enabling us to make more complex and more varied discriminations about actions than may occur in ordinary experience" (p. 272). This is obviously a traditional humanistic claim: judging from his "Preface to Shakespeare," Dr. Johnson would have accepted it without hesitation. What is different here is the basis for the claim. Altieri borrows Nelson Goodman's view of a work of art as a sample: the work is a sample of the terms we would use to talk about it. Grasping a work deeply is something like learning a new word. Reading "This is Just to Say," for example, brings before the mind a specific notion of apologizing. While this notion stays tied to the work's exemplification of it, it has enough generality to let us bring other cases, including those from life, under its influence. One feels here the pressure of Derrida, among others, modifying the grounds of Altieri's defense of poetry and, finally, the defense itself. Altieri is not trying to resurrect the claim that poetry tells us directly and reliably about the world. Rather poetry gives us means for understanding the world; in particular, since in poetry characters and authors perform themselves, poetry provides us with types for assessing the range and quality of human purposes.

Since Altieri takes poetry to be an aspect of culture and regards culture as at bottom something people *carry on*, he is in no position to assert with Shelley that a poem "is the very image of life expressed in its eternal truth."[1] Nonetheless, in his closing discussion of Hegel, one hears an echo of the commonplace in the defense of poetry tradition that poetry provides a universal perspective on human affairs. The discussion, as usual, is dense, but this is what I take the basic claim to be: literary study enables us not only to use cultural types, but also to reflect on them. This reflection lifts us up above the level of the purposes we just happen to have and lets us judge the seriousness of our purposes against a spectrum of possible alternatives. Moreover, this reflection lets us see the intrinsically social or communal nature of our purposes. Culture may have no deeper foundation than the activity of persons who sustain it, but what they bring into being flows back into and links individual lives: "Expressive acts at once bring a world into being and become constituents of self-understanding, which, in turn, involves recognizing what one shares with other consciousnesses" (p. 327). Shelley thought that all creative acts, literary and otherwise, would turn out to be "episodes" in a single "great poem."[2] While lacking the metaphysical ground for Shelley's confidence, Altieri can still find in literary study a glimpse of the possibility that the human purposes most worth pursuing are to a significant extent compatible.

The scope of this book is such that virtually everyone with a developed interest in critical theory will find that interest spoken to at some point. We are witnessing, for instance, a strong revival of interest in rhetoric. While most of such work is still concerned with the teaching of writing, there have been several attempts to describe the procedures of literary criticism from a rhetorical point of view.[3] Altieri recognizes that he also rhetoricizes his subject by taking the literary realm as a whole to be sustained by our powers of expression and comprehension. It is less clear that he sees the kind of rhetoric his theory makes criticism out to be. In one place, he compares a critic presenting a reading to a lawyer addressing a jury. This comparison directly suggests that we are dealing with forensic rhetoric, but this seems finally not to be the correct placement. The dominant element of the rhetoric of Altieri's poet is *ethos*: the poem is a display through choices of poetic making of qualities of mind and self. Altieri's critic tries to convince others "that a particular way of conceiving the performance in the text articulates the fullest possibilities inherent in the words, situations, and formal patterns" (p. 234). The emphasis here and throughout the book on richness is a sign that the critic's rhetoric is epideictic: the critic's goal is to exhibit maximally the praiseworthy or blameworthy qualities of the self implicitly displayed in the work. The significant alteration that Altieri makes in the standard account of epideictic rhetoric is, as we have seen, to stress the reflexive nature of the activity: through the activity of construing the work, the critic/reader cultivates his own powers of judgment, rather than merely applying them. *Act & Quality* is a book that will be mentioned in essays on critical theory for a long time. Perhaps the relatively modest notice it has thus far received may be attributed to the fact that there is much more to come to terms with here than our experience with recent books in the genre has led us to expect.

Notes

1. Shelley, "A Defence of Poetry," in *The Great Critics*, ed. James Harry Smith and Edd Winfield Parks (New York: Norton, 1951), p. 561.

2. Ibid. p. 569.

3. Two of the more important of these attempts are Wayne Booth's *Critical Understanding: The Powers and Limits of Pluralism* (Chicago: Univ. of Chicago Press, 1979) and Stanley Fish's *Is There A Text in This Class? The Authority of Interpretive Communities* (Cambridge: Harvard Univ. Press, 1980).

Arthur Koestler, A Half-Life

Reed Merrill

Iain Hamilton. *Koestler: A Biography*. New York: Macmillan, 1983. 398 pp.

From the beginning of his writing career, which now stretches over fifty years, Arthur Koestler has been obsessed with mending the rift between feeling and knowing, metaphysical speculation and scientific "fact." In *Bricks to Babel* (1980), an anthology of his writing, Koestler describes his lifelong search for a unifying principle which will synthesize man's dissociation of sensibility and serve as an integrative systems theory capable of structuring the pluralism of existence. *Bricks to Babel* is divided into two sections which mark the two phases of Koestler's life and indicate the radically varied thrusts of his intellectual efforts: from a dedication to finding, through political action, a cure for what he refers to as "the disease of absolutism" (this period ending about 1950), to a focus on discovering the common relationships between the arts and sciences and a return to the concept of wholeness and organic completeness represented by natural philosophy. Koestler calls these two periods "In Search of Utopia" and "The Act of Creation." In the first volume of his two-volume autobiography, *Arrow in the Blue*, a work which, in conjunction with *The Invisible Writing*, remains one of the most informative and readable of modern autobiographies, he describes the schism which has fired his creative interests and structured every volume of his *oeuvre:*

If I am to remain truthful, the separate existence of the two souls in my bosom must be emphasized, for the split has remained with me, and the resulting tug-of-war is one of the recurring *leit-motifs* of this report. It is reflected in the antithetical titles of my books: *The Yogi and the Commissar, Insight and Outlook, Darkness at Noon, Le Zéro et L'Infini, Arrival and Departure*, and so on. The choice of these titles was more or less unconscious, and the underlying pattern only dawned on me much later.[1]

In his extraordinarily diverse search for meaning and consistency, whether the writing has been fiction, pure theory, quasi-scientific tract, or reportage, Koestler has placed a hypothetical *Gestalt* at the core of each of his books. This organic system would necessarily replace dualistic thinking— for instance the standoff of the mind/body schism—would respond affirmatively to the pessimism of determinism and absolutism by asserting the freedom of humanistic endeavor, and would demonstrate purposiveness through a reevaluation of evolutionary theories from Lamarck and Darwin. At first his search was reflected in Koestler's studies of religious and political ideologies which might disclose intellectually tenable concepts of belief and action. When he became disenchanted with ideologies as absolutistic ends (a direct result of his personal involvement in Zionism and Communism) he turned to ideas rather than actions for his researches. This quest for a comprehensive descriptive metaphor which could disclose the complexity of any given organic system is evident as early as *Insight and Outlook: An Inquiry into the Common Foundations of Science, Art, and Social Ethics* (1949), a work which is now of mostly historical interest, having been superseded by *The Act of Creation, The Ghost and the Machine,* and *Janus: A Summing Up.* In *The Invisible Writing,* Koestler refers to his newfound interest in heuristic theory as "the reality of the third order," a three-layered ontological system (later to be more rigorously developed in his theory of "bisociation," a term created in *Insight and Outlook*), the "trivalent creative process," and his "Holon" and "Open Hierarchic System" theory. This trivalent ontology is divided into a first order, the world of sensory perceptions; a second order, abstract concepts such as "gravitation, electromagnetic fields, and curved space . . . which filled the gaps and gave meaning to the absurd patchiness of the sensory world"; and what Koestler refers to as a third and "higher order of reality," which gives meaning and essence to the second world of non-sensory phenomena:

The third order of reality enveloped, interpenetrated, and gave meaning to the second. It contained "occult" phenomena which could not be apprehended or explained either on the sensory or on the conceptual level, and yet occasionally invaded them like spiritual meteors piercing the primitive's vaulted sky. Just as the conceptual order showed up the illusions and distortions of the senses, so the "third order" disclosed that time, space and causality, that the isolation, separateness and spatio-temporal limitations of the self were merely optical illusions on the next higher level . . . . Just as one could not feel the pull of a magnet with one's skin, so one could not hope to grasp in cognate terms the nature of ultimate reality. It was a text written in invisible ink; and though one could not read it, the knowledge that it existed was sufficient to alter the texture of one's existence, and make one's actions conform to the text.[2]

Much of Koestler's output of the past thirty years has been dedicated to justifying this triadic system, to demonstrating how all creative activities function according to common procedures, and to explaining how an ethic free from determinisms of one kind or another can function within this creative, constantly changing natural process. While one might have doubts concerning some of Koestler's conclusions about ESP, pharmapsychology, and the "occult," he has still grounded his ideas in sensible and demonstrable theory, much of which is still to be extended and examined, and all of which is dedicated to Koestler's desire to systematize artistic and scientific principles into a common humanistic ethic.

"Bisociation" is Koestler's term for the associative process of uniting two seemingly incompatible contexts. According to Koestler, every organism (social, artistic, or natural) has its own set of laws, its own systems and methods of operation. However, when an organism discovers and creates new procedures, it must move outside the confines of previous laws and standards as a result of having brought together, through conscious or unconscious bisociation, what seemed to be dissimilar or even antithetical concepts. The result of a bisocation is an organism's crucial period of adjustment in which it adapts to new conditions and extends its previous field of operation. When it fails to adjust and adapt, the effect can be disorientation or even destruction of the organism's organizing principles. On the other hand, a state of disequilibrium and tension exists as a constant in any organism, a conflict between what Koestler calls "self-assertive" (aggressive and defensive), and "self-transcending" (integrative) tendencies. These illustrate the polarization of any organism and also describe its tendency to conserve the status quo and, at the same time, evolve and change into something better, worse, or at least different. In *The Act of Creation*, which is subtitled "A Study in the Conscious and Unconscious Processes of Humor, Scientific Discovery and Art," Koestler continues his study of the creative organic process but with the focus now upon the neuropsychological consequences of his theory and with the supplemental concept of the "trivalent creative process" which he characterizes as the "discovery of hidden similarities":

> All patterns of creative activity are tri-valent: they can enter the service of humour, discovery, or art; and also . . . as we travel across the triptych from left to right the emotional climate changes by gradual transitions from aggressive to neutral to sympathetic and identificatory—or, to put it another way, from an absurd through an abstract to a tragic or lyric view of existence.[3]

The Ghost in the Machine is essentially two books, the first of which must be the most humorous and destructive attack on behaviorism in print, the second a continuation of Koestler's theory of creativity and evolution in which he discusses man's "urge to self-destruction." It is difficult to agree with Koestler's conclusion that, because of the radical and manifestly destructive split between man's evolved and refined brain and his archaic neocortex, chemotherapeutic measures should be taken to protect him from himself. Still, this book remains Koestler's most important theoretical work. He is proposing a substitute for what he calls, in reference to behaviorism, "ratomorphism" (Koestler has a genius for creating metaphors) and mechanistic determinism. In this book, Koestler extends his concept of bisociation and the trivalence of the creative process to a larger context which includes the working of the individual psyche and the functionality of organisms in nature. His concept is called the "Open Hierarchic System" (O.H.S.); it is an ontological and epistemological structuring principle for natural phenomena. It is based upon the organic entity he calls "Holons." These are "double-faced entities which display the characteristics both of independent units and interdependent parts."[4] Holons are Janus-like in that they face "upwards" and "downwards," and move equally across an operative field as polarities. They are "levels of hierarchies" which, on the lower levels, are subordinate to higher and more sophisticated levels of organization. The subordination of the Holon to higher levels corresponds to Koestler's idea of integration and self-transcendence; the Holon's "freedom" and autonomy are an analogue for the self-assertive and aggressive tendency of the individual Holon to adapt or to reject the laws and parameters of operative fields. This theory also serves to explain continuity, in its adaptation to higher forms, and creativity, in its tendency to reach new dimensions through self-imposed change. It is Koestler's belief that the tendency of an organism toward integration presents a greater danger to the organism's potential and future than its self-assertive movements. He concludes that "the glory and the tragedy of the human condition both derive from our powers of self-transcendence. It is a power which can be harnessed to creative or destructive purpose."[5]

Janus: A Summing Up is Koestler's attempt to bring his Holon and bisociation theories up to date with current speculation in the sciences and humanities. The basic premise of the book remains what Koestler refers to as man's "schizophysiology," the ever-dangerous consequence of mankind's conflict between rationality and irrationality, and "the resulting paranoid streak in history."[6] *Janus* has created some controversy, but Koestler's assessment of man's inherent inability to restrain his self-destructive nature is difficult to refute.

Koestler's early years are comprehensively described in his volumes of autobiography, which are themselves valuable chronicles of the twenties, thirties, and forties by a person who was actively involved in many of the major events of those times. In addition to *Arrow in the Blue*, which concerns the period 1905-31, and *The Invisible Writing*, 1932-50, *Scum of the Earth* and *Dialogue with Death* are also autobiographical works, as are many of the essays published in additional volumes. On the basis of such a detailed and comprehensive documentation of a life by the author himself, the writing of a biography of Koestler will necessarily entail a number of formidable obstacles, few of which Iain Hamilton has overcome in his study. Since Koestler has so thoroughly dealt with the ideological search-for-utopia period, it would follow that a biographer should place greater emphasis on Koestler's theoretical and philosophical endeavors since then. However, Hamilton does not do so. His justification for covering basically the same material Koestler has treated in his early volumes is that he finds many of Koestler's later theoretical ideas personally uninteresting:

> My (no doubt unfortunate) lack of interest in the so-called 'Psi-factor' in such alleged paranormal phenomena as psychokinesis and the like effectively disqualifies me from dealing in detail with his late works. Even if I had the competence to find my way through those murky and tangled thickets, I should refrain from doing so. As I write in my final chapter: " . . . I hope that I may be forgiven if the last part of my biographical account is offered in summary form. That there is a book to be written about Koestler's researches and speculations in this field I have no doubt. But I am not the man to write it." [pp. xvi-xvii]

The biographer of a man who has never flinched at controversy and who has consistently defended his case persuasively, and with admirable intellectual vigor, should not resort to this kind of "preferring not to." Instead he should respond to those ideas in Koestler's writing which he found questionable. The result of this opting out is a book which concerns only part of the subject. Hamilton recapitulates much old material to which he adds occasional anecdotes and journalistic gossip, far too much of it culled from the letters of Mamaine Koestler, Koestler's second wife. The structure of this biography mirrors Hamilton's biases and deficiencies: pages 3-311 concern Koestler's life from 1905-59, already covered in depth in the autobiographies. The balance, pages 312-64, covers 1959 to the present, Koestler's most prolific and important creative period. During this time he has published seventeen books, including what surely must be at least four of his major works, but none is discussed in detail. The biography is thus half a life. There is virtually no discussion, and no critical analysis, of Koestler's work or of his important theories outside the realm of the "pseudo-science" which Hamilton condemns. Nor is there an examination of Koestler's views on behaviorism, determinism, indeterminism and reductionism, Lamarckian versus Darwinian evolution theory, British economics, the psychology of creativity, the philosophy of science, the Holon theory, or bisociation. Whether one agrees with Hamilton about the nugatory value of some of Koestler's speculations and investigations, it should have been Hamilton's responsibility to show cause for his disagreements. In consequence, Hamilton fails to deal with his subject on the subject's own ground.

In fairness to Hamilton it must be said that he does mention an important facet of Koestler's life which Koestler, for obvious reasons, has not discussed—his compelling humanitarianism and his dedication to important causes. Koestler's contribution to the abolition of capital punishment in Britain and his attempts to improve the penal system, as well as his patronage for artistic and creative endeavors by prisoners in the system, are only a few of his efforts to put his humanism to practical use.

However, rather than concerning himself with evaluating Koestler's ideas or assessing his intellectual contribution to the age, Hamilton recites journalistic tidbits from the private and public life of Koestler, some of which for lack of taste and discretion might better have been left out. These events do show the variety of activity in Koestler's life, but none of them serves to illuminate his concepts.

When Hamilton does attempt to evaluate and analyze Koestler's achievement, he often resorts to subjectivism instead of persuasive argument. For instance, although his animus for Sartre and de Beauvoir is eminently clear, it is never logically justified. The result is a jarring change in the tone of the book: "He [Koestler] knew also (enough of the English temper of pragmatism having rubbed off on him) that he would never again feel entirely at home in the intellectual life of Paris, among people like Sartre and Simone de Beauvoir, so wilfully abstract and, at bottom, frivolous, nihilistic and irresponsible" (p. 118); or, "I think it not unfair to assert that in his development as a 'thinker' (to put it in a simpler, old-fashioned way) Koestler has been more successful than Sartre, who suceeded only in reducing to venomous rabble-rousing absurdity his synthesis of atheistic existentialism and neo-Marxism after the school of Frankfurt-am-Main" (p. 347). Such unsupported value judgments and political biases are seldom convincing and generally self-defeating.

There are some fascinating anecdotes in this book which are not, in my memory, included in Koestler's own works. These help explain his disdain for living in the United States and at the same time justify his dubiety about the intellectual climate here since the McCarthy era. There is an amusing description of Koestler's meeting with Adolph Zukor and Alfred Knopf on the *Queen Mary*. Both Zukor and Knopf attempted to persuade Koestler to come to Hollywood to write screenplays with Isherwood and others. And there is an interesting retelling of Koestler's battle with Sidney Kingsley over Kingsley's inept dramatic interpretation of *Darkness at Noon*—a hit on Broadway and a disaster as a play. There is an account of Koestler's agonizing struggle to gain landed immigrant status in the United States, and there is a particularly amusing reference to Koestler's on-going skirmishes with academics. Hamilton calls this Koestler's *"odium academicum,"* and includes Koestler's explanation to Cyril Connolly of the purpose of his writing. He wishes to reach a large audience without using academic double-talk:

It was a misunderstanding when I gave you *Insight and Outlook* to read. You then said, I remember, "Why do you waste your talents writing popular science?" But *The Sleepwalkers* is not popular science, it is a reinterpretation of the history of philosophy of science written with as little jargon as possible, and as little technicality as possible. And *The Act of Creation* is, on the one hand, a frontal attack on that school of psychology and philosophy which dehumanises man's behavior and on the other on logical positivism. But on the positive side it is, for better or worse, an orginial theory." [p. 380]

A word about the sources for this book. Hamilton includes no footnotes to primary and secondary sources, claiming that most of his information comes from Koestler's own papers and from Mamaine Koestler's letters. However, that does not excuse the absence of references to other texts. It is difficult, for example, to locate quotations such as the one from William James, a statement especially pertinent in these days of the decline of the humanities:

Of all the insufficient authorities as to the total nature of reality, give me the 'scientists' . . . . Their interests are most incomplete and their professional conceit and bigotry immense. I know of no narrower sect or club, in spite of their excellent authority in the lines of fact they have explored, and their excellent achievements there. [p. 309]

Koestler's friends and associates know that he became disenchanted with the direction and method of Hamilton's work some eight years ago, the time at which this biography was supposed to have been published in honor of Koestler's seventieth birthday, and that a considerable conflict has resulted. This difficulty is explained in a recent article by Harold Harris, Koestler's long-time friend and editor. In commenting on Hamilton's biography, Harris refers to his role as mediator between Hamilton and Koestler, a role which resulted in the publication of the book in spite of Koestler's deep dissatisfaction over its content. Harris' final assessment of the book seems accurate and bears repeating: "There is no comparable figure of this century who combines to the same extent a life of action with a life of contemplation. It is sad to see it reduced to a patchwork, a random selection of extracts, reviews, jottings, journalism." One might add that for a reader who has no knowledge of Koestler's life, the book does at least provide an introduction to one of the most powerful humanistic voices of this century. But as a work which evaluates and assesses Koestler's valuable contribution to human understanding and ethical behavior, Hamilton's book is incomplete and unsatisfactory.

Notes

1. Koestler, *Arrow in the Blue* (New York: Macmillan, 1952), pp. 106-07.

2. Koestler, *The Invisible Writing* (New York: Macmillan, 1969), pp. 431-32.

3. Koestler, *The Act of Creation* (New York: Macmillan, 1964), p. 27.

4. Koestler, *The Ghost in the Machine* (New York: Macmillan, 1968), p. 68.

5. *The Ghost in the Machine*, p. 245.

6. Koestler, *Janus: A Summing Up* (New York: Random House, 1978), p. 11.

Deconstructive Reading of Eighteenth Century Texts: Dilemma and Insight

Richard H. Dammers

G. Douglas Atkins. *Reading Deconstruction Deconstructive Reading*. Lexington: University Press of Kentucky, 1983. x, 158 pp.

Reading Deconstruction Deconstructive Reading, G. Douglas Atkins's second book, offers a challenge and a call to the reader. The challenge demands a new way of reading literature, a new way of examining the process of thought, and a new way of looking at life. The call invites the reader to accept this "new way" as salvation. Most literary critics call the reader to accept a certain vision or way of looking at literature, but this book goes further. On his second page Atkins announces that "some of the most important, perhaps even revolutionary, implications of deconstruction are for theology and religion." Obviously committed to deconstruction, Atkins persuasively tries to explain in Part One and demonstrate in Part Two his reading of literature. The reader should, I think, find refreshing the polemical intent of this book. Even an unsympathetic reader ought to discern the compelling honesty, clarity, and directness of Atkins's presentation. Both in style and in content, this is a remarkable book.

The challenge from Atkins to the reader in *Reading Deconstruction Deconstructive Reading* emanates from his belief in the need for "an exposition of deconstructive principles and practices" (p. 1). He senses that certain readers either will show no interest in or will demonstrate lively antipathy to such a project. Writers on deconstruction are often associated, rightly or wrongly, with obfuscation. And, for a number of readers, deconstruction threatens long-held opinions. James Sloan Allen expresses familiar objections to deconstruction in his article "The Humanists Are Guilty of Betraying Humanism":

> The humanists have betrayed humanism by converting education—and most egregiously the teaching of literature—into a pseudoscientific labor over technical issues set forth in a jargon that baffles common understanding. One does not talk about novels or stories, poems or plays any more; one "decodes" or "deconstructs texts." One does not explore and evaluate an author's thoughts and perception for the purpose of strengthening mind and illuminating life; one seeks clues to "performative linguistic acts" for the purpose of achieving "critical enablement." Literature, after all, we are told, is "primarily about language, and not much else."
>
> The infatuation with esoteric questions and cant has turned the MLA convention into a circus of professional hokum, which may be no great loss, but it is also turning humanistic education into a funhouse mirror's image of science comprehensible only to an initiated elite. This is a loss. By rendering the study of literature (as well as history and culture generally) arcane and exclusive the humanists deprive us of the education we most need—an education in mental discipline, intellectual autonomy, moral judgment, emotional response and the like.[1]

Admitting that "deconstructionists have been loathe to provide" an exposition of the principles and practices of deconstructionism, Atkins takes up the challenge of providing an "exposition of deconstructive goals and principles and so a defense of deconstruction against mistaken and distorting polemics" (pp. 2, 3). He challenges the reader to walk with him in tolerance and in understanding through the complexities of deconstruction and the application of deconstructive principles to three eighteenth-century literary masterpieces.

Atkins begins by asserting the importance to him, as well as to fellow deconstructionists, of the traditional close reading of a text. "There can be, then, no question of jettisoning, or being able to do without, the traditional or unequivocal reading" (p. 8). Then he presents his declaration of deconstructive understanding and methodology: "As my readings of *Religio Laici, A Tale of a Tub,* and *An Epistle to Dr. Arbuthnot* show, texts can be seen as moving dynamically beyond and even against or counter to any purposiveness that can be attributed to their authors, textual description being precisely a deconstruction of declaration. Due attention to the text's immanent purposiveness, its 'dynamic progression,' thus may lead *both* to the author's apparent purpose as worked out in the text *and* to the deconstruction of that purposiveness of the text's language (p. 11).

Notice an important similarity between Atkins's position and that of Geoffrey Hartman. Hartman, too, locates deconstruction with past critical reading. "Deconstructive criticism does not present itself as a novel enterprise. There is, perhaps, more of a relentless focus on certain questions, and a new rigor when it comes to the discipline of close reading. Yet to suggest that meaning and language do not coincide, and to draw from that noncoincidence a peculiar strength, is merely to restate what literature has always revealed."[2] Hartman's emphasis on the noncoincidence of language and meaning indeed matches Atkins's statements on the importance of the trace, of *differance*, in the text and on the opposition of textual description and declaration. On this point at least Hartman, Atkins, and J. Hillis Miller agree:

> The ultimate justification for this mode of criticism, as of any conceivable mode, is that it works. It reveals hitherto unidentified meanings and ways of having meaning in major literary texts. The hypothesis of a possible heterogeneity in literary texts is more flexible, more open to a given work, than the assumption that a good work of literature is necessarily going to be "organically unified." The latter presupposition is one of the major factors inhibiting recognition of the possibly self-subversive complexity of meanings in a given work. Moreover "deconstruction" finds in the text it interprets the double antithetical patterns it identifies, for example the relation of parasite to host. It does not claim them as universal explanatory structures, neither for the text in question nor for literature in general. Deconstruction attempts to resist the totalizing and totalitarian tendencies of criticism.[3]

Hartman and Atkins place emphasis on the importance of the trace or *differance*, so that certainty of meaning becomes an impossibility. Deconstruction, says Hartman, "refuses to identify the force of literature with any concept of embodied meaning and shows how deeply such logocentric or incarnationist perspectives have influenced the way we think about art. We assume that . . . the 'presence of the word' is equivalent to the presence of meaning. But the opposite can also be urged, that the word carries with it a certain absence or indeterminacy of meaning. Literary language foregrounds language itself as something not reducible to meaning: it opens as well as closes the disparity between symbol and idea, between written sign and assigned meaning."[4] There, in the religious echoes of Hartman's declaration, appears another similarity of thought between Atkins and Hartman. The final statement of Atkins's first chapter delineates his interest in deconstruction beyond literature and his call to the reader to follow, even if with doubtful steps. "Since it is unlikely that either benign neglect or wishing will make deconstruction go away, we must come to grips with it, explore its implications, and evaluate it fairly. There are signs that just this kind of thoughtful analysis is under way in religion and theology as well as in criticism and philosophy" (p. 33).

Atkins stresses the connection between deconstruction and recent developments in theology and philosophy. He devotes a considerable part of his second chapter to a discussion of this linkage. With praise for Thomas J. J. Altizer, Atkins announces that "Altizer embraces Nietzsche as a guiding spirit and celebrates the very chaos Gerald Graff fears" (p. 42). The decentering occurring in criticism, says Atkins, has already occurred in theological discussions and the decentering of criticism is a part of, as well as a result of, that larger decentering movement. Atkins quotes Altizer: "'Nietzsche's vision of Eternal Recurrence records the chaos of a world that has fallen away from its original center. It reflects a totality of perpetual and meaningless flux; no longer is there a beginning or an end, or, for that matter, a purpose or goal of any kind.'"[5] Although major deconstructionists do not particularly link their work to religious speculation, Atkins attempts to bridge these two foci by demonstrating their essential similarities. This part of Atkins's book allows the reader to understand his overarching vision of deconstruction's role not only in criticism, but in life.

After presenting Altizer, Atkins turns to John Dominic Crossan, who has affirmed, says Atkins, "that 'the Holy has no such plan at all and that is what is absolutely incomprehensible to our structuring, planning, ordering human minds.' Crossan's various efforts are directed at countering 'the classical vision of a fixed center out there somewhere.'"[6]

Crossan describes his perception of existence: "I have accepted play, well known to us in the microcosm of game and sport, as a supreme paradigm for reality. Reality as the interplay of worlds created by human imagination. . . . Comedy is the conscience of play. The comic vision is our consciousness and awareness of the inevitability and ubiquity of play." The reader recalls that Atkins, too, had considered "play" with regard to language. Play, then, emerges as one of the linkages between literary/critical and theological deconstruction. Crossan calls language "our supreme play."[7] He goes on to claim that it is only in language that we know reality. We know reality in language, not through language. He insists on the unknowableness of reality. "What is happening here before our eyes is the death of mimesis. When reality was thought of as existing out-there by itself prior to and independent of our knowledge and our language, this latter could be considered as groping more or less effectively to describe that reality, and one could then claim that literature was where it was grasped the best of all."[8]

With an amazing compression of thought and language, Atkins presents, unthreateningly, the challenge of deconstruction. In no sense, and Atkins postulates this himself, does he complete the work which this book begins. He has produced, as he tells the reader, a series of essays, ongoing in nature. One may expect, from the nature of the book, a continuation of his presentation.

Atkins devotes his sixth, seventh, and eighth chapters to deconstructive analyses of three eighteenth-century works, Dryden's *Religio Laici*, Swift's *A Tale of a Tub*, and Pope's *Epistle to Dr. Arbuthnot*. His argument in each of these three chapters focuses on the separation between the text's declaration and its description: "Texts can be seen as moving dynamically beyond and even against or counter to any purposiveness that can be attributed to their authors, textual description being precisely a deconstruction of declaration" (p. 11). In the sixth chapter, "Reading and/or Swerving: The Quest(ion) of Interpretive Authority in Dryden's *Religio Laici*," Atkins claims that "Dryden's text will reveal a description that fundamentally challenges his declaration" (p. 92). Such analysis leads the reader to a position where the text is "unreadable in the sense that no complete understanding, no fully present comprehension is possible." The cause of Dryden's swerving remains in his figurative language. "Dryden can only be indirect and figurative in describing the 'Letter' and the supposed directness of God. That is, in spite of his desire and his expressed intention, Dryden writes figuratively about the putative plainness of Scripture, swerving from the desired literalness that supposedly characterizes the Bible" (pp. 104, 99). The application of the effects of figurative language, or swerving, he projects beyond Dryden's *Religio Laici* to the Bible, the subject of Dryden's poem. "Figuration, or swerving, subverts declared meanings, and so reading as commonly understood plainly is made both impossible and possible" (p. 104).

In chapter 7, "Allegory of Blindness and Insight: Will and Will-ing in *A Tale of a Tub*," Atkins suggests that the *Tale's* frequent contradictions, "or at least the Hack's contradictions of himself, will immediately suggest to the reader familiar with deconstruction 'the critical difference' that is inevitable in all texts, made of language and so bifurcated and dialogical (p. 107).[9] Atkins claims that in *A Tale of a Tub* the figurative language reverses the meaning of the literal language. Agreeing that Swift preferred the literal and worried about the disturbing and disrupting power of figurative language, Atkins again posits a description of the text in opposition to the declaration of the text. The description of the text points to the insight of the Hack, even though the satirist presents the Hack as mad. Atkins indicates a debt to Ronald Paulson, whose *Theme and Structure in Swift's* Tale of a Tub (Yale University Press, 1960) he finds especially useful in helping him through Swift's complex text. Paulson's sections on "The Converting Imagination" and "The Hack's Battle with Reality" demonstrate extraordinary sensitivity to Swift's text, and Atkins refers directly to Paulson's discussion of "The Converting Imagination" in a 1981 article. There he also discusses the dilemma that he sees confronting both himself and other scholars in the last decades of the twentieth century. He admonishes the reader: "The current battle of books between the so-called humanists and the deconstructionists raises the most insistent and crucial questions now facing critics . . . . If, amidst the problems and contradictions, *A Tale of a Tub* has anything to teach us in this sophisticated critical age it may be that such choices are not simple, are not simply either/or . . . . Differences within perhaps mitigate differences between, turning what appears to be an either/or choice into a both/and situation."[10] One notices, both in Atkins's essay and in his book, a sense of toleration, a desire to communicate with scholars in general rather than with only the disciples of deconstruction.

In his final chapter applying the principles of deconstruction to eighteenth-century English literature, "'Grac[ing] These Ribalds': The Play of Difference in Pope's *Epistle to Dr. Arbuthnot*," Atkins focuses on "that external form consisting of difference between (say) Pope and those he indicts, and the internal form representing self-division and rendering certain conventions problematical (pp. 118-19). Here Atkins argues that Pope's attempts to insist on absolute difference are doomed to failure, because difference can only exist in relation and because the trace or *differance* always already exists in whatever position Pope posits. "From the very beginning," Atkins suggests, "Pope is concerned to draw straight, distinct, and unmistakable lines between himself and those others (p. 121). Atkins indicates here a debt to J. Paul Hunter's essay "Satiric Apology as Satiric Instance: Pope's *Arbuthnot*"; Hunter rigorously examines Pope's poem and Atkins's reference to it indicates his thoughtfully considered connection to traditional scholarship at its best. Hunter's position differs from Atkins's, for the former believes that "Pope is always in control."[11] Atkins says that despite "Pope's desire for, and efforts toward, absolute difference, he is finally and always already related to all those from whom he would distance and differentiate himself." Atkins claims that "absolute difference such as Pope sought . . . must result in loss of difference; only relation preserves difference." If true, then it naturally follows that "there appears to be no undoing, or satirizing, that is not also a preserving" (pp. 134-35). The description in the text negates what Pope declares in his poem.

In a stinging indictment of certain representatives of post-structuralist criticism, Gerald Graff argues that today's critic does not feel bound by traditional restraints. "In an age of self-absorption, he may claim his right—and who is to stop him?—to let it all hang out in his critical works, to make his agony as a critic the main focus of his criticism."[12] Graff attacks the self-reflexive focus on self of such critics and offers instead a call for "a certain self-effacing detachment and objectivity." He concludes: "This is what the malaise of criticism finally amounts to: modernism weary of itself and knowing it, but not ready to strike out in a different direction."[13] And Harold Fromm in a recent essay expresses additional concerns about the directions of post-structuralist criticism.

If in our lives we are afforded only a limited number of pulse-beats, it is not frivolous (however unfashionable) to ask about the priorities of the use of those beats; and *within* the professions, questions of priority need to be raised as much as do questions from without concerning the validity of the activities of these professions as a whole. And, so the current democratization of readers' responses to literary work together with the imaginative new works based upon them that have resulted from the repudiation of the substantial reality of texts necessarily leave us with practical and ethical dilemmas. How can one hope to read all of those proliferating responses to literary works (when ultimately they don't apply to oneself anyhow)? And how can an individual or a profession justify even trying to do so without, however unwittingly, also justifying what amounts to an insidious sort of idolatry?[14]

Such concerns cannot be ignored or repudiated with ease. Unquestionably we are in the midst of a large on-going debate. It is one of the particular merits of Atkins's book that, while it clearly argues for a deconstructive reading of three eighteenth century texts, it addresses the interests and needs of a general audience of scholars. Atkins emerges not as a weary modernist without direction; in fact, his book provides a clear direction which readers can accept or reject as they please. Among the proliferation of books and articles on critical theory, Atkins's communicates successfully in brief compass to a reader who wants to know. *Reading Deconstruction Deconstructive Reading* is extraordinarily concise, but for the purpose of precise communication, not obfuscation or opaqueness. Founded on sound and thorough scholarship, this book does not assume the reader's familiarity with all of its supporting resources. It provides a worthwhile introduction to deconstruction; and, even as it proselytizes, it demonstrates a noteworthy tolerance. The reader, of whatever critical persuasion, will find his time with this book well spent.

Notes

1. James Sloan Allen, "The Humanists are Guilty of Betraying Humanism," *Wall Street Journal*, 2 February 1982, quoted in George L. Geckle, "Heuristics and Schemata: Some New Problems Concerning Texts and Readers," *The CEA Forum*, 13, no. 1 (October, 1982), 7.

2. Geoffrey Hartman, "Preface," *Deconstruction and Criticism* (New York: Seabury Press, 1979), p. viii.

3. J. Hillis Miller, "The Critic as Host," *Deconstruction and Criticism*, p. 252.

4. Hartman, "Preface," p. vii-viii.

5. Thomas J. J. Altizer, *The Gospel of Christian Atheism* (Philadelphia: Westminster, 1966), p. 149.

6. John Dominic Crossan, *Raid on the Articulate: Comic Eschatology in Jesus and Borges* (New York: Harper and Row, 1976), p. 44, and Crossan, *The Dark Interval Towards a Theology of Story* (Niles, Illinois: Argus Communications, 1975), pp. 42-43. Crossan explains his perception of the loss of reality outside language as follows: "Emily Dickinson makes me shiver in a way that Nietzsche has never been able to do. Her version: 'Finding is the first Act / The second, loss, / Third, Expedition for / The 'Golden Fleece.' / Fourth, no Discovery— / Fifth, no crew—Finally, no Golden Fleece— / Jason—sham—too.' In that 'sham' one hears the chilling slam as the door closes on the classical vision of a fixed center out there somewhere. What had died was the fixed center outside language."

7. Crossan, *Raid on the Articulate*, pp. 28, 38.

8. Ibid., p. 40.

9. Atkins here directs the reader to Barbara Johnson, *The Critical Difference: Essays in the Contemporary Rhetoric of Reading* (Baltimore: Johns Hopkins Univ. Press, 1980).

10. G. Douglas Atkins, "Interpretation and Meaning in *A Tale of a Tub*," *Essays in Literature*, 8 (Fall 1981), 238.

11. J. Paul Hunter, "Satiric Apology as Satiric Instance: Pope's *Arbuthnot*," *JEGP*, 68 (October 1969), 625.

12. Gerald Graff, "Fear and Trembling at Yale," *American Scholar*, 46 (Autumn 1977), 467-68.

13. Graff, 478.

14. Harold Fromm, "Sparrows and Scholars: Literary Criticism and the Sanctification of Data," *The Georgia Review*, 33 (Summer 1979), 258.

CONTRIBUTORS

BRUCE BASHFORD is Assistant Professor of English at the State University of New York at Stony Brook.

GUY CARDWELL is Professor of English Emeritus at Washington University, St. Louis.

ROBERT CASILLO is Assistant Professor of English at the University of Miami.

PAUL CONNOLLY is Director of the Institute for Writing and Thinking at Bard College, on leave from Yeshiva University.

RICHARD H. DAMMERS is Professor of English at Illinois State University.

LENNARD J. DAVIS is Assistant Professor of English at Columbia University.

PAMELA DUNBAR is Lecturer in English and Comparative Literary Studies at the University of Warwick.

W. L. GODSHALK is Professor of English at the University of Cincinnati.

DAVID LEON HIGDON is Paul Whitfield Horn Professor of English at Texas Tech University.

SUZANNE H. JUHASZ is Associate Professor of English at the University of Colorado.

JACOB KORG is Professor of English at the University of Washington.

GEORGE P. LANDOW is Professor of English and Art at Brown University.

VERONICA MAKOWSKY is Assistant Professor of English at Middlebury College.

JAMES MCKINLEY is Associate Professor of English at the University of Missouri, Kansas City.

NOEL POLK is Professor of English at the University of Southern Mississippi.

ROBERT C. SCHWEIK is Distinguished Teaching Professor of English at Fredonia State University.

GERALD TRETT is Editor at the University Press of Virginia.

JAMES L. W. WEST III is Professor of English at Virginia Polytechnic Institute and State University and co-editor of *Review*.

WAYNE W. WESTBROOK is Associate Professor of English at Husson College.

CALHOUN WINTON is Professor of English at the University of Maryland.

CHRISTIAN K. ZACHER is Associate Professor of English at Ohio State University.